Conversations with

Yogananda

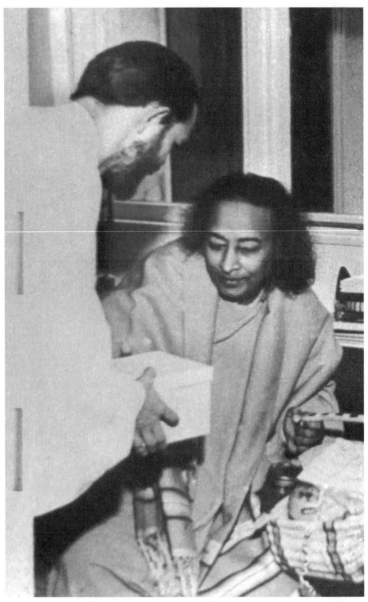

The author presents a gift to Paramhansa Yogananda on
the occasion of the visit to Mount Washington in March 1952 by
Binay R. Sen, India's Ambassador to America.

Conversations
with
Yogananda

Recorded, with Reflections,
by his disciple
Swami Kriyananda (J. Donald Walters)

Crystal Clarity Publishers
Nevada City, California

Cover and interior design by Christine Starner Schuppe

Printed in Canada

Crystal Clarity Publishers

14618 Tyler Foote Road

Nevada City, CA 95959

530.478.7600

fax 530.478.7610

www.crystalclarity.com

clarity@crystalclarity.com

Library of Congress Cataloging-in-Publication Data
Walters, J. Donald.
  Conversations with Yogananda / recorded with reflections, by his disciple Swami Kriyananda (J. Donald Walters).-- 1st ed.
      p. cm.
  Includes index.
  ISBN 1-56589-202-X (trade paper)
  1. Yogananda, Paramahansa, 1893-1952. 2. Self-realization. 3. Spiritual life. I. Title.
  BP605.S43Y68 2004
  294.5'092--dc22

                                        2004013138

Dedicated to the sincere truth seeker,
whatever his religion.

Preface

It has taken me over fifty years to publish these conversations. For all that time, the notebooks containing them were my most precious possession, and their protection my first care. In the Sierra Nevada foothills of California, where I resided for many years, forest fires are a major threat. I therefore kept in mind always that, should my home ever be threatened by fire, my first duty would be to save this material. Everything else was secondary. I kept the notebooks locked securely in a safe. When, eventually, I moved to Italy in 1996, I brought the notebooks along with me, taking the loving care of them that a father would devote to his only, delicate child.

Now at last that responsibility has been discharged. You would certainly be justified, dear reader, in asking me, "What on earth took you so long?" My answer, however, would be equally justified: It takes time to excavate a diamond mine. Discipleship is a long-term commitment. To convey to others the wisdom of a great master requires a certain maturity in the disciple also.

I've been a disciple of Paramhansa Yogananda's since 1948. I was twenty-two when I came to him. In May of 1950, he began urging me to record our conversations. I couldn't, however, contemplate publishing them soon; I was hardly more than a boy then. The spiritual value of his words, however, was not limited to the time when they were spoken. The conversations are as immediate today as they were then, over fifty-three years ago. Indeed, they will remain so thousands of years from now. Meanwhile, my memory, fortunately, remains fresh; I have not had to depend exclusively on my notes, and have even added material to them, from memory. I present them here as clearly as if they had occurred yesterday. I believe, friend, that you will find many new insights in these pages. Some of them may be unexpected by you, for the life and actions of my great Guru followed no well-worn rut, and were never ruled by conventions that he considered pointless. He was a way-shower, not an institution.

Some of this material has already appeared in two others of my books, namely, *The Path,* and *The Essence of Self-Realization.* A few other sayings have appeared also in print, notably in the book *A Place Called Ananda.* The first of those three, *The Path,* was published in 1978. I gave it an autobiographical form, to help others to know something of what the life of discipleship was like under that great master. The reason I made it an autobiography was that I felt incompetent, still, to write about him with any authority, and wanted to give discerning readers a chance to separate whatever they might deem unworthy of the Guru from the imperfect instrument who was trying with his pen to do him justice. I hoped also that others would find in my own search for truth, leading as it did to the feet of Paramhansa Yogananda, answers to their own spiritual seeking. To my great satisfaction, this latter hope has been realized in many thousands of readers.

There remained much material that was not used in *The Path,* or that I quoted there only partly, in the hope of using the rest of it again later to better advantage. My thought was, Let me advance further on the spiritual path; perhaps in another twenty years I'll be able to present this material with greater wisdom.

In February, 1990, I abstracted selections from those notes for a second book, which I titled, *The Essence of Self-Realization.* The material I chose was limited to that theme. If, therefore, a quotation contained other teachings which weren't relevant to the subject, I omitted those portions. In some cases, that material has been included here in its entirety. There remained much more material, covering a wide range of topics. Most of it— leaving out any conversations that might hurt or offend living persons—appears in this volume.

A quarter of a century has elapsed since *The Path* was written and published. Since then, I have prayed for guidance as to when I should release the rest of the material for publication. Always the response I felt intuitively was, "The time will come. Be patient."

As one's life slips by, increasing age forces on him an awareness that his time on earth is growing steadily shorter. How long would this body live? Hundreds of years might be desirable for a work of this nature, but if I put it off too long it would have to be finished by someone else, and under the considerable disadvantage of not having even known the Master. I had to accept that my position for undertaking this labor was unique, however incompetently I did it. In 1996, I passed my Biblically allotted threescore and ten years.* Increasingly, the completion of this book was becoming a top priority. To be fair to these conversations, I couldn't simply toss them out disjointedly, without any commentary or explanation. They needed to be presented in their proper setting, and not left dangling in midair, like an abused participle.

A gemstone's beauty is enhanced when it is set in a piece of jewelry. Thus too, the clarity of these sayings would be enhanced if the reader could know, wherever possible, to *whom* the Master was speaking, *when* he spoke, and *where* and *why*. The perceptive reader, moreover, would have no difficulty in detecting any artificial *mise en scène* in this regard. Here again I was, in most cases, the only one who knew the whole "picture."

Recently, the guidance came to me at last to begin this work. Though I saw it as a labor of love, the magnitude of the challenge had always, I confess, daunted me. Not only did I expect it would take at least two years—

*Psalm 90:10.

not so very long a time, perhaps; others of my books have taken longer. The really daunting part, for me, was that I had no idea how to arrange these conversations into any logical sequence. I had been accustomed, when writing, to develop a theme gradually. My mind resisted the idea of simply scrambling groups of unrelated thoughts together randomly. Yet randomness proved, in the end, the best way. Indeed, it was the only possible way. The conversations were simply too varied, and in many cases too brief, to be put in any sequence.

To my astonishment, the work simply flowed. Much of it entailed, of course, simply transferring to my computer what existed already in my notebooks. I found, however, that apart from grouping a few of the conversations together I could leave the sequence more or less as it was already, or heed an inner guidance that said, "Why not put this one here, and that one there?"—without effort on my part. It has taken me hardly two months to finish the entire book.

Throughout these pages I've referred to myself, when necessary, in the first person. This method seemed to me simpler and clearer than the common, and perfectly legitimate, third-person device. To help the reader to distinguish when the first person refers to me and not to Paramhansa Yogananda, I've occasionally inserted parenthetically the name by which he himself used to call me, "Walter."

Conversations
with
Yogananda

1

A professor from Columbia University came to lunch with the Master in his third-floor interview room at Mount Washington. I served them, and was able afterward to sit in the room and take notes while they conversed. At a certain point in their discussion, the professor asked, "Do your teachings help people to be at peace with themselves?"

"They do indeed," the Master answered, "but that is the least that they do. We teach people above all how to be at peace with their Creator."

2

The Columbia professor had a probing mind. Among many questions, he asked, "How do you distinguish between yourself and your followers?"

"All are waves on the same, one ocean," the Master replied, "composed, as ocean water is, of the same substance: Spirit. Some of the waves are higher than others. Some waves don't even want to distance themselves from the ocean. All waves, no matter how high, are in essence one and the same. The difference between the guru and the disciples, then, lies only in their respective closeness to the ocean: in how conscious each one is of his essential reality. The greater the sense of ego, the taller the wave, and the greater, in consequence, the ignorance. The greater one's awareness of the ocean as one's sole reality, the smaller the wave, and also the less his sense of having a separate individuality."

Professor: "Is there a difference, then, of evolution?"

The Master: "That much is true, if we understand evolution to mean a progressive refinement of awareness. The tall waves participate more exuberantly in the play of delusion. The little waves, which are more enlightened, are no longer excited by the play. Enlightened beings enjoy everything, not for itself, but as a 'play' of God's."

Professor: "Is there any end to evolution?"

The Master replied, "No end. You go on until you achieve endlessness."

꒰ 3 ꒱

"Is man important in the scheme of things?" the professor asked.

"Man is important in one sense only," the Master replied. "He was made in the image of God: That is his importance. He is not important for his body, ego, or personality. His constant affirmation of ego-consciousness is the source of all his problems."

4

On another occasion, the Master told us, "Man was given ego-consciousness to inspire him to seek God. That is the only reason for his existence. Job, friends, personal interests: these things, by themselves, mean nothing."

5

"What is the difference," asked the professor, "between science and religion in the search for truth?"

"True religion," the Master replied, "is not theology. It is born of deep, inner communion with God. True religion teaches us, for example, how to *become* the atom, whereas theology at most only discusses the atom. Science studies the nature of the atom outwardly, proving its existence by experimentation. Inner religion, however, goes beyond experimentation to actual *experience*. It helps one to cognize, by direct experience, his oneness with the atom at its vital center."

6

It was that same professor, I believe, who posed a classic question: "Which came first: the tree or the seed?"

"The tree came first," the Master answered without hesitation, "as the idea of a deed precedes the deed itself. The tree was, in this way, a special creation. God, when He set the process in motion, gave the tree seeds that it might produce other trees like itself.

"Everything, at first," he added, "is an idea, a special creation."

7

"People spend too much time fussing over their persons and possessions. What a waste it is, to devote so much energy to polishing, polishing, polishing this little body, home, and belongings—all of which, so very soon, must be abandoned forever!"

❦ 8 ❧

"If you go to a doctor and get a prescription from him, but after you return home you tear it up and toss it away, how will you expect to get well? The guru is your spiritual 'doctor.' It isn't sufficient merely to *have* a guru: You must do what he tells you. If you follow his prescription even a little bit, your life will be transformed. Everyone who practices what he learns here will pass through the portals of death into the radiant kingdom of light. Don't expect to get there, however, if you merely depend passively on the guru—like a superstitious patient whom one may imagine framing his prescription and hanging it on a wall—as if expecting the writing itself to make him well! And don't think to get there by merely 'hanging on' grimly to the end! Go on with steadfast faith, devotion, and joy. Long before you reach your divine goal, you will have realized how very sweet life can be when it is lived rightly. You will be glowing with inner radiance, vitality, and happiness!"

❦ 9 ❧

The Master used to tell us, "If you practice even a hundredth part of what I teach you, you will reach God."

.

↝ 10 ↜

Toward the end of the Master's life, he experienced a prolonged illness. One afternoon, when he had begun to come out of his quarters again, he was getting into his car. I and another monk were helping him. "You are getting better, Sir!" I exclaimed gratefully.

"Who is getting better?" The Master's tone was impersonal.

"I meant your body, Sir," I replied. I knew, of course, that he had no attachment to it.

To him, however, the very distinction was superficial. "What's the difference?" he asked. "The wave belongs entirely to the ocean from which it protrudes. This is God's body. If He wants to make it well, all right. If He wants to keep it unwell, all right.

"It is wisest to be impartial. If you have health, but are attached to it, you will always be afraid of losing it. And if you fear that loss, but become ill, you will suffer. Why not remain forever joyful in the Self?

"Man's greatest problem is his ego—his consciousness of individuality. Whatever happens to him, he thinks it affects *him,* personally. Why be affected? You are not this body: You are *He!* Everything is He: All is Spirit.

"Unfortunately, mankind sees everything as separate and individual. The Lord had to create that appearance. Ask yourself, however: *Why?* Why is this a tree, and you, a human being? The answer is simple: Without that variety, there would be no play! It wouldn't interest you. If people saw that there was only one essence in everything—painting all the scenes, directing all the action, and acting all the parts—they would quickly tire of it. For 'the show to go on' there has to be activity, interest. It all has to *seem* real. Hence this appearance of individuality.

"As long as man enjoys the play for its own sake, he will go on birth after birth, experiencing life's pleasures and pains. The Bhagavad Gita describes it as a wheel, constantly turning.

"To get off the wheel, you have to desire freedom very intensely. Then only will God release you. Your longing has to be fervent. If it is, and if you are determined no more to want to play, the Lord *has* to release you. He tries to keep you here with tests, but in His higher aspect, as the Cosmic Lover, He hates this show, and wants you out of it. Why shouldn't He release you, once He sees that you really want Him alone, and not His show: that you want only freedom in Him?

"The same essence—conscious life—is in you and in that tree over there. The tree, however, was put there, whereas some free will on your part made you who and what you are. Only the wise know just where predestination ends and free will begins. Meanwhile, you must keep on doing your best, according to your own clearest understanding. You must long for freedom as the drowning man longs for air. Without sincere longing, you will never find God. Desire Him above everything else. Desire Him that you may share Him with all: That is the greatest wish.

"And try, meanwhile, to rise above the pairs of opposites: pleasure and pain, heat and cold, sickness and health. Free yourself from the consciousness of individuality, of being separate from everyone and everything else. Keep your mind fixed steadfastly on Him. Remain inwardly as unaffected as the motionless Spirit you want to become. *He alone* is what you really are. His bliss alone is your true nature."

❧ 11 ☙

Ted Krings, a new disciple, asked the Master, "Can you tell just by looking at a person how spiritually advanced he is?"

"At once!" replied the Master with a gentle laugh. "I don't talk about it, however. I see inside people, because that's my job. One who boasts that he knows these things, knows them not. And one who says he knows not, also knows them not! One who truly knows doesn't talk about it. Wisdom keeps its own counsel."

Master with a tiger skin. Advanced yogis sometimes meditate sitting on a tiger skin, a practice which they say heightens the sense of determination and self-control.

〜 12 〜

The Master was talking to a small group of disciples, of whom all were monks except one, an older nun. The Guru decided to have another nun summoned for the purposes of the discussion. I promptly offered to fetch her.

"You stay here!" He commanded me almost peremptorily. Turning to the nun who was present, he said, "*You* go get her."

When she'd left the room, he said to me, "Keep your distance, and they will always respect you."

For years, my assumption was that he'd meant only, "keep your distance *from women,* generally," since he taught that, also. The woman he wanted called, however, was someone in authority with whom, as he knew, I had often to discuss official matters. Lately, I've asked myself whether he wasn't foreseeing another kind of problem altogether between the two of us—one which did, in fact, arise some years later. For there was nothing between us to suggest even slightly the kind of attraction that can develop between men and women. The problem, however, when it did arise, might have been avoided had a greater mental distance been kept between us. What developed was a somewhat condescending attitude on her part toward me—a consequence, I now believe, of insufficient reserve between us.

13

Divorce is widely considered, by Christians, to be contrary to the teachings of Jesus Christ. In the Catholic Church it is not even permitted. In matters of this nature, however, affecting as they do a person's own life, one should be guided by intuition, and not only by church policies. This is to say, also, that one should inquire what the wise, rather than any mere institution, have said on the subject.

Paramhansa Yogananda did not see marriage as being necessarily "made in heaven," even when it had been blessed in a church. To him, the sanctity of marriage depends on the degree of a person's spiritual awareness.

The following story was one he told about Amelita Galli-Curci, the famous Italian opera singer, who was also his devoted student. It illustrates the importance of soul union, as opposed to merely institutional or legal sanction. This inner union was, to him, the true meaning of the ceremonial phrase in the marriage service, "Whom God hath joined together. . . ."

"Mme. Galli-Curci," the Master said, "was married first to a drunkard who, when he drank to excess, used to beat her. One day, he raised a chair to strike her. She looked him straight in the eye, with calm inner strength. Then she turned away, and walked out of his life forever.

"Years later, she married Homer Samuels, her accompanist. Theirs was a true soul-union."

Divorce, the Master felt, is not necessarily in conflict with spiritual law, or with the teachings of Jesus Christ. If marriage obstructs a person's spiritual development, it may be his spiritual duty to leave it. As the Indian scriptures teach, "If a lower duty conflicts with a higher one, it ceases to be a duty."

14

The Master wouldn't, as a rule, perform weddings if he saw that a couple were not suited to one another— though circumstances forced him, sometimes, to relent in this respect.

"A couple once came to me," he told us, "and asked me to marry them. I could see at once that they were unsuited to each other, so I refused their request.

"'Let's go, dear!' the man said angrily. [I remember with delight the Master's Bengali inflection as he imitated that word, wrathfully delivered: 'De-ahr!'] They'd reached the door when I added, 'Please allow me to give you this one piece of advice: Just don't kill each other!'

"'Let's get out, de-ahr!' the man repeated furiously. He thought I was deliberately insulting them.

"Well, two months later they returned. 'Thank God you sent us away with that warning!' they cried. 'If it hadn't been for that, we might well have ended up killing each other!'

"They hadn't realized what a cauldron of rage boiled within them. Marriage removed the lid from that pot. The steam, once let out, scalded them."

⋇ 15 ⋇

The subject of vows is quite subtle; it depends above all on inner *intention*. More is involved also, however. I mentioned "other circumstances," above, that sometimes forced the Master to perform a marriage of which he didn't really approve. A good example springs to mind: a couple whose wedding the Master regretted, for he saw it would block the man's spiritual development. Yet the Master himself performed their wedding ceremony. Why, one may ask, did he do that?

There are two answers. First, he wanted them to know that they had his blessing no matter what, and even though they were acting in opposition to his will.

Second, by emphasizing strongly, in the vows he had them take, their continued loyalty above all to God and Guru, and by virtually insisting that the man repeat that vow despite his clear reluctance to do so, the

Master sought to implant in their consciousness a deeper commitment to God. He must have seen that their marriage would cause the man, in the future, to turn away from him, and even to try (ineffectively, as it turned out) to damage him with a lawsuit. The Master wanted to save his disciple from the serious sin of betraying his guru. Thus, he got him to affirm his divine loyalty. Knowing, moreover, that the betrayal was karmically possible, he wanted to sow deeply in the man's consciousness an awareness of where his highest duty lay.

16

On the subject of vows, there is more to be said also. To some extent, obviously, the Master saw vows as an affirmation. One of the monks, who had come to the Master while very young, was a sweet, simple soul, deeply devoted to the Guru. The Master showed him special love, in response to his purity of heart. One day, however, a sister of this boy, who also lived at Mount Washington, found the Master deeply sad.

"What's the matter, Master?" she inquired anxiously.

"Your brother is going to leave this path," was the reply. As I understand the story, it was not necessarily in the boy's karma to leave. Rather, it was mass karma that drew him downward, as if into a vortex, for lack of sufficient resolve on his own part. His weakness was that he depended too heavily on others' good will.

This boy once told me, in a somewhat puzzled tone, "Master had me repeat my vows of renunciation and discipleship to him—he even did it more than once!"

The interesting point here is that the Master knew the boy was going to break his vows. Obviously, what he wanted was to help this disciple to affirm his spiritual commitment, hoping that the affirmation itself would at least strengthen his future understanding. Whether or not the attempt worked, I don't know. I, too, was anxious for the boy's future, for I knew him to be sincere and goodhearted. Evidently the Master felt there was still a chance to avert that negative karma, which must not have been strong in him.

Master said once, "I saw this young man laughing superficially with some of the other men one day. Later I told him, 'This is the first time you have cut off my vibrations by your lightness.' I wanted to see him become stronger in himself."

After the boy left, he became a policeman. This was consonant with his need for inner strength. Later—it can only have been under the influence of others—he became a Christian fundamentalist of the kind that would never, I imagine, accept the Master. I never heard from the man directly, but I cannot believe he lost the love he felt for the Master in his heart. And at least—in fact, importantly—he made a spiritual, not a worldly, choice, even if his church affiliation took him into a narrower vision.

17

In another story in connection with vows, one of the younger monks pleaded with the Master to give him the vows of *brahmacharya* (renunciation). Several others joined him later in the brief ceremony. The Master was clearly not happy about it.

"You must take this vow very seriously," he said, "Remember, God is here; He is listening to you. Some of you will fall. When you break this vow, because you took it here today, all the forces will be upon you. The responsibility is yours, not mine. Don't take this event lightly. Please, heed what I say."

The Master saw those vows, in other words, as more than a mere affirmation. Spoken before him, and administered by him, they had the power either to uplift or to destroy—destroy not in an eternal sense, to be sure, but in the sense of attracting great suffering to the failed disciple.

One thinks again, however, of that young man he'd had repeat his vows more than once, knowing that he would break them. Was it in reaffirmation of vows he had already taken, earlier? Or was the Master trying to hold the disciple to a soul-commitment, hoping that it would be reawakened, years later?

Sister Gyanamata, the Master's most advanced woman disciple, once stated in a letter that a master doesn't try to spare his disciples suffering, if it can be a means, eventually, of helping them toward their ultimate attainment of God.

Strange are God's ways, and strange the ways of a God-realized master.

Never, however, will God turn his back on the devotee, so long as he keeps on trying. "As often as you fail," the Master used to say, "get up and try again. God will never let you down, so long as you don't let Him down, and so long as you make the effort." What he saw in some of those monks, I think, was that they would fail in their *intention*. He wanted to spare them the suffering that would be consequent on that failure.

✣ 18 ✣

To return to Mme. Galli-Curci, the Master said, "I was talking with her one day, and she said to me with conviction, 'I have no desires!' A little while later, however, she remarked enthusiastically, 'In heaven, I will sing and sing!' I commented with a chuckle, 'Didn't you just tell me you have no desires?'

"The sense of being a separate, egoic self," he explained on other occasions, "begins with the astral, not with the physical, body. The soul is individualized spirit. It comes into separate existence with the causal body, when the universal 'I' first conceives this particular expression of itself. The soul then energizes that expression, clothing it first in an astral body of light. When, further, it assumes a physical body, its appearance of individuality becomes—though still only in appearance—fixed and permanent.

"People who think to merge into the Infinite by committing suicide only break their outer shell temporarily. They are still locked in the ego, which is implanted in the astral body and is the source of all their troubles. They must return, ego-bound, to the material plane, burdened additionally with their karmic sin. Self-murder is a greater sin even than murder, for it springs from a desire to destroy not only another person's right to live, but life itself. One can never succeed in this attempt. Life is God. And God is life."

~ 19 ~

Concerning Mme. Galli-Curci, again, I once asked the Master, "How is she faring, spiritually?"

"She is soaring in God," he replied blissfully.

~ 20 ~

The Master had me join him on a number of occasions when he was receiving guests. One visitor came several times, always with great enthusiasm. When it came to learning the teachings, however, his exuberance was less in evidence. The Master asked me to instruct him in the techniques, but after this man had missed several appointments and hadn't even explained the reason for his absence, I decided that what he was interested in was more the glamour of being with the Master than absorbing the substance of the teachings.

"He isn't sincere," I said to the Master the next time this man had scheduled a visit.

The Master smiled. "Well, we'll have fun today!" was his only comment. What followed was the usual enthusiasm on the visitor's part, and the Master's smiling acceptance of him for who he was. I'm afraid that, for my part, I was far from being so accepting.

Later, the Master remarked to me, "How dry you

were toward him! How many would be left here, if I had behaved toward all of you that way—so unforgivingly?" Throughout that man's long life, in fact, he retained toward the Master, in a rather unusual fashion, the attitude of a devoted disciple.

❧ 21 ☙

On the importance of attunement, the Master once remarked, "When I help somebody, I forget everything else. If one wants to benefit spiritually, however, he must do what I say.

"Look at Bernard. For years I had him doing all that heavy work in his frail body, and he thrived." (Bernard had only one lung, and double curvature of the spine.) "He built that large dome-tower in Encinitas, and even that hard work didn't hurt him.

"Then he began thinking that so much hard labor was too much for his body, and asked to be relieved of it. I did as he asked. I gave him a large, comfortable room, and got it fixed up especially for him. And yet, look at him: He keeps on getting worse!

"You have to be in tune with Guru, and do what he says. If, then, you risk even being hurt working for God, He will protect you."

These words of the Master's must be seen in the

context of his spiritual power. He himself told me, in speaking of his Ranchi school, that he used sometimes to lead the boys above a dangerous waterfall. "Do you believe in God?" he would cry loudly. "Yes!" came the shouted reply. No one was ever hurt. The Master related to me, however, an unfortunate sequel to that story:

"Years later, after I'd come to America, one of the teachers tried to do the same thing: He took boys over the waterfall as I had done. He lacked spiritual power, however. One of the boys slipped, and fell to his death.

"True faith," the Master concluded, "comes only from actual spiritual experience. It cannot be presumed."

To return to Bernard, he was very sincere. For years, he followed the Master faithfully. After some time, however, concern for his own physical well-being—and even more so, I'm afraid, a growing self-assurance on his part that, in practical matters, he knew more than the Master (a self-assessment that, as was obvious to me, was entirely illusory)—caused him to withdraw proudly into his own ego. The sad ending to his story is that he fell, spiritually, and left both the Guru and the teachings. I had noticed earlier, to my regret, that the more Bernard opened himself to other lines of thinking from the Master's, the farther he withdrew onto a kind of mental peak. Finally, he grew attuned entirely to worldly ways, with their unceasing emphasis on the ego. Bernard's thinking became twisted to conform with those ways. Truly, as the Master wrote in *Autobiography of a Yogi* (quoting his guru), a keen intelligence is a two-edged sword. It can be used either to lance the boil of ignorance, or to decapitate oneself.

22

Several of the monks were reading the lives of saints. At this time, the Master gave us the following recommendation as to what we should read of those lives:

"Read the lives only of those in our own line: Saint Francis of Assisi, for example, and Saint Teresa of Avila."

His expression, "those who are in our own line," was one I pondered for a long time. The Master could not have meant, "those who are directly connected with our line of gurus," for we'd have had no way of knowing who such persons were. He could only have been referring, then, to saints who had attained deep states of inner communion with God. Not all saints, certainly, even among those canonized by the Church, belong in this higher category.

⟡ 23 ⟡

"A visitor," the Master told us, "asked me yesterday, 'Who made God?' Many ask that question. That is because they live in the realm of causation. Everything, to their way of thinking, must have a cause since that is how everything happens in this world. God, however, is the Supreme Cause. He has no need of being caused, or created. He is the very cause of causation. The truth is, nothing is really *created* anyway! The Spirit simply *manifests* the universe. Ultimately, nothing causes anything, for nothing, in actuality, is even happening!"

⟡ 24 ⟡

The Master was reminiscing with me about his early years in America. "Ralph," he said, "was a man who chauffeured me on my first cross-country lecture tour. There was another driver with us also, Arthur Cometer, who was a good and sincere devotee." (Mr. Cometer visited Mount Washington shortly before the end of Master's life. I had an opportunity to meet him there.) "Ralph, on the other hand," continued the Master, "was arrogant and had a skeptical nature. When he drove on country roads, he would go out of his way to run over rabbits, killing them. He refused to listen when I asked him to stop doing so. I then warned him, 'You'll draw a severe karmic lesson for the heartless slaughter you are committing.'

"'Oh yeah, prophet?' he sneered. 'Leave off! I'm having a good time.'

"'You'll see,' I repeated, very seriously. 'Your action is an offense against karmic law.'

"One day, all of a sudden, I ordered him to stop. So firm was my tone of voice that he obeyed. The car had barely come to a halt when a wheel rolled off. It had been working itself loose; if we hadn't stopped just at that moment, we would have had a serious accident. After this experience, Ralph stopped his sadistic 'entertainment.'

"Because of Ralph's skepticism, I played up to it, hoping to draw this delusion out of him. Before giving a lecture, for example, I would primp, combing my hair with exaggerated care, and pretending in other ways to be inordinately vain.

"Whoever comes to me finds me a mirror to whatever is in his heart. Thus, I try to help him to see qualities in himself that he needs to overcome. In Ralph's case, I wanted to bring out his vanity so he could see it clearly and work to overcome it."

From my (Walter's) understanding of this account, the end of Ralph's story may have to await telling at a future date, for, so far as I know, he played no further role in the Master's life. I did, however, see the Master

38

sometimes play up to people's delusions, exaggerating them in order to bring them to a head and thereby free those people of their errors. In some cases, the healing process took a very long time. I remember him telling one disciple, "I lost sight of you for a few incarnations." He then added a deeply inspiring promise: "But I will never lose sight of you again."

Reflecting also on the unusual promptness with which Ralph attracted his karmic retribution, I realize that the Master had simply allowed the karmic law to operate without what he called, in *Autobiography of a Yogi,* in referring to Trailanga Swami, the "thwarting crosscurrents of ego."

It is against karmic law to take life in any form with deliberate intent and without cause, especially for mere pleasure. People who engage in what they like to call the "sport" of hunting would do well to reflect on this truth. How innumerable, indeed, are the lessons implicit in the least words and actions of a great master!

✧ 25 ✧

Paramhansa Yogananda demonstrated no respectful solemnity toward religious practices that he considered false or merely emotional, rather than devotional. Indeed, he could make very merry at their expense. He once told us, laughing, about a "holy roller" gathering he had witnessed.

"There they all were, fat ladies, old men, all rolling about on the floor in their zeal. They thought they were being inspired by the Holy Ghost, but what really moved them was the 'unholy ghost' of emotions! Devotion must be internalized. When it is allowed to flow outward, it becomes emotion. Emotional devotion, by its very exuberance, takes one further into delusion. Excitement only extinguishes the lamp of pure love.

"God, too," he commented, "has a sense of humor! All men are His children, but why shouldn't He have fun when He sees them acting comically?"

⚡ 26 ⚡

"There was a preacher many years ago in Harlem," the Master told me. "He was well known as 'Father Divine.' Father Divine once wrote me a letter suggesting that we 'team up.' He signed his letter, 'I am healthy, energetic, and happy in every muscle, bone, molecule, AND ATOM!' Those last two words he underlined vigorously three times. His official chair, I was informed, bore the word 'GOD' carved across the back!" The Master chuckled in amusement at the memory.

Yogananda at the Palace of Fine Arts in San Francisco, California.

ᔥᐧᕉ 27 ᕉᐨᕽ

Concerning orthodox religion in America, the Master said, "It needs improvement. Its present focus is on training the ministers intellectually. They learn to speak well, but don't meditate or try to attain spiritual realization. In our churches, the ministers are committed above all to their own Self-realization. When I appoint someone a minister, I look first to see what degree of spiritual progress he made in a former life."

The Master then declared very seriously, "We are on the eve of a great change in the churches. Real seekers will go there. The church will become a spiritual laboratory, where people will be encouraged to test the teachings they receive, and to judge for themselves what works and what doesn't work, instead of accepting emotional declarations of untested dogmas."

ᔥᐧᕉ 28 ᕉᐨᕽ

The Master was standing out of doors at Mount Washington with a small group of us, discoursing at length on spiritual matters. At a certain point he looked at me and said, "Hey, Walter! Write that down. I've never said that before." What follows is, as nearly as I could recall, what he'd just finished saying:

"In meditation, you must go beyond thought. As long as you are busy thinking, you are in your rational mind, on the conscious plane. When you sleep and dream, you are on the subconscious plane, and in your astral body. And when your mind is fully withdrawn in superconsciousness, it becomes centered in the bliss of the spine. You are then in your ideational, or causal, body. That is the level of the soul."

29

In lectures, the Master would sometimes address a question people often ask concerning the nature, and even the existence, of evil, and its purpose in the great scheme of things. "There needs to be a villain," he explained, "so that people will be inspired to love the hero. If you act the villain's part, however, you will have to suffer his punishment.

"Joseph Stalin," he continued, "was one such villain. [The name *Stalin* means *steel*. Stalin's actual name at birth was, Yosif Vissarionovich Djugashvili.] I had an opportunity once to meet his former chauffeur, who told me, 'When I was driving Stalin, I would often hear him repeat with great firmness the affirmation, "I am Stalin! I am Stalin! I am steel!"'

"For the bad karma he acquired in this life, and also

in previous lives, he will have to suffer a hundred thousand years."

On several occasions the Master told us, "Stalin, in a recent incarnation, was the ruthless conqueror Genghis Khan."

Debi Mukherjee, a Bengali disciple, responded to the Master's prediction regarding Stalin's punishment for past sins by exclaiming, "Only so long, Master?" (As if a hundred thousand years were nothing at all!)

"How long do you want someone to suffer?" asked the Master. "God is no tyrant. He loves all His children equally."

30

The Master responded to people according to the energy they projected. Often what they projected, and the way he responded, were very subtle. He once refused the application to the monastery of a young man who, some of the monks felt, was very sincere. "If you could see his karma!" was all the Master said.

❦ 31 ❧

"I usually know when God wants me to save some-one," he said. "I then show particular interest. If that person doesn't respond, I accept it as God's will [that is to say, as that person's non-acceptance of God's will]. But if he accepts the help God extends to him through me, I know he will be saved. God teaches through those who love Him purely and have surrendered themselves completely to Him. The end of every person's story, however, depends on that person himself. Everyone has the sacred right of free will."

❦ 32 ❧

In the above connection, I remember the Master one afternoon devoting a considerable amount of time to a casual visitor. He answered all the young man's questions, and gave him more words of advice than I'd ever heard him share with a newcomer before. As far as I know, the man never returned. My "reading" of that situation was that the man felt in his heart, and indeed demonstrated outwardly, a certain openness to the Master's vibrations, but after his departure worldly desires reawakened within him, enclosing him once again in the fog of delusion. Delusion it is that causes people to cling to their old "comfortable" ways of thinking and living.

Still, the Master must have seen in that visitor some potential for awakening, for it was never his way to speak of these matters casually.

The minds of most human beings are like the sky on a partly cloudy day. The mental clouds may part for a time, and let in the sunlight of clarity, but unless those people deliberately seek out the bright spots and bask in their warmth, the clouds close in again, and hide behind mists of worldly karma the sunlight of clarity.

⟡ 33 ⟡

Some of the monks at Mount Washington once sent a petition to the Master, requesting a change in their diet. They asked that their food be more "scientific." They submitted their demand, unfortunately, in a spirit of self-righteousness.

It must be admitted that the diet could have been improved. It was excessively starchy, and emphasized heavily such foods as macaroni and cheese. The Master's answer, however, was scornful.

"You have given your lives to God," he said. "As devotees, you should not worry about what you eat. Be concerned, instead, that your love for God be deep enough."

❧ 34 ☙

The Master was, at various times, either lenient or
severe in his training. Since the goal of the spiritual life
is the perfection of bliss in God, he didn't want us to
develop a grim attitude. "Always remain in the Self," he
counseled me one day. "Come down, as necessary, to
eat or talk a little bit; then withdraw into the Self again."

At the same time, I recall asking him, when I was
new on the path, to bless me that I overcome my liking
for good food. With an indulgent smile he replied,
"There is so little outwardly that you, as a yogi, can legit-
imately enjoy that you might as well enjoy what you eat!

"When ecstasy comes," he added, "everything goes."

What he counseled us to do was ever-increasingly to
develop inner non-attachment. "Be even-minded and
cheerful," he would say to us, adding, "What comes of
itself, let it come." That advice embraced both the
happy and the sorrowful experiences of life. "Refer
every joy and even pleasure back to the joy of the inner
Self," he said, "and let every sorrow remind you that
your home is not here, in the world of sensory experiences, but in the eternal joy of the soul.

"Don't worry about the little things," he said also. It
is, I believe, clear from the above that what he was
scolding in those monks' demand for a better diet was
their *self-righteous attitude,* more than their request for

better food. For him, however, it must have been a consideration also that it was no easy matter to feed, clothe, and house a constantly growing family of monks and nuns.

35

"A visitor to Mount Washington Estates," the Master told us, "once inquired of me superciliously, 'What are the assets of this organization?'

"'None!' I promptly replied. 'Only God.'

"Divine Mother once told me, 'Those to whom I give too much, I do not give Myself.'"

36

1949 saw a worldwide "stir" of recent sightings of "flying saucers," or UFOs (unidentified flying objects). The newspapers generally made light of the reports, but Paramhansa Yogananda's brief comment was: "What people have seen is true. Those phenomena are not imaginary."

About interplanetary travel, he once said, "Modern man thinks that everything must be accomplished by physical force. There are many subtler forces in Nature.

These will come to light as the general sensitivity of man becomes more refined. Someday it will be a simple matter to travel from Earth to Mars, or to other planets. If man can progress from the bullock-cart method of traveling to flying at hundreds of miles an hour, it will be easy for him, in future, to find ways of locomotion that will take him, like electricity, from planet to planet."

❧ 37 ❧

"The universe," he once commented, "is teeming with life. Even what people think of as 'barren' planets are manifestations of consciousness, and therefore are not really 'dead.' God's consciousness is at the heart of every atom, ever seeking to express itself outwardly. All life gradually evolves toward outward expression. Materialistic science believes that life appears only by accident, out of a mere combination of chemicals. Spiritual 'science,' however, discovered long ago that, at the heart of everything, dwells the infinite consciousness."

✿ 38 ✿

In Los Angeles—perhaps during the month of February, 1951—there was a succession of unusually heavy rains. One day the Master commented, "Well, this is better, at least, than worlds where it is always raining, or where the sun never stops shining."

✿ 39 ✿

All creation, he taught—and as the Bhagavad Gita states also—is a mixture of the three *gunas,* or basic qualities of consciousness. The lowest of them is *tamo guna* (the darkening quality). Next comes *rajo guna* (the activating quality). The highest of the three is *sattwa guna* (the spiritually clarifying, or elevating, quality). The universe everywhere manifests predominantly one or another of these qualities. Indeed, the Master told us that entire galaxies manifest primarily one or another *guna.* I must paraphrase here, for although I am quoting, my recollection of his actual words is somewhat vague:

"There are entire galaxies where *tamas* predominates. The inhabitants of the planets in those galaxies are for the most part brutish and incapable of aspiring to spiritual heights. Fierce animals abound there, and cannibalism. The inhabitants are constantly in a state of conflict and warfare. Lust and every animal pleasure are considered the best that life has to offer.

"Again, there are galaxies where *rajo guna* predominates. The planets in them are peopled by more self-aware beings, whose primary concern is with self-advancement, self-aggrandizement, and self-importance. Our own 'Milky Way' galaxy is such a system."

I (Walter) should interject here the personal supposition that this Earth, situated as it is near the outskirts of our galaxy, may receive less of the spiritual power that Swami Sri Yukteswar said emanates from the galactic center. Thus, we on Earth may be even more *rajasic* than the majority of those rajasic planets, which are closer to the center.

"There are, finally," the Master continued, "entire galaxies where *sattwa guna* predominates. The planets there resemble legends of the Garden of Eden. The people there can communicate easily with beings in the astral world. Harmony and beauty are prevalent everywhere.

"One should always bear in mind, however, that whatever the predominating *guna,* intelligent beings are still confined in their egos. Perfection cannot be attained except in the infinite Self. For that true Self, the ego is a prison. The soul's eternal longing is ever, and never ceases to be, for freedom and perfect Bliss. The infinite Self not only permeates all manifested existence, but lies beyond all manifestation and is its ultimate cause.

"Even to contemplate the cosmic vastness is expansive to the mind. Dwell always on the thought that, in your true Self, you are infinite and eternal! Memorize also my poem, 'Samadhi.' Repeat it every day, when you meditate."

ᗡᑎ 40 ᑎᗡ

The history of the world is very different from the version official archeology presents. As Swami Sri Yukteswar, Yogananda's Guru, explained, the Earth passes through great cycles of time as the solar system's position changes relative to our galactic center, and to certain so-called "fixed" stars. The galaxy itself rotates very slowly—if a hundred and seventy miles a second can be called "slow"!—over a period of 200 million years. The sun, again, as Sri Yukteswar explained, moves in orbit around a dual. This dual has yet to be discovered by modern astronomy, but so many other facts he claimed have been verified since his book, *The Holy Science,* was published in 1894 that one would be safe, I believe, in accepting his explanation in its entirety.

The time required for the sun to orbit around its dual is, Sri Yukteswar stated, approximately 24,000 years. The general level of human consciousness changes according to the sun's position, during this orbit, relative to both its dual and the galactic center.

Swami Sri Yukteswar found, by careful study, and also by deep intuitive perception, that major errors had crept into the Hindu almanacs during a time when the earth was passing through the darkest of four ages, called *Kali Yuga*. During that period, human awareness was at its dimmest. We are now ascending again, he said, toward increasingly clear understanding and sensitivity.

This fascinating claim corresponds with many more-recently discovered facts in astronomy and physics, and also with known facts of human history. The whole concept cannot be explained here at length, for it is incidental to the subject of this book, but it is important enough to our theme to merit at least brief explanation. It figured largely, though sometimes only as a backdrop, in what the Master taught. For more information, the reader is referred to Sri Yukteswar's book, *The Holy Science,* and to Paramhansa Yogananda's *Autobiography of a Yogi.* Byasa Steinmetz is also writing a whole book on this subject. Suffice it here, then, to point out a few of the many corroborations of Sri Yukteswar's discovery. In terms of mankind's increasing awareness, these include:

1. man's ever-broadening perception of the universe, which, before the Twentieth Century, was limited to a relatively small star system of which our own sun was, until the 1920s, considered the center;

2. the discovery, at the beginning of the Twentieth Century, that matter is a vibration of energy, and

people's growing awareness and acceptance, since then, of this fact;

3. man's rapidly increasing ability to banish space by rapid travel and instant communication—a capacity that has been increasing exponentially since the beginning of the Twentieth Century;

4. people's growing awareness—since the development of radio communication and airplane travel, and man's ability to leave the atmosphere of the earth and move into outer space—that our planet is relatively small, and that we need to find ways of living together in global harmony;

5. the rapid increase in human awareness, especially since the start of the Twentieth Century, of realities—radio and television waves, for example—that are subtler than sensory perception;

6. a growing dissatisfaction with anything that merely *seems* reasonable, but that lacks the support of either experience or experiment, and an increasing tendency to challenge all *a priori* assumptions and dogmas;

7. an awareness, rapidly becoming worldwide, that the goal of all religions is personal enlightenment, rather than some merely outward, social upliftment.

The *descending* dark age of *Kali Yuga* lasted 1,200 years, ending in the year 500 A.D. It was succeeded by an *ascending* dark age—the same *yuga* in reverse—lasting another 1,200 years. This ascending *Kali Yuga* ended in the year 1700 A.D., since when there have been countless developments throughout the world, including the following:

1. a revolution toward the use of labor-saving machinery, and toward private enterprise, which replaced a basically agrarian and landholding, or so-called aristocratic, society;

2. the discovery, and the increasingly widespread use, of electricity;

3. the growing use of atomic power;

4. a complete revolution in man's ways of thinking, and a perception of the universe as no longer earth-centered, but far, far vaster than even a single star system, as well as a perception of reality that is, essentially, non-personal.

5. countless revolutionary discoveries, previously unimaginable, including radio, television, electronics, laser surgery, and other breakthroughs in every field— so many, indeed, that it would be impossible to list them all, even if one tried.

This new age, named *Dwapara Yuga,* began in the year 1700. *Kali Yuga* ended with a hundred-year "twilight," or interval, between the years 1600 and 1700, during which time the discoveries of Galileo, Newton, and others were made, heralding already the coming new perceptions of reality.

Dwapara began with a *two*-hundred-year "dawn," or interval of adjustment to the new cosmic rays. It became fully expressed in the year 1900, and will last another 2,200 years. The centuries immediately before us will be increasingly characterized by a general awareness of, and command over, the forces of energy.

So different from its predecessor is the age we now live in that people's thinking is already being affected on every level of their lives. Realities that once appeared to be fixed and immutable are perceived, now, as endlessly mutable. It is possible today at least to envision a loaf of bread being "dissolved" into the energy of which it is a manifestation, and remanifested as a bar of gold.

In religion, theology-dominated churches, with their rigidly formed systems and dogmas, are yielding increasingly to a more flexible view of truth. *Kali Yuga* consciousness is gradually fading, as night fades to dawn and then daylight. With this change, man is beginning to consider his former anthropomorphic concepts of God as too droll to be taken seriously.

It was only recently, in the Twentieth Century, that the Roman Catholic Church "forgave" Galileo for his claim that the earth moves around the sun rather than the opposite. In 1633, the Church had condemned him for heresy. The differences between science and religion are being perceived less and less as absolute. Church dogmas, of which a prime example is the Christian Trinity, are no longer so tightly "packaged" as to exclude any possibility of a broader, more universal explanation. Can the "Father" really be a human figure, like that bearded Creator whom Michelangelo depicted on the ceiling of the Sistine Chapel, in Rome? Can the "Son" really be someone who lived only thirty-three years on this little mud ball of a planet, in a universe so vast as to be no longer conceivable? And can the "Holy Ghost" really be, as I've seen it depicted, another young man, seated reposefully on a stone wall?

Mahatma Gandhi, by means of the song *Ram Dhun,* popularized the concept in India that Ishwara (a Hindu name for God) and Allah (the Moslem name) are appellations for the same Supreme Deity. Paramhansa Yogananda showed that the Christian Trinity has its counterpart in the Hindu term, *AUM-TAT-SAT.* He explained that both stand for cosmic realities.

A growing number of people today are finding it absurd to think that a universe containing at least a hundred billion galaxies, each one with some hundred billion stars, can have been brought into existence by an anthropomorphic Deity. Everywhere the question is asked, "Isn't it possible that every religion worships the same God, and aspires to the same lofty truths?" No longer is there a general willingness, today, to accept what was long held as the justification for all dogmas: "It *ought* to be true: therefore it *must be* true." The elegance of a theory has ceased to be its supreme justification. The question asked increasingly is, "Does it work?"

Because our present entry into a new age was fundamental to much of what Paramhansa Yogananda taught, I have included this discussion here, making it as brief as possible. New ideas always encounter resistance before they are generally accepted. The very concept of cycles of history is foreign to the West. Even in the East, where it has long been accepted, it is new as Swami Sri Yukteswar explained it. In India, the entrenched notion is that the world is at the beginning of a long descent into an ever-darker *Kali Yuga,* expected to last another 430,000 years!

In March of 1900, Sri Yukteswar organized a procession through the streets of the city of Serampore, Bengal, announcing the advent of the new age of *Dwapara.* Certain bystanders actually protested by throwing stones! Even today, it is difficult to get his unorthodox explanation widely accepted in India. The resistance in that country is on dogmatic grounds.

In the West, the objection is more to the fact that Sri Yukteswar's astronomical explanations do not correspond in every respect to the modern scientific perception of the universe. Yet his claims are supported by an ever-growing body of scientific evidence.

The first objection modern astronomers make is to his claim that a dual exists to our sun. Numerous other stars in our galaxy, however, have been found to exist in pairs. The possibility that our own sun has a dual is not dismissed in modern astronomy, and has actually come under discussion by serious scientists in recent years.

The second objection in modern astronomy is Sri

Yukteswar's identification of the sun's revolution around a dual with the phenomenon known as the "precession of the equinox." His explanation is at variance with scientific orthodoxy, which states that this precession is due to a wobble in the earth's axis.

It seems premature to be too dogmatic about anything science claims, since it has had too often to revise even some of its basic tenets. There seems little point, therefore, in insisting strongly that these two differences must be resolved before Sri Yukteswar's "theory" can be given a respectful hearing, especially since some of his even more startling claims have been completely justified, after the fact, by modern science. For what he wrote in 1894 was at variance with numerous other beliefs of the scientific orthodoxy of his day, yet on these points he has since been thoroughly justified.

1. Sri Yukteswar wrote—in 1894—that matter is really energy. This fact was discovered by science only eleven years later, in 1905.

2. Sri Yukteswar described a distant center for the visible stars. The astronomers of his time still believed the universe to be heliocentric; they continued to hold this belief until the 1920s.

3. Sri Yukteswar correctly stated that the sun moves. The scientists of his day had no such idea, supposing it to be standing stationary at the center of everything.

4. Sri Yukteswar also described the sun's movement as a sweeping arc, its present direction being toward the

center of our star system. Astronomers have since discovered, first of all, that the sun does move, and second, that its direction of movement is substantially as Sri Yukteswar claimed.

Sri Yukteswar's claim, of course, that human consciousness is affected by rays of energy proceeding from the center of our galaxy seems, to modern-day thinking, impossible of rational demonstration. Yet astronomers have in fact discovered that there *is* a powerful energy issuing from the center of our galaxy, which affects planets even as distant from it as our own. Subtle influences of an energetic and magnetic nature are being constantly discovered in science, a fact which suggests that all natural phenomena are in some way interconnected. This interrelationship was undreamed of even as recently as eighty years ago.

The facts most clearly known to us today concern the events of relatively recent earth history. They point to a steadily increasing enlightenment in every sphere of activity. Even the increasing licentiousness that is so evident today, which might point to a general moral and spiritual decline, seems even more explicable as being due to man's inner struggle to come to grips with so many new perceptions of reality.

In one of my books, *Out of the Labyrinth,* I have explained that the moral dilemma introduced by Einsteinian relativity, far from proving (as some writers have claimed) that moral values are subjective, is being resolved in a growing perception that *relativity is not chaotic, but directional.* The truths that are being perceived nowadays have been leading mankind toward ever subtler insights that seem, increasingly, to have universal validity.

This rapid advancement of knowledge during recent centuries, and especially today's increasingly widespread reliance on energy, suggest forcibly that what Sri Yukteswar wrote—and bear in mind that he was a great master with spiritual insight, and no merely intellectual theorist—should be considered no mere theory, but revelation.

Yogananda sometimes remarked, quite casually, that in future mankind would see innumerable changes in its way of thinking, living, and behaving: a change toward international and interreligious unity, interplanetary travel, and countless new ways of dealing with reality.

⚶ 41 ⚶

I once asked the Master, "Sir, as we progress into the higher *yugas* [ages], will the people now on earth continue to be reborn here?"

"No," he replied. "I've stated before that there are many populated planets in the universe. When a soul returns from the astral world to the material plane, there are many planets available to it. Where it reincarnates depends on its own level of spiritual development."

He added wryly, "If they always returned here, they might find out too soon!"

That last comment must seem strange to anyone who imagines God as eager for man to be redeemed. And, man thinks, how could He not want that, if He loves us? In this perception too, however, man's perception of the cosmic verities needs expansion. The truth is, the cosmos was designed by God. His plan was for us not to "find out too soon"—that is, realize our need to return to our Source in God until we decide to do so of our own free will.

Many incentives are given us, outwardly, to inspire us to seek a higher reality. There are Nature's countless beauties. There is the amazing adaptability and precision evident in the natural order: the signs of a mighty, guiding Intelligence. And there are inspiring qualities in human nature, which sensitive people, as they become aware of them, want to develop in themselves.

On the negative side, the incentives are suffering, and the repeated disappointment of all worldly hopes. The ignoble qualities in human nature, also, cause anyone of refinement to repudiate such qualities in himself as base and ugly, and to aspire to the spiritual heights within.

There are, of course, also many incentives for continuing to play in delusion. The divine spark within man must be kindled by his own personal longing for the truth, and not by mind-numbing proofs of God's existence. The Lord wants each individual to desire Him alone. Salvation is not served on a silver platter by smiling angels. Each person must strive by arduous effort to become worthy of it. The self-sacrifice demanded of those who seek truth is perceived at last as being no sacrifice at all, but the eternal fulfillment of perfect bliss. First, however, one must accept joyfully that nothing, anywhere in this world, exists that is worth the seeking.

The thought that this earth can ever be perfected is, finally, one of man's greatest delusions. What this world is, simply, is a school through which the soul passes on its upward evolution. As in any school, one can also "flunk out" of it and move downward for lower education elsewhere, in order to become better grounded in what life is really all about.

Perfection is, in other words, an ideal to be sought for the benefit of the students, not of the school. Were this school, our earth, to complete its educative purpose, by means at present unimaginable, it would mean simply that souls still in need of its instruction would have to be "enrolled" elsewhere. No outward improvement will ever guarantee a corresponding improvement of the individual. Ultimately, man's betterment depends, always, on his own recognition of his need for it.

᠁ 42 ᠁

Of India's riches in a higher age, the Master once told me, "In those days, people used to eat off of golden plates, then cast them into the Ganges. Such was their wealth. And such is the rise and fall of civilizations.

"Never be attached," he then said, "to the passing scenes of life."

᠁ 43 ᠁

One night, those living near the Master's apartment at Mount Washington heard a loud sound of clanking metal. The following morning they learned the cause of that tumult.

At this point, I must back up a space. The Master had told some of his disciples that he had lived, centuries ago, as a military commander in Spain. His divinely appointed task at that time had been to help liberate that country from the Moors, in order to protect the integrity of Christianity. The noise that previous night had been caused by a Spanish soldier who had been under his command at that time. He had materialized in full armor to ask for the Master's blessing that he be released—in what way, I've no idea. From what I understand, the Master gave him the release he sought.

In the present lifetime, the Master knew no Spanish. I remember him greeting me once, however, with a big smile, in Spanish. Señor Cuaron was visiting Mount Washington from Mexico City. What the Master said was, *"Cuál es su nombre?"* (What is your name?) I answered in Spanish, upon which the three of us had a good laugh.

44

Several of the monks at Mount Washington had read a book claiming that certain masters from ancient Lemuria (a continent said to have existed in ancient times in the south Pacific) still lived inside Mt. Shasta near the northern California border. Intrigued, a little group planned to travel north and see if they could meet these legendary people. (How strange, I thought, that even though they were living with a true master, they could entertain such a fantasy! To me, their curiosity seemed merely a mark of inner restlessness.)

When the Master heard of their plan, he told them, "There are no masters living there." He added an interesting comment: "There *have* been colonists. However, no masters." That final comment intrigued me— not because I felt any personal attraction to going there, but as a possibility for future investigation on someone's part.

❧ 45 ❧

Several of the monks persuaded me—against my will, as it happened—to go with them to a spiritual movie. They were so eager for my company that I finally relented.

"That's wonderful!" they exclaimed. "Now then, would you please ask Master for his permission?" I realized at once, of course, why they'd been so anxious for my company! I did ask him, and he gave his consent, albeit reluctantly.

"Don't waste your time going to movies," he told us. "Even when the movie concerns the life of a saint, it must be filtered through those who write it, then through the director and the producer, and finally through the (usually) far-from-saintly actors. What comes out in the end is a very diluted, and even distorted, version of the true story."

❧ 46 ❧

I once inquired of him, "Do many Christian monks and nuns attain high spiritual levels?"

"Very few," he replied. "Of those who do, moreover, almost none reach the heights achieved by the great yogis of India.

"Monks and nuns generally find inner peace as a consequence of their renunciation. Christian monastics, however, are not encouraged by their orders to seek spiritual realization. Few reach it, therefore, unless they were born with already very good spiritual karma from the past.

"The problem is, the approach in those monasteries is negative. It is what I call the 'bullock cart' method of seeking God: plodding along with earnest petitions for redemption, but without any understanding of how one can assist in the process. Kriya Yoga, by contrast, is the 'airplane route,' for it teaches the seeker how to withdraw his energy into the spine, and then to direct it up the spine to the brain. By following this inner route, one cooperates with the way divine grace actually works. In this way, one can achieve realization much more quickly."

From these words, and from others that I heard from him occasionally, I came to understand that orthodox Christian monks and nuns, by their concentration on attaining "perfection" outwardly by such matters as "comportment," miss the true point of the spiritual path, which is to seek deep, inner communion with God. Even the practice of kneeling, though an outward gesture of humility, prevents the inward withdrawal of energy and consciousness from the senses. This obstacle can be overcome by intense devotion, and may in fact help to fan an attitude of humility, but it poses an unnecessary obstruction to the inwardness so necessary to divine contemplation.

Western monastic discipline approaches the question of perfection by suppressing one's natural inclinations. This may sometimes be correct, if the inclinations are harmful, but only if it is balanced by directing one's aspirations also positively, toward bliss.

Bliss, on the other hand, is no mere mental concept. It is God's very nature. We must *cooperate* with bliss, and not merely pray that it be given to us. We must not hope to be its merely passive recipients. Indeed, we should pray *with bliss*. Suppression, even of wrong desires, can easily result in blocked energy.

How many pitfalls there are on the spiritual path! Most of them the ego itself digs! Few spiritual aspirants, in either West or East, shine with that radiant inner glow which comes from the actual experience of divine love and bliss.

47

"What about monastic obedience?" a disciple once asked the Master.

"Obedience is important," he replied. "If it is given unconditionally, however, it should be given only to one who is wise—preferably to the guru, who is sent by

The Master blesses his disciple Rajarsi Janakananda at a
Kriya initiation in 1951.

God. Otherwise, obedience may actually weaken, not strengthen, the will. If the devotee suppresses his nature, instead of trying to expand it, he diminishes himself as a human being, with no corresponding increase of spiritual awareness.

"Wise guidance never violates people's free will. A superior who demands obedience of his subordinates should show respect for their capacity to understand, and also for their innate right to their own free will."

It seems to me (Walter), as I reflect on this advice, that subtly included in it also is the suggestion that obedience must be given *willingly* and *joyfully*. Indeed, the Master always said it should be. With that combination—willingness and joy—even if something one is asked to do conflicts with his own desires, and, more fundamentally, with his actual needs, obedience to others can help one to develop great spiritual strength. This felicitous result can be reached, however, only if one offers his every action to God. For the goal of the spiritual path is self-transcendence, not self-suppression. It implies, that is to say, ever-diminishing identification with the little ego, and ever-increasing expansion in infinity.

Ego-motivation, Paramhansa Yogananda taught, is the supreme obstacle on the spiritual path. The true benefit of obedience, for the devotee—leaving aside, that is to say, any question of benefit to an organization—is that it helps one to overcome attachment to littleness.

This is the negative, but ever necessary, side of renunciation. The positive side is its encouragement toward channeling all one's aspirations to God. The addition of a positive direction is essential. The prayerful plea that God do all one's redemptive work for one encourages passivity. One's will must be strengthened, rather than quashed. Never has there been a true saint whose will was flaccid.

After the Master's words on the contrast between the bullock cart and the airplane approaches to spiritual development, he added, "To attain spiritual realization, effective meditation techniques are necessary."

ᘏᘓᑑ 48 ᘔᘐᘏ

The Master did not belittle the importance, however, of bringing the ego "to heel." Often he even played with us, so to speak, to help us not to take the ego too seriously.

Once, he and Dr. Lewis spent the night in a hotel. The next morning both of them, with the Master's encouragement, went out of doors to practice the energization exercises. The layout of the hotel was such that these exercises would have to be done in full public view. Doctor Lewis was always the "proper Bostonian," and felt intensely sensitive to the social "proprieties." It embarrassed him, therefore, to be doing anything so unusual in public. The Master took this opportunity to help him conquer his exaggerated sensitivity. His way of doing so was, first, to *increase* his embarrassment!

A policeman walked by on his beat. The Master ducked hastily behind a pillar, as if anxious not to be seen. The man glanced over, but said nothing. A few minutes later he returned. Once again the Master stepped hastily behind the pillar. This time, the policeman stopped, his suspicions aroused. "What's going on here?" he demanded.

"Oh, *nothing,* Officer. Nothing at all!" The Master smiled winningly, as if anxious to convince the policeman of his complete innocence. "We're just exercising. See?" He repeated one or two movements as if in hope of a reprieve.

"Well," growled the policeman, "see that you don't get into trouble."

Doctor Lewis, who had been thinking he might die of shame, at last saw the fun of the situation, and accepted it with good humor. Often he related this story later on, to delighted audiences. Together, they always laughed heartily.

49

Sri Das, a man from India, was commissioned by the Master to teach on his behalf. Sri Das had a weakness, however: He was inordinately fond of women. The Master often scolded him for this shortcoming.

Sri Das was bald, and very sensitive on the point: He wanted the ladies to think him handsome. Master played on this sensitivity with a view to curing him of it. It wasn't the baldness itself the Master made fun of. Saint Lynn, for example, was also quite bald, and the Master never even alluded to the fact. He teased Sri Das, however, relentlessly.

He also worked, much more seriously, to help him overcome his tendency to view women as all that different from men, when the difference was only biological.

In telling me (Walter) about Sri Das, the Master said, "I said to him very frankly, 'What you find attractive are only the grossly physical differences. You demean not only them, but yourself, when you view women in that way. Learn to see everybody as a soul. No one is his or her mere body!'"

✿ 50 ✿

The Master, on one occasion, also deliberately embarrassed Bernard for the same reason. Bernard was an SRF minister who, when I knew him, conducted services in the SRF Church in Hollywood. Certain women in the congregation had been saying they thought he would look well in a turban. The Master made no comment on the point. He determined, however, to quiet this little ripple of interest before it grew to become a wave.

A formal Indian gathering had been scheduled. For the event, the Master dressed Bernard in a turban. He wound a long strip of cloth with great care on the disciple's head—arranging it in such a way, however, that although the turban managed to stay on, it would slip lopsidedly over one eye, then over the other eye, and manage always to look ridiculous.

Did Bernard enjoy the comedy, as Doctor Lewis had? The fact that he never told me about it makes me suspect that he didn't relish it at all! He was the sort of person who might well have responded, with Queen Victoria, "We are not amused." It was an elderly nun who, gleefully but not unkindly, told me the story.

51

One time, while traveling by car with a group of nuns, the Master made them stop by the roadside on a main highway, get out, and consume a large, very juicy watermelon. He cut it into unwieldy pieces which made sure the juice got all over their arms, hands, and faces: not the sort of spectacle that women—especially young ones—like to present for public inspection. The Master was unconcerned for their embarrassment. They too, after their initial shock, accepted the situation with good humor.

52

In disciplining his disciples, the Master tried always to lead them toward their own inner freedom and joy. Often the discipline in traditional monasteries is administered with the intention of suppressing people's pride. The Master sought, instead, to *expand* people's sense of self into a greater awareness of their true, infinite Self. Sometimes, in the process, he could appear quite harsh though always he had an expansive purpose in mind, and certainly he never spoke out of anger or personal displeasure.

For some time he made a point of scolding one of the nuns every time they met. She had a proud nature, and, predictably, resented his treatment of her. Sometimes he reduced her to tears of frustration. His scoldings seemed to her both unfair and unreasonable. Sometimes, indeed, they may have been, for what he was trying to change, particularly, was her reactions.

At last the woman concluded that it didn't really matter. Perhaps, she reflected, he was only trying in some obscure way to help her! At any rate, since she'd come there to find God, she realized that his smiles of approval were beside the point.

The next time he scolded her, she took his words calmly, even pleasantly. In the midst of what had started as a tirade, he stopped, smiled with approval, and said, "I see you are learning. That's good. I've wanted to make you more malleable." From then on, he rarely scolded her again.

❧ 53 ❧

Sometimes, when I hear the Master described as a harsh disciplinarian, I remember with a smile the following story. For he wasn't harsh: he was only *appropriate,* which is quite another thing. He was kindly disposed toward everyone. His only aim was to *help.* He never corrected anyone, moreover, unless that person *himself asked* to be guided. Otherwise, he might overlook even the most glaring defects.

One day he visited the monks' dining room. The luncheon dishes hadn't yet been washed, and the table, besides, was an utter mess. In our defense, I might add that the dining room itself was no inducement to housekeeperly pride, situated as it was in the basement, without windows. A single light bulb dangled loose on a wire from the center of the ceiling, and provided the only light. In an attempt to create a cheerful atmosphere, someone had painted the walls an almost painfully bright yellow.

Had the Master been the stern disciplinarian, however, that superficial people sometimes considered him, he would certainly have seized on this situation to give us a thorough scolding for this disorder. Instead, he gazed about him with a kindly expression and remarked, "It could be worse."

༄ 54 ༂

The Master's reactions were, as I said, *appropriate,* never motivated by personal feeling. Once, when he was still relatively young, he was late for a lecture and set off at a run to keep his appointment. Someone urged him, "Now, don't be nervous."

"One can run nervously," the Master replied, "or one can run calmly, but not to run when one has to is to be lazy!"

55

His way of training included helping people to work out their own wrong attitudes, rather than merely telling them they must change.

"At our Ranchi school," he said, "two of the boys were always fighting together. Finally, in order to cure them of this tendency, I had them sleep in the same bed. From then on, it was either constant war, or grudging peace. In time, they learned to get along reasonably well together.

"When I saw they'd become friends, more or less, I decided to try them a little further. One night, as they were sleeping soundly, I stole to the head of their bed, stood silently, then reached down and rapped one of them sharply on the forehead.

"He sat up angrily. 'Why did you do that?' he demanded of his companion.

"'I didn't do anything!' the other protested indignantly. A few more sleepy words, and then both of them lay back again. When they were once more asleep, I gave the other one a smart rap on the forehead. This time it was he who sat up, furious.

"'I *told* you I didn't do anything!' he shouted. They were all set to do battle when, looking up, they saw me smiling down at them.

"'Oh,' they exclaimed sheepishly, '*you!*' From then on, they became the best of friends."

⁎⁓ 56 ⁓⁎

"Another boy at our Ranchi school liked to smoke. I didn't forbid him to; that would only have made him 'sneak behind the barn' for a puff. Instead I said to him, 'Smoke if you like. It is all right. All I ask is that every time you feel the desire, come and smoke in my presence.' Well, he did in fact come once or twice, to test me. After that, however, he simply couldn't go on, and dropped the habit completely."

⁎⁓ 57 ⁓⁎

When it came to living for God, the Master could be quite austere. Heber Kimball, a tall, dignified young man, visited Mount Washington with the intention of joining the monastery. The Master had put me in charge of the monks, so I mentioned Heber's interest to him.

"Tell him from me," the Master replied, "that if he stays here he can find salvation in this lifetime." This was no mean promise!

I encouraged Heber to remain, therefore. The next day, he said to me, "Please ask the Master what I should do about this problem: My parents are growing old. Is it better that I go back, find a job, and take care of them? Or should I remain here?"

I reported the question to Master, who replied very sternly: "That is for him to decide. We want only those here who are a hundred percent for God!"

Did Heber stay? Yes, but he didn't remain very long.

✺ 58 ✺

A young woman once addressed a similar question to the Master. "My mother needs support," she said. "Ought I to leave here for her sake, and take a job?"

"Leave at once!" the Master ordered her peremptorily. "Get out! You aren't needed here!"

So dismissive was he that she burst into tears. "Master," she pleaded, "my place is with you. I don't want to leave! I will just practice faith in God, that He will attend to her needs."

"That is the right attitude," he replied with a kindly smile. "When a person gives his life to God, the Lord takes care of every aspect of his life." The mother came, later on, to Mount Washington, and lived there happily until her death many years later.

✺ 59 ✺

"A young boy came here years ago with his mother," the Master told me. "She generously asked me to help with his upbringing. I did my best, but every time I said anything to correct him, he would pucker his lips and cry, 'Mommy, he's scolding me!' At last I gave him a toy airplane. He fell in love with it. After growing up, he left and became an airplane engineer, where he found whatever happiness his karma permitted him.

"People have to ask me, themselves, to discipline them. Otherwise, it doesn't work for me to try to teach them."

✺ 60 ✺

The Master once, in speaking of a certain woman disciple, told me, "I used to call her 'Great Mother.' She had given all her children here for training. They weren't all ready for our way of life, but she had great faith in me. The oldest boy was very sincere, though he lacked the spirit you all show. If, for instance, I asked him to fetch me a glass of water, he might reply, 'I'm busy now. Can you get it yourself?'

"He returned once from a long voyage. A young woman 'fell for him,' as the expression is. She saw him through a romantic haze as 'the great world traveler.' He and I were together in New York when he announced to me one day, 'I have to make a short visit to Philadelphia.'

"'To buy a ring?' I challenged him.

"'You don't know *anything* about her,' he replied defensively, well aware of whom I was referring to.

"I said, 'I know *everything* about her!'

"Well, he found out. He hasn't had a day of happiness since he got married. It will take him incarnations to become freed of this karma.

"His mother, when she saw his desire to get married, sided with him against me. My wish was to spare him great suffering, but her reaction was what most mothers' would have been in matters like this. Since then, I have never called her 'Great Mother' again."

The Master meditating in the Temple of Leaves at Mt. Washington.

61

"Marriage is seldom the beautiful thing it is popularly depicted. I smile at the typical movie plot. The hero is so handsome, and the heroine so lovely, and after all kinds of troubles they get married and (so we are supposed to believe) 'live happily ever after.' And then I think, 'Yes, with rolling pins and black eyes!' (The producers, however, don't let us see that part!)"

62

The Master was commenting to the monks on the high divorce rate in America. "Too many people marry for the wrong reasons: sex and physical beauty, usually. I sometimes think of it as a union between an elegant bow tie and a nice shade of lipstick!

"In India, there are many more happy marriages. Marriage there is arranged by the parents, whose first concern is for their children's happiness. The hypnosis of adolescent infatuation isn't a factor. It is different, of course, when parents want to marry their children off for mercenary reasons, such as the bride's dowry. Money is as much a hypnosis as sex. If, however, the parents are sincerely interested in their children's happiness, there is a greater likelihood that the marriage will be a success. Physical attraction is both superficial and fleeting.

"Marriage in America today is a gamble: like going to Las Vegas, or playing the stock market. In India, there are many 'Romeo and Juliet' marriages."

The Master paused, then added wryly, "In a way, the system here is better: At least they find out more quickly!"

❧ 63 ❧

Michelle Evans had studied under Doctor Lewis. (As it happened, she was the first person I ever initiated, at the Master's request, into Kriya Yoga.) She kept a photograph of Doctor Lewis on her altar. The official SRF altar, however, was designed by the Master to hold only the photos of the five gurus. Mrs. Evans's addition of Dr. Lewis was unorthodox, and was seen therefore as being opposed to the Master's wishes. Someone reported the matter to him.

"That is her own altar," he replied, "and therefore her private matter. What she does there is her affair. I designed our altars for public display."

64

"My Master [Sri Yukteswar] once asked me, 'Do you love people?' I answered, 'No, I love only God.'

"'That isn't enough,' he replied.

"Later he asked me again, 'Do you love people?'

"I smiled blissfully this time, and said, 'Don't ask me.' He could see that my love, now, was too broad to be spoken about. This time, therefore, he only smiled."

65

I had been with him about five months when he invited me to a meeting at which he instructed another of the monks, Harvey Allen, on his wishes for the work in India. The plan at that time was to send Harvey there. (Harvey, unfortunately, though a good person and earnest, wasn't able to tune in to the Master's consciousness, and a year or two later, caught up in opinionated attitudes, his very earnestness became his undoing. Desires for the world did the rest.)

The thought came to me as Master was speaking that, even though he had said nothing about sending me to India, my work might lie there someday. I therefore took notes of everything he said. Here below is what I wrote:

"There should be a Bengali, and later a Hindi, correspondence course.

"The teachings [presumably the correspondence course lessons] should be a benefit of membership.

"A history of the work should be published in Bengali.

"The magazine should be in two languages, Bengali and English. In the beginning, it should comprise about twenty-five pages."

(At this point I wrote down, "Revelations of Self-Realization." I am no longer clear as to what he meant here. Did he intend this as a name for the magazine? for the correspondence course lessons?)

"There should be monthly festivities," he continued, "and, once a year, a congress of all the centers. Winter is the best time in India to hold such a congress: January 2nd–6th, more or less, would be a good time, lasting one week and ending on a Sunday. It would be good also to revive Sri Yukteswar's four annual festivals, on the solstices and equinoxes.

"A teacher should be sent around to the centers on a regular basis, as a means of keeping them bound together.

"Recorded talks should be sent out regularly to the centers.

"Keep the organizations in India and America united. A good way to do so would be to make them financially interdependent." (I will return to this point at the end of this section.)

He then spoke of the larger picture. "Because, in the divine plan, materialism was intended to be manifested in the West, and spirituality in the East, Krishna came first to teach the fundamental principles of spirituality. Later, Jesus Christ was sent to the West. The Eastern is the more ancient of the two civilizations. It was therefore right for the West's development to *follow* that of the East: Material realities come after the spiritual. The teachings which God is sending now through this work provide a balance between East and West: between Eastern spirituality—that of India, in particular—and Western material efficiency—that of America, especially."

Not long after that meeting, the Master, to whom my interest in India could not but be obvious, commented, "I have plans for you, Walter." He didn't say what they were, but I took him to mean that his thought was to send me, too, to India someday. I was delighted. Later on, however, I fell into a deep depression. "Here," I thought, "I have only just found my Guru. *He* is my India! Oh, don't let me be sent away from him so soon!"

A day or two later, the certainty came to me that he would never ask anything of me that was not in my highest spiritual interest. Thus, I fought my way out of this temporary mental morass. The next time I saw him, he gazed at me penetratingly, and said, "No more moods now, Walter. Otherwise, how will you be able to help people?"

From 1950 to 1952, he planned every year to go to India, and to take me with him, along with several others. That trip never materialized—in the end, because he left his body.

Because my activity, over the years, has entailed creating a missionary work in America and Europe, the same question has arisen in my mind: How can two separate works be kept tied together: the branch to the parent body? (I would have loved for my work to be tied also to Self-Realization Fellowship, but that door, so far, remains closed. Ananda, therefore, is a separate organization from SRF, though it is one with SRF in its dedication to serving the Master.)

The Master had suggested that his works in India and America be made financially interdependent as a means of tying them together. Realistically, however, the financial flow was, and would have to remain for many years, entirely one-directional: from America to India, not the reverse. This situation might change in time, but from my experience I think the three best ways of keeping two separate works interdependent are:

1. to have a frequent interchange of personnel;

2. to arrange for frequent visits, both ways, by the leaders in the two works; and,

3. to include every leader in whatever deliberations concern the work as a whole.

These are the practices we follow at Ananda. As a result, the financial flow, also, is becoming increasingly reciprocal.

ᘓᕽ 66 ᕽᘐ

"Master," I said to him one day (at that time, I was working in the correspondence department), "what letters we are receiving from Germany. Such sincerity and devotion! It is thrilling to see."

"Yes," he replied, adding softly, "They have been hurt, that's why. All those wars and troubles over there. What they need is Kriya Yoga, not bombs."

"How wonderful it would be," I exclaimed, "if Henry could be sent there some day, with his knowledge of German." (Henry was a disciple from Zurich, in German Switzerland.)

"Well," the Master replied, "maybe I will send you there someday."

His reply surprised me. "I thought you had other plans for me, Sir." (I was of course thinking of India.) "I'll be happy to go wherever you send me, however. Certainly I have a natural rapport with Europe, having, as you know, been born and raised there."

"There is a great work to be done there," he said in conclusion.

For years I thought he had been referring to Germany, since that was how our discussion began. I'd spoken German as a boy, moreover, almost as well as English. Where God finally took me, however, was to Italy. The Master's words, "over there," must have been a general reference to Europe, and not specifically to Germany. In fact, it was in Italy, years later, that I met with the greatest receptivity. In Germany I encountered less openness to what I had to give. They seemed contented with their own way of doing things.

The Master once made an interesting comment:

"You can practice yoga better in California than anywhere else on earth. The climate is more conducive."

68

During his first years in Boston, the Master studied the American ways of doing things, worked on becoming fluent in English, and gave classes to a few students. Doctor Lewis would sometimes talk with me about that period. "The people were slightly disappointed," he said, "in the Master's explanations, which to them seemed too 'down-to-earth.' They wanted something more exotic! A few of them once complained to him, 'Couldn't you go a little deeper into the Indian teachings?' For his next class, accordingly, the Master delved into some of the philosophic subtleties of the ancient teachings. Soon, the students were all asleep!"

❧ 69 ❧

The Master told us of a community experiment that a few people had tried. "Two ex-members of that community," he said, "came to me later. The community itself no longer existed.

"'Things were going along so harmoniously,' they lamented, 'and then came an evening when half the community wanted custard for dessert, and the other half wanted tapioca pudding. The disagreement became so emotional that at last the community was disbanded!'

"'Why,' I inquired, 'didn't half of you simply have custard, and the other half, tapioca pudding?'

"'Oh!' they exclaimed in surprise. 'We didn't think of that!'

"Artificial principles—in this case, an *a priori* commitment to consensus—never work. A community must accept the diversity of human nature. Room must always be left for compromise. Rigidity, like a dry twig, is fragile and easily broken. Under stress, it will simply snap."

70

Master remarked to me once out in the desert: "I used to have many friends, and I enjoyed their company. Then someone said to me, 'I once had lots of friends, and was sure I would never forget them. After I married, however, I forgot them all. I then realized that my dependence on them had actually been a desire for a companion of the opposite sex.'

"On hearing those words I said, 'Thank you very much. You have taught me an important lesson.' Since then, I have always kept myself somewhat apart."

71

"Think how, for thousands of years, human lovers have vowed under the moon to love each other eternally. And the moon looks down and laughs to see their skulls strewn over the sands of time! Such is human love. This body seems so permanent, but life is brief! The love entertained by people for one another is an abstraction. Only love itself, like life itself, endures for eternity. Its forms change constantly. Outward attachments also change. God's love alone is eternal."

72

"Master," I said one day, "what is the reason you have accepted many into the monastery who obviously weren't suited to the life here?"

"It is because I came with a special dispensation," he replied. "There have been times, I admit, when some of those I accepted were very hard on the organization!" He didn't add, what I now believe to be true, that he'd made a commitment to those individuals in former incarnations, and wanted to encourage them toward their own eventual salvation. Indeed, it was constantly impressed on me that, far from being merely the president of an organization, he was the loving father of a family of spiritual seekers, many of whom were still wandering in delusion.

I asked him, next, "Do you want us to be as lenient in accepting people after you are gone?"

"No," he replied. "You must be stricter."

73

Bernard asked the Master, "What is the best way to transform emotion into devotion?"

"The company you keep" the Master replied, "will determine in what direction your feelings develop. In the company of devotees, those feelings will more easily become devotional."

"Master," pursued the disciple, "what if I am alone—for instance, when I meditate?"

"Am I not always with you?" the Master replied with a loving smile.

74

"It isn't enough merely to live in this holy place [Mount Washington]. Some people who live here waste their time playing the organ and engaging in other idle pursuits. There are many rats and mice in the canyon on this property: they aren't progressing spiritually! To develop spiritually, you have to make a deep, individual effort."

75

One day a new disciple, in a fit of emotional frenzy, cried, pleaded, and shouted to God to appear. Others were meditating with him, and felt intensely embarrassed by his emotional outburst. One of them wrote the Master a note afterward, inquiring whether it is all right, spiritually, to be so outwardly expressive.

"By all means it is all right!" replied the Master. "Cry to God. Roll on the ground in your fervor of longing for Him. Halfheartedness will never take you to God."

The Master had taken this opportunity, however, to fan the fire of devotion in those disciples' hearts— especially in the one who had written that note, who tended, himself, to be rather lukewarm. As a rule, the Master never counseled emotional displays unless they proceeded from an uncontrollable inner fervor. On another occasion, he told that same emotional disciple:

"Don't be like a straw fire in your devotion. Enthusiasm is good, but keep it under control. Otherwise, you will merely scatter its power.

"If you explode dynamite high in the air," he continued, "it will only make a loud noise. If you bury it in the ground, however, its explosion may make possible the building of highways, or the construction of tall buildings. Enthusiasm, similarly, is wonderful, but learn to be enthusiastic about the right things, and in the right way. Feeling should be calmly focused. Don't burn away its intensity as if in a straw fire.

"To demolish the mountain of delusion before you," he continued, "inwardness is necessary. Devotion must be kept under control. It should be a secret between you and your Beloved."

ᘰᕢ *76* ᕥᕟ

"A rich man visited a farmhouse. The farmer gave him a piece of cake and boasted, 'This is the best cake in the whole world!' The rich man tasted it, and commented, 'It is all right. I would like, however, to invite you to my home and let you taste the cake we serve there.' The farmer returned his visit, later on. When he'd tasted the rich man's cake, he exclaimed, 'I never knew there was such good cake in existence!'

"The other replied, 'I didn't want to hurt your feelings, but you were familiar only with that dry cake of yours. I know many varieties. That is how I knew that yours was by no means the best in the world.'

"So it is when you get a taste of divine bliss: You know immediately that nothing else in existence can equal it. Temptation then becomes dry and loses all its attractiveness. The best way to conquer temptation is to have something better to compare it with."

ᘰᕢ *77* ᕥᕟ

"Did the Master ever sleep?" someone asked me recently. I replied, "All I can say for sure is that I remember hearing him tell us once, 'I experimented last night with going into the subconscious. It was like being

In public in the West, the Master favored Western clothing. He pulled his long hair back into a knot to give the appearance of short hair. For spiritual occasions he wore Indian clothes and let his hair hang loose.

hemmed in by a heavy wall of flesh. I didn't like the feeling at all!'"

"Sleep," he used to tell us, "is the semiconscious way of knowing that we are Spirit. We would not have been able to bear life without it. Even though subconsciousness can be pleasant, however, it is also a sort of drunkenness. Much, much more enjoyable is superconsciousness."

Often he commented, "Sleep is counterfeit ecstasy."

ॐ 78 ॐ

There are two aspects to the following stories. One is the petty opposition the Master had to face continually in his life: a common phenomenon, unfortunately, in the life of every great human being, especially in the lives of saints and masters. The other aspect is the unfailing charity the Master always displayed before opposition. These stories were not ones he would have told generally. He did tell them to me, however, perhaps to encourage me always to keep a nonsectarian attitude. I hesitated, at first, to include them in this book. Yet they convey salutary lessons on an all-too-common human trait. Sectarianism is one of the "meannesses of the heart," as Sri Yukteswar called them: "pride of pedigree." Even among the followers of great men—and

Sri Ramakrishna was certainly a great man, and also a great master—sectarian attitudes are, unfortunately, all too common.

In niches along the side walls of his little church in Hollywood, the Master placed sacred images to represent other religious paths. Thus, he underscored the truth he'd proclaimed in the very name of the church: "Self-Realization Church of All Religions."

To Debi Mukherjee, an Indian disciple, he said, "I would have liked to have a representation of Sri Ramakrishna in one of those niches, for although he isn't in our line of gurus, I have always had deep devotion to him, and would have liked to honor him. In this country, however, too many of his disciples display a sectarian intolerance toward other expressions of India's teachings. Only because of their attitude, I have omitted him."

The Master was concerned, evidently, that those disciples might protest. He didn't want his sweet act of devotion to become a cause for disharmony from others.

 79

Often, when the Master and I were alone, he would reminisce about episodes in his life. He made it clear, among other things, that he deplored sectarianism, which, as he indicated, is all too prevalent among even the sincere followers of good paths. Once he told me:

"A group of monks from the Vedanta Society arrived in America from India. Out of love and devotion for their Master, Sri Ramakrishna, I wanted to make them feel welcome, and invited them to a lunch at the Encinitas hermitage. We gave them a good Indian feast. As they were leaving, I asked them if they would like to sign our guest book. They looked at one another hesitantly, as if asking whether, by signing our book, they might in any way compromise themselves. They resolved their dilemma by signing their names in Bengali.

"Seeing them do that, I felt like saying to them, 'Please, don't sully your names!'"

I (Walter) remember thinking when the Master told me that story, Such narrowness of spirit could *never* enter the hearts of Master's disciples! He has trained us too clearly in attitudes of universal generosity and love.

Has this remained so? I only ask the question.

❦ 80 ❧

The Master faced opposition from several of the Indian swamis in America. He told me, "The Vedanta swami in Hollywood once told someone about me, 'Oh yes, I know Yogananda. He's a very good—cook.'"

How it saddened the Master to relate this story. He himself had such deep devotion for Sri Ramakrishna.

"One day," he said, "I met that swami at a public function. He came over to me and said, 'Here is a line. On one side of it is Sri Ramakrishna; on the other side'—he concluded with a look of contempt—'*you!*' How Ramakrishna would have grieved over such absence of generosity among his own disciples!"

⬥ 81 ⬥

Yogi Khagen was from India, and was the Master's disciple. Motivated by the common failing, envy, he eventually turned against his Guru. He continued to teach, however, and was lecturing one evening in Phoenix, Arizona when, "out of the blue," he asked, "Is anyone here a member of Self-Realization Fellowship?" Several of those present stood up, expecting to hear words of appreciation for the Master and his work. Instead, what they got was a tirade against the Master and his organization. Deeply offended, several of them telephoned the Master that evening in Los Angeles and reported this outrage.

"Thank you for telling me," the Master said. "I will take care of the matter." Thus, he relieved them, graciously, of any further responsibility in the situation.

Next, he telephoned Yogi Khagen. What he said to him, however, was not at all what anyone expected.

"God bless you," he said, "for the good that you are doing. I bless you; our gurus bless you." He said nothing about the episode of the previous evening.

Always, when facing negativity, his way was if possible to emphasize something positive.

❧ 82 ❧

Many people—some of whom, unfortunately, were Indians—spoke against the Master during his lifetime. Why Indians? Perhaps they didn't like his having brought the spiritual teachings of India to the materialistic West, especially since they themselves were trying to adjust to Western ways! Or perhaps they didn't like the fact that the Master *adapted* those teachings to the West, instead of keeping them rigidly orthodox. Or perhaps—indeed, most probably—his enormous energy made them simply uncomfortable. For people of low energy always tend to resent people of high energy, especially if both of them are in the same field.

Dr. Haridas Chaudhuri told me in San Francisco, in 1962, "When I first arrived in America, I met a number of people in the Indian community who spoke against Swami

Yogananda. I finally got to meet him myself, and found that, for his part, he had nothing but good to say about his critics. I knew, then, 'on whose foot the shoe fit'!"

༺ 83 ༻

Master had given me and others for Christmas a copy of *The Imitation of Christ,* by Thomas à Kempis. When I thanked him, he said, "That is a wonderful book. It is no mere *imitation* of Christ: It *is* Christ. I don't often encourage people to read other books, but this one I recommend unreservedly."

"Thomas à Kempis," I remarked, "must have been a great saint. Is that so?"

"A very great saint," he replied.

༺ 84 ༻

In an episode described in my book, *The Path,** someone tried by underhanded means to create a serious problem for one of the SRF churches. The Master was physically incapacitated at the time. As he explained to us later, a guru sometimes assumes onto his own body some of the karma of his disciples. His

*In the chapter titled, "Attunement."

illness was not caused by any karma of his own: It was to lessen the karmic burdens of others. He told a small group of us afterward, "During that trial in the church, I was lying helpless in bed. Divine Mother appeared to me as a little girl, and stood on my forehead. I understood from Her, then, that everything was going to be all right."

Mr. Jacot, a devoted student of the Master's, was the person who had resolved that situation. He'd done so by publicly denouncing what, as he had soon realized, was a dishonest trick. Later on, the Master thanked him. He added, however, "The good that you did would have been greater had you employed more harmonious means. It is never good, even with good intentions, to create wrong vibrations by anger and harsh words."

❧ 85 ❧

On the subject of renunciation, the Master said, "If you forsake truly for God, you will receive a hundredfold, as Jesus promised—and, as Jesus said also, persecution. No one escapes persecution, for God wants to be sure of his devotee. One has to be willing to suffer opposition for choosing the spiritual path over the ways of the world."

ᗰᐁᗴ 86 ᗴᐁᗰ

"Desires," the Master said, "are the greatest obstacle on the spiritual path. I see it," he added, "as a war, with people fighting to achieve victory. Some are killed by bullets of desire, and must be reborn to renew the struggle. Others, after great difficulties, win through to victory, and have no need to return to this material plane."

Another time he said, "I see the spiritual path as a race. The devotees are running, running. Some of them, their strength sapped by desires, drop out of the race. Some of them even begin running in the opposite direction! When someone wins at last, however, he achieves eternal blessedness in God."

Desires come, of course, in differing degrees of intensity. All of them, the Master said, must eventually be fulfilled. I once asked him, "*All* desires, Sir—even trivial ones, unfulfilled at the time, that one later forgets about? What about such insignificant desires as the mild wish for an ice cream cone? Must even that idle wish be fulfilled, eventually?"

He shocked me by answering quite seriously, "Oh yes!"

Doctor Lewis once told me he had been glancing over a new car one day. "Watch your desires, Doctor!" the Master warned him.

It may seem, considering the infinite number of desires that ripple across the mind, that liberation must remain eternally an "impossible dream." Fortunately, such is not the case. For one thing, as the Master once told me (and as I've quoted earlier), "When ecstasy comes, everything goes." For another, as he explained to us more than once, "It is possible even during one deep meditation to be freed, through visions, of the karmas of many lifetimes."

✧ 87 ✧

"Very few saints, even," the Master once told me, "have attained final liberation."

I exclaimed in dismay, "What about all those saints in the *Autobiography*? Are all of them dead and gone, with no one to take their place?"

(In *Autobiography of a Yogi,* Paramhansa Yogananda makes it clear that final liberation is usually attained from higher astral worlds, not from this material plane. It seemed to me at the time, however, that that goal must be virtually impossible of attainment.)

"Very few even of those saints," he replied, "were fully liberated."

I named a few of them specifically from his book. In each case, his reply was, "No." At last he said, "Only Babaji, Lahiri Mahasaya, Sri Yukteswarji, and two of Lahiri Mahasaya's disciples: Swami Pranabananda [the

"Saint with Two Bodies" as he is described in the *Auto-biography*] and Ram Gopal Muzumdar [the "Sleepless Saint"]." On the occasion I quote here he didn't name himself. At other times, however, he told us he had come into this body fully liberated.

"I also met another fully liberated soul," he told me. "His name was Yogi Ramiah. He was a disciple of the great master, Ramana Maharshi. It does happen, occasionally, that a disciple becomes more highly advanced than his guru." (Yogi Ramiah, when I myself met him in 1960, was known by the name, Sri Rama Yogi. He is mentioned again later in this book.)

"Why can't a master simply dissolve all his karma," I asked, "the moment he realizes his oneness with God?"

"Well, in that state you don't really care. You see all this as a dream. You may even go on for incarnations that way, returning to earth to help free your disciples. Masters, at that level of development, may even keep a little bit of karma deliberately, as a means of holding them down to this plane for that higher purpose for a while. Once you've attained the highest state, *nirbikalpa samadhi,* there is no ego-consciousness left. You are essentially free anyway."

"What is it, Master," I asked, "that draws a soul back to earth after he has attained final liberation?"

He replied, "He still keeps the 'desireless desire' to help others."

"To those who think me near, I will be near."

In his correspondence course lessons he explains the difference between the rebirth of a fully liberated soul, and that of a master who has a little karma of his own remaining to be worked out. The latter, after he attains full liberation, becomes an "ascended master." If, as rarely happens, he returns to earth, it is as a full manifestation of God—an *avatar*—with divine power to shower blessings, generally, on all mankind. Those who still have some past karma of their own to work out, return primarily to help their own disciples. These saints, called *jivan muktas* ("freed while living"), are able to uplift a few, but cannot carry innumerable disciples to God. Those, on the other hand, who return without any karma of their own, having become *param muktas* ("fully liberated") in a former life, come as *avatars*. Whoever comes to them for help can be saved, though his salvation is not necessarily immediate.

I asked the Master once, "Are you an avatar?"

"It would take such a one," he replied quietly, "to bring a mission of this importance."

When his mother took him, while he was a baby, to be blessed by his guru's guru, Lahiri Mahasaya (*Yogavatar,* or "Incarnation of Yoga," as Paramhansa Yogananda called him), that great master said to her, "Little mother, thy son will be a yogi. As a spiritual engine, he will carry many souls to God's kingdom." Those words could not have been spoken of a lesser master; they could only have been spoken of an *avatar.*

❧ 88 ❧

In the above discussion, after the Master said, "You can go on for incarnations," he added, "Or you can say 'I am free!' right now. It's all in the mind. As soon as you say you are free, you *are* free."

Boone, who was present, raised the objection, "Sir, if I said I was free, I wouldn't be, would I?"

"Oh yes!" the Master replied. "But the thing is, you answered your own question! You said, 'I wouldn't be.' The trouble is, you see, that the mind is already poisoned with the delusion it wants to overcome. It lacks force.

"There was a man," he continued, "who wanted to rid himself of a demon. He decided to perform a certain *Vedic* ritual for that purpose. Taking up a handful of powder, he chanted the prescribed incantation over it, then cast the powder onto the demon. The demon only laughed. 'Before you could say your incantation,' he said, 'I got into that powder myself. How, then, could it affect me?'

"The thing is, the demon of delusion is already well settled in the mind. That is why guru's help is so necessary. He empowers the mind to banish its demons. Therefore it says also in the Bible, 'As many as received him, to them gave he power to become the sons of God.'" *

*John 1:12.

111

89

"Practice Kriya so deeply that breath becomes mind," the Master said to us one day. He added, "The breath is a gross dream of the mind. It can be rubbed away by superconsciousness.

"True Kriya Yoga practice takes place in the deep spine, the *sushumna.*"

90

The Master was truly an embodiment of compassion. No matter how much anyone wronged him, he remained ever his spiritual friend. And no matter how far a disciple strayed from the path, he sought always to bring that person back to God.

In the West, the word "disciple" suggests discipline, but in India the word often used is *chela,* suggesting a beloved son or daughter.

There was one disciple to whom the Master gave a very serious warning: "If you leave this life here, it will take you two hundred more incarnations to return to it." The disciple, to his own great misfortune, did leave. Later, he returned for a visit. The Master said of him afterward, "He sobbed before me, 'Why did I ever leave? The moods I had here were as nothing compared to what I've experienced since I left!'"

On another occasion the Master said, "Some people who leave here criticize us, reporting that we do not live the spiritual life. That's because they themselves didn't live it! They spread evil gossip about us. Well, so long as they hold that attitude I can't help them. But if they leave and, afterward, come running to me for help, I do everything I can for them. It isn't that I condone their delusion. I am, however, as the saying goes, 'in this for the long haul.'

"Norman, after leaving, came to me crying. 'Why did I ever leave this place?' I said to him, 'Wasn't it a paradise?'

"'You bet it was,' he replied, and wept so long that I wept with him. If only he had listened before getting burned!"

Of Swami Dhirananda, a disciple who had left years before I (Walter) came to Mount Washington, and had then turned against his Guru, the Master wrote in a letter about him, "It will take him another three lifetimes, now, to be liberated."

Carole Nealey, an editor-student of his, was present during a discussion in the living room at the Master's desert retreat. She asked about Sadhu Haridas, about whom the Master had spoken. This well-known eighteenth-century saint, though he had spiritual powers, had fallen from the path and had gone to live with a woman. He'd returned to his disciples, later. The Master had just finished telling us that Haridas attained final freedom at the end of his life. Mrs. Nealey asked him, "Isn't the punishment for a spiritual fall much greater, if one is highly advanced?"

The Master shook his head. "Mm-mm. God is no tyrant. Once one recognizes his mistake, and realizes deeply that God was all he ever really wanted, he will be taken back. One who has been accustomed to drinking nectar, and then eats stale cheese, soon grows dissatisfied with it and throws the cheese away, crying for nectar again. If he longs with all sincerity for God's love alone, the Lord won't reject him.

"Sadhu Haridas, at the end of his life, said, 'I have committed many wrongs, but now my Beloved is calling me. I am going home.'"

(What a blessing, I thought, that, however far a soul strays from God, the Lord will always love him, and will never turn His back on him if he cries for Him sincerely, no matter what he has done! As the Master said, "Pray to God in this way: 'Divine Mother, naughty or good I am Thy child. Thou *must* accept me!'")

Some disciples, like Dhirananda, actually turned against the Master. Of such fallen ones, the Master said, "If my child falls from a rooftop, I rush to pick him up, and will do everything I can to help him. But if, as I draw near, he starts shooting at me, what can I do? I must put my hand in my pocket and leave him to his own devices. I respect his free will. If he would allow me

114

to help him, however, I would at once forget that he ever disobeyed me or turned against me."

The Master was a spiritual doctor: His one aim was to heal suffering.

Once, after he'd scolded a disciple, the young man asked, "But you will forgive me, won't you?" The Master's reply, accompanied by an astonished look, was, "What else can I do?"

≈ 91 ≈

Doctor Lewis told me, "I once said to the Master, 'One thought is troubling me, Sir. Supposing, after long effort, I attain liberation. Is the freedom I'll attain good for this one Day of Brahma only?* What if, when Creation is remanifested after the next Night of Brahma, I, along with everyone else, get sent out again and have to go through the long, painful struggle all over? Wouldn't all these present efforts, then, seem almost futile?'"

"Never fear," the Master reassured him. "Once the soul becomes free, it remains so for eternity. Never more will it have to roam the long, winding road of evolution."

"That answer," Doctor admitted to me, "came as a great consolation!"

---

*A "Day of Brahma" is described in the Indian scriptures. It is one complete period of cosmic manifestation, lasting billions of

92

I (Walter) was having great difficulty in quieting the mind in meditation. I felt an inner rebellion against the very idea of inner peace!

"Don't fight your mind," counseled the Master. "Treat it like a donkey. That beast is so stubborn that, sometimes, it won't budge even when it is beaten repeatedly. If its owner lets it stand still for a while, however, the donkey finally resumes walking again of its own accord. The best thing, when your mind rebels, is to let it stand awhile. Don't be too hard on it. Let it 'make its point.' After that, it will resume advancing of its own accord, without being forced."

---

years. The "Day of Brahma" is followed by a period of equal duration, called the "Night of Brahma." During Brahma's "night," all creation is withdrawn from outward manifestation. Beings that are not yet liberated rest in "seed form" for that time, in the consciousness of Spirit, awaiting the Creation's next manifestation. When the following Day of Brahma dawns, they resume whatever state they attained formerly.

93

The Master was a strong advocate, at the same time, of self-discipline. "You must be tough on yourself!" he used to say to us. He described a boyhood friend of his, whose mother was raising him in a hard school. "He was also hard on himself," the Master said. "His mother would beat him regularly, and he had come to look upon her beatings as simply a fact of life! One day he climbed a tree, and fell off it. He was able to cling to the tree trunk, and slide down it to the ground by keeping his arms wrapped around the trunk. When he reached the ground, his chest was all shredded and bleeding. We gazed at him in horror. All he said, however, was, 'What are you staring at? Hurry and cover me up! Get some dust. Get anything. Plaster me over. My mother will beat me up!' That's what I mean: Be tough! Don't baby yourselves."

94

"My Master [Sri Yukteswar] was often harsh with me, even in public," the Master said. "His intention was to discipline me so I'd become indifferent to public opinion. One day, before hundreds, he asked me to fetch him a glass of water. I went at once. As I returned with the glass, my foot caught on the corner of a carpet, and flipped it over.

"'Look at that clumsy oaf!' scoffed my Master. Everyone there laughed. I looked at them and thought, 'Not one of you has attained what I have!' But he succeeded in hardening me so I wouldn't be affected by anybody's opinions." (For one who loved people deeply, as the Master did, it was important that he become immune to the hurts they dealt him, their callousness, and even their hatred.)

Even with that hard training, the Master loved his Guru deeply. A picture of Sri Yukteswar hung in the hallway outside his apartment at Mount Washington. Whenever he passed it, he would pause a moment in silent prayer.

"Very few," he told me, "were able to bear Sri Yukteswar's discipline. Once, the others in the ashram came to me in a body and said, 'Let us leave here. We've decided to follow you instead.'

"'You leave,' I replied. 'I stay with my Guru!' Many fled. He didn't even want disciples. But just see: By converting me, he converted thousands."

"Sir," I once asked him, "was it because he knew he wouldn't be coming back to this world that he didn't want disciples? Was it because he didn't want the responsibility for anyone else on this plane?"

"That's right," the Master replied. "He had a few stragglers this time, that's all."

95

"Sir," I asked, "what stage must one have reached to be called a master?"

"He must have attained Christ consciousness. The stages of enlightenment," he continued, "are, first, to be conscious of the *AUM* vibration throughout the body. Next, one's consciousness becomes identified with that *AUM* vibration *beyond* his body, and gradually throughout the universe. One then becomes conscious of the Christ consciousness *within* the *AUM* vibration— first in the physical body, then gradually in the whole universe. When you achieve oneness with that vibrationless consciousness everywhere, you have attained Christ consciousness.

"That final stage lies beyond vibration itself, in oneness with God the Father, the Creator beyond the universe. When, still in that highest state of consciousness, you can return to the body without losing your inner sense of oneness with God, *that* is complete freedom. All true masters, even those who are not yet fully liberated, live in that *nirbikalpa samadhi* state. That is what Jesus Christ had. It was what he meant by perfection, in saying, 'Be ye therefore perfect, even as your Father which is in heaven is perfect.'* To be a Christlike master, one must have attained that state."

*Matthew 5:48.

On another occasion, the Master gave this very simple explanation: "You are a master when you can use your senses, but they don't use you."

🌸 96 🌸

Dr. Lewis told me, "The Master was reminiscing with me the other day. He spoke as an intimate friend of our years together. 'We've had a good life,' he said. 'It seems only yesterday that we first met. Soon we will be separated, but in a little while we'll be together again.'"

🌸 97 🌸

"Years ago," Dr. Lewis told us, "my mother suffered a severe stroke. The doctor said she might not live until morning.

"The Master was in Cuba at the time, and couldn't be reached. I prayed to him mentally for help, and my prayer was answered: My mother recovered.

"A few months later she again fell ill. This time I was able to speak to the Master and ask him in person for help. He replied, 'The Lord has spared her life quite some time now. If she lives another four months, we must be satisfied.'

"It was four months later to the day that she left her body.

"Several years afterward," Dr. Lewis continued, "the Master said to me, 'Your mother has been reborn.' I inquired immediately, of course, 'Where is she living now, Sir?' He told me where she was: up north in the state of Maine. After some time I had an opportunity to visit her family. Their little girl—my mother—was three years old by this time. The resemblance was uncanny. There were many little mannerisms, gestures, and movements—all exactly as they had been! The child didn't remember me, but she showed an instant affection for me, and I, quite apart from my special knowledge, felt a natural affection for her."

☙ 98 ❧

Samadhi is no "Sunday outing," no lark one experiences for the mere fun of it! It creates an absolute revolution in one's consciousness. *Samadhi* is altogether different from anything the ego can possibly imagine.

Dr. Lewis once told me, "I kept asking the Master to give me a *samadhi*. One day I backed him into a corner, so to speak, and insisted that he give me *samadhi* 'this very minute'!

"The Master looked at me deeply, demanding almost fiercely, 'Are you ready for it, if I give it to you "this very minute"? Can you accept a complete change of outlook on everything?'

"My will faltered. I looked down. 'No, Sir,' I had to confess. 'I guess I'm not ready yet.'"

I (Walter) am reminded of something Boone told me. "I once asked Saint Lynn to give me a taste of ecstasy. He answered, 'If I gave it to you now, you would not be able to bear your life as it is.'"

❦ 99 ❧

Rumors and gossip tend to flourish when groups of people are gathered together. The Master once made the following comment on this tendency: "My Master [Sri Yukteswar] used to say, 'If it is not something I can say to everybody, I don't want to hear it.'"

The Master often warned us not to go to worldly places for relaxation and enjoyment, not even for milk shakes (though this he said only to a few of the younger ones). He said also, "You must report it when you see anyone here commit a serious offense against our rule."

Someone once reported to him, "I saw So-and-so going into an ice cream parlor."

The Master dismissed the statement impatiently, "I didn't mean that kind of infraction! Don't bother me with such petty gossip. Report *serious* infractions, however—those which might harm others in our way of life. If someone does something seriously wrong, to say nothing about it would be treachery. Supposing someone put poison in another person's drink, and you knew about it, wouldn't you speak out? Were you to rationalize, instead, 'Well, it wasn't I who poisoned that drink; it isn't my business,' you'd be as guilty as the poisoner. When anyone here goes *against* our way of life, it is, in a way, poisoning it. When you know of any serious wrong, you *must* report what you know. It would be shirking your own responsibility not to do so.

"Some people think, 'Oh, he knows about it.' Naturally, God sees these things. He doesn't always talk, however. My role here is very difficult: I have to play both divine and human parts. My inner and my outer natures are different. In my divine Self I see these things, but sometimes that Self remains aloof until something is called to my attention. My outer self plays a human role. It is not easy to play both roles at the same time, though I do my best to live as God wants me to. But you mustn't assume, thinking, 'Oh, he knows,' that it will always be all right. You, too, have to behave responsibly. Irresponsibility is not the way to grow spiritually. Always speak out, therefore, when something serious demands your involvement."

These important points are touched on again later in another context, close to the end of this book.

⚜ 100 ⚜

People in groups tend to develop a special "in" vocabulary, almost a jargon. The words can be used almost mindlessly, like waving a flag absent-mindedly. The Master gave us the following example of that tendency:

"A fundamentalist Christian once announced to me fervently, 'You must be saved by the blood.'

"'Produce a quart!' I challenged her.

"She was so astonished. How could she respond to this literal demand? The fact is, she had no clear idea what she was talking about. She had been merely quoting a phrase, repeated mindlessly by other dogmatic, so-called 'believers.'"

⚜ 101 ⚜

The Master's approach to truth was pragmatic. During his early years in America, certain persons were claiming in public that they would live forever.

"Study them," the Master advised when someone asked for his opinion. "Look for a few obvious signs. Is their hair falling out? Is it turning gray? Do they wear dentures? Are their faces becoming lined? If they manifest any of the common symptoms of mortality, how can they be believed when they claim they'll live forever? Ignore those claims! Those people are counting on not being around when the time comes for proving their claim. They'll have slipped away, conveniently, to the astral world, and won't have to face the people they've hoodwinked! Meanwhile, they enjoy the glitter of a false notoriety!

"What is the use, anyway, of keeping the physical body indefinitely? Even were it to remain in perfect and glowing condition, the body—or, rather, the very ego that constructed it—is a prison! You aren't this body. You aren't this ego. You are the immortal soul. In superconsciousness alone does immortality exist."

༄ 102 ༄

Many people of "New Thought" persuasion place exaggerated emphasis on "manifesting" health, wealth, and other symptoms of material success, which they see as outward demonstrations of high spiritual development. The Master's attitude toward these things was qualified.

On the one hand, he considered that seeking such things for themselves could demand more energy than they are worth—like devoting the wealth of a nation to preventing snow from falling in the mountains in January. For the devotee of God it is, he felt, a waste of energy to strive too assiduously for outer perfection, which is ever and cannot but be evanescent. He counseled people, "Do what you can, within reason, to remain healthy and to achieve the worldly success you need, but remember, it is better to rise above outer conditions altogether, so that they cannot affect you."

He accepted that, since people live on many different levels of awareness, no one teaching in this respect can, or even should, be applied to everyone. "Illness," he said, "can be a serious obstacle on the spiritual path. So also can poverty. Do your best—again," he repeated, "within reason—to achieve health and prosperity, and to succeed at whatever you set your mind to do. On the other hand, keep those efforts proportionate to the true, long-range goal of life, which is to find God. To devote all your energy to fulfilling your material desires, as so many people do even in the name of spirituality, distorts their values, for it deprives them of the time they need for more important things."

He never accepted any material blessing as *proof* of inner development. Yet it can be an *indication* of such development. We should be grateful to God for blessings, he said, but we should be equally grateful to Him if he *removes* them. For it is not material things that should command our gratitude. We should be grateful

126

The Master with American Indians of the Yakima tribe
from Washington State.

for—nay, exult in—life itself in its many costumes, re-membering always that one of those "costumes" is death. We are the immortal offspring of Infinite Bliss. In bliss lies our true reason for eternal gratitude.

Some of the Master's most spiritually advanced disciples were highly successful businessmen. The ability to succeed at anything is an aid in life, certainly, not a liability. The question is one only of proportion. We should give our energy where it is needed first. Many saints, he pointed out, have had serious illnesses. Many others have lived in poverty. The test of spirituality is one's inner *state of consciousness,* and above all the purity of one's love for God. The test of one's spiritual refinement, moreover, is his degree of freedom from ego-consciousness.

He once related the following story: "There was a saint who fell ill. His disciples pleaded with him, 'Master, so many have been healed by your intercession. Why don't you pray to the Divine Mother to heal you, too?' This seemed to him not a bad idea; he accepted their suggestion. When he prayed, the Divine Mother appeared to him.

"'Of all things!' She rebuked him. 'You, who have realized your oneness with the Infinite, and who have so many bodies you live through, want now, by praying for this one little form, to limit yourself to it? For shame!' The saint deeply regretted his error, and prayed, ' Mother, Your love alone is all-sufficient!'"

103

I suspect the Master was showing me, amusingly enough, another aspect of the above teaching one day. It was after a luncheon guest had left, and I was sitting alone with him at the table. Idly he tried to flip a fork into an empty glass by striking downward on the curved prongs. Several times his attempt failed, but he persevered. On about the fifth try, the fork finally went into the glass—which broke! The Master looked at me, smiling almost like a child. "But it went in!" he said, as if proudly.

He seemed to be telling me that, whatever one sets his mind to, it should be carried through to completion—even if, in the process, the glass gets broken!

How often in my life have I had to resolve to carry something through even though I knew the very attempt would cause me, personally, great hardship. I've reminded myself with a smile, "Even if the glass breaks, my duty, which I've accepted, is to flip the fork in!"

ᡐᡬᢁ 104 ᢁᡬᢁ

"We must strike a balance," the Master said, "between non-attachment to outer things and sensible concern for our present realities. So long as a person is centered in body-consciousness, he must take sensible care of his body. It is important spiritually, also, to take reasonable physical precautions. Proper diet, proper exercise, fresh air and sunlight: These things are necessary for a well-rounded existence."

The Master once wrote me, "Keep exercised and body fit *for God-realization*." (I've added the italics.)

He also scoffed, however, at excessive preoccupation with one's own health. Perhaps partly to encourage us not to be over-concerned over it, he would sometimes give us money for ice cream—a thing that health faddists would frown upon. "Make God, not food, your religion," he said. "Many faddists only weaken their systems by depending excessively on dietary principles. 'Oh!' they'll cry, 'I didn't get my avocado today; my spine feels weak!' That very preoccupation with secondary matters only weakens their will power. Their very attitude toward life becomes spineless! Such concern for superficialities is like working to seal the cracks in a plaster wall when termites are eating away at the foundation!"

✦ 105 ✦

Saints often adopt extreme measures in their search for God—virtually starving themselves, for example, or going for long periods without sleep, or deliberately creating discomfort for their bodies. Many devotees wonder if it wouldn't help them to adopt similar practices, even if they are following the more moderate path of meditation and Kriya Yoga. With such aspirants in mind, the Master, who himself had undergone severe austerities during his youth, counseled people generally, "It is best not to be fanatical in your search for God. Only those with some measure of realization can safely afford to risk their health and physical well-being in seeking Him. Without realization, such practices make one fanatical."

One time, Henry, who had been reading the life of Saint Francis, and was comparing the austerities of that great saint with the more moderate lifestyle the Master provided for us, asked him whether it wouldn't be a good thing for us to be more austere. The Master answered him, "When God gives more, take it. *He* knows what is right for you."

Indeed I've experienced that, perhaps because the present age is less heavily burdened with physical deprivations than the days of Saint Francis, even our tests, however intense, tend to be more psychological in nature.

106

"The medical doctors," the Master said, "have discovered God's laws on a certain level of reality. Respect them for their knowledge; don't ignore them. On the other hand, don't lean on them too heavily. If you continue using a crutch when you no longer need it, you'll never develop your own strength."

One evening, he was deploring the fact that, during his illness and subsequent seclusion, people had taken to going to doctors every time anything went wrong with them. "When I was more actively involved in things," he said, "no one went to doctors. They depended more on God. Now that I've been out of things a little bit, I find them going all the time. Learn to rely more on God. He is ever within you, watching over you."

107

Karle Frost, a middle-aged and kindly man who lived for a time at Mount Washington, fell ill. The Master agreed that a doctor should be summoned. He also prayed for Karle. Later, when this student was well enough to get up, he was able to look out the window and wave at the Master as he was going out. The Master called back cheerfully, "Ha! Ha! The doctors get all the credit, when it is God who heals!"

108

Speaking of his own illness, the Master said, "When the wisdom dinner has been eaten from the plate of life, one may break the plate or keep it: It no longer matters."

109

In his later years, the Master, like many other masters, experienced physical illness. He explained that a master, according to the law of karma, although free from personal karma may take onto his own body the karmic debts of others, and in that way free them for more rapid spiritual growth. This loving sacrifice was the true reason for his own illness.

"Carry my body," he cried happily to us one day as we carried him up a flight of stairs, "and I will carry your souls!" On another occasion as we were carrying him, he said, "You are stealing lots of magnetism. That's good! It will help you."

When, after a long illness, he had recovered sufficiently to take short walks in the garden, I said to him one day, "It's so good to see you walking again, Sir."

"Yes," he replied, "it's good to be out again. But this body is not everything." Smiling cheerfully he added, "Some people have the use of their legs, but can't walk all over!"

༄ 110 ༅

He was describing to some of us, for our benefit, what he had undergone during his recent illness. "This experience was not physical. Though it affected the physical body, it was astral in nature. Demonic entities were torturing me. Some of them were shaped like saws; others, like corkscrews. They were working on the legs of my astral body. Christ's crucifixion was bad, but at least it was over in a few hours. This torture went on for months. Sometimes I kept my consciousness down to the physical body, so that I might experience suffering as others do.

"A nurse was hired to care for me. She was completely materialistic, and was actively hostile to the truths we teach here. Every time she turned me over— as she had to do because I couldn't turn myself—she did it with deliberate, unnecessary force, heedless of the pain it caused. At one moment there appeared in my forehead the blue light of destruction. Divine Mother's voice told me, 'Give it to her!' I could have destroyed that woman with a glance. But I knew this was God's test. 'Do as You like, Mother,' I prayed. 'It is all Your play.'"

꩜ 111 ꩜

He counseled us on what it was better to read, and not to read. One evening he said, "Why read the books of other paths? Too many people here read endlessly from the writings of others, while neglecting our own. You shouldn't mix your studies. If you do that too much, it becomes a kind of spiritual prostitution. The mind gets diluted by so many teachings, and is easily confused.

"We had a lady living here once who read other teachings all the time. She was very nice, always kind and polite to everyone. But I used to tell her, 'Why don't you read your own?'

"'Oh, all teachings are the same,' she said.

"'That's true,' I said, 'but just the same, if you keep reading everything you will get confused. You have to *realize* the truth behind those teachings. Only then will you know *from realization* that they are the same. Until that time, however, it will be like trying to cross a river in two boats, one foot in each of them. When the boats separate, you will fall between them and drown. Some differences do exist between the various teachings. With wisdom, they can be resolved. To the unenlightened mind, however, though they are superficial, they can be a cause of confusion.'

"Well, she didn't heed my advice, but kept on with her eclectic reading. After a time, she drifted off. People must learn loyalty to one path."

℘℘ 112 ℘℘

I once asked him, "Sir, if the thing that keeps us bound to this world is worldly desires, why don't those who commit suicide become liberated? Obviously, considering the extreme measures they've adopted to escape this world, they have no desire to remain in it!"

The Master chuckled as he contemplated this seeming paradox. "But there must also," he replied, "be a positive *desire* for God!"

The Master, a flawless mirror, reflected the consciousness
of those around him.

🙢 113 🙠

The Master was speaking about someone to whom he had given divine love. That person later turned against him, and in consequence suffered greatly. "When you give someone divine love," he commented, "and he goes against it, he crucifies himself."

🙢 114 🙠

"I met an eighty-year-old woman in Seattle," he told me, "who had been an atheist all her life. She was completely changed by our meeting. Thereafter, she would listen all the time to a recording of my voice. She kept orange flowers on her altar as a reminder of our meeting. In the few years that were left to her, she attained salvation.

"So you see," the Master concluded, "it isn't only a matter of when you come onto the path. Above all, it is a question of how much energy you devote, once you actually set foot onto it. As Jesus said, 'The last [whether coming last in time as disciples, or continuing to the last of their lives] shall be first, and many that came first [or early] shall be last.'"

༼ 115 ༽

The following story was told to me by Kamala Silva, a disciple of the Master's who lived in Oakland, California, when I knew her.

"I went once with Master," she said, "to the island of Santa Catalina off the coast of southern California. Master was a very fast runner when he was young. For our visit there, a young man accompanied us who was a good athlete. When he heard that Master was a fast runner, he challenged him to a race. The young man himself ran in college competitions. Well, they started out even, but by the time the youth had finished the first block, Master had almost finished the second one!"

Sananda Ghosh, one of Yogananda's younger brothers, told me, "Paramhansaji had a very unusual style of running, as if slightly angled. But his legs moved like pistons, and he won every race!"

I was told that on the tennis court also, the Master was amazingly fast on his feet. I forget who told me, but that person said, "Master just seemed to appear wherever the ball landed! One might have thought his movements were supernatural, but of course they weren't. How could they be, for a mere game?"

The Master himself told two of us the following story. We were at his desert retreat:

"There were some stray dogs at our Ranchi school that caused a lot of trouble. One day they killed a horse.

I decided they had to be captured and taken away. Taking up a few gunny sacks, I chased after them so quickly that I was able to seize them and put them, one by one, into those sacks. We then took them far away. They never returned."

As he told this story, the Master's speech, too, became very rapid. He was not only laughing merrily over the memory, but he acted out the episode with animated gestures and facial expressions. That acting, and the breathless way he told the story, made me miss much of what he said, though it was great fun listening to him. I'm sure he spoke longer than I've indicated here.

Another person, as I've said, was present on that occasion, It was Laurie Pratt, his chief editor. Laurie maintained throughout the telling an air almost of disinvolvement. "Well, well," was her somewhat distant comment when he finished. To me, it seemed as though she were thinking, "This isn't the Master I know!"

I've always remembered the contrast the three of us made in that relatively brief encounter: Master, exuberantly reminiscing; Laurie Pratt, somewhat distant, and smiling only vaguely—if at all; and myself, laughing but not wholly understanding everything the Master said. He was delighting in his reminiscences, but there was something about the whole scene that seemed to me almost surreal. Did he have a hidden purpose in telling the story, and in the exuberance he showed in the telling? He spoke less clearly than when the two of us were speaking alone. Of course, he was reliving an exciting moment, and communicated its drama successfully. It almost seemed, however, as if, perhaps only by the rapidity with which he spoke, he was deliberately garbling his English.

I've often wondered about that occasion since then. It seems to me, now, to have been fraught with meaning. Was he subtly telling Laurie, for instance, "Don't imagine that you've ever really known me; I am not who I seem to be"? Was he saying to me, "Know me for your own Self; don't let anyone try to tell you who I am"?

Laurie, many years later, dealt me the severest test I've ever had to face in this lifetime. It began with her insistence that I didn't know the Master at all; that she alone, and others who agreed with her, knew him. She said I would never be able to serve his work in the way he wanted.

That occasion at his desert retreat was the only time the three of us were ever alone together. Was the Master merely relating an amusing—and, let's face it, quite amazing—story, rather incomprehensively?

I cannot but think, as I look back on that occasion, that it *should have* held, and *also did* hold, a deep significance. For he must have known what the future held for Laurie and me. Perhaps his message had to do with our attunement with him. Was he saying—perhaps more for her sake than for mine—"I am not who you think I am"?

How subtle was his way of teaching! Often it wasn't even verbal. I soon came to realize, in Laurie's and my relationship together as editors, that although we were friends, we were also poles apart in our perception of the Master's mission. He must have known these differences existed long before they surfaced, though he said nothing about them. He also spoke to me about Laurie in such a way as to ensure that I would always hold her in high esteem, though in later years she tested that esteem to the utmost.

This is a fascinating subject. Because the present book concerns the Master, however, I cannot explore the theme further, here, nor offer any further comment.

✺ 116 ✺

The Master told me the following story about his visit to India in 1935.

"Because it was a time of political agitation in India, when the country was making increasing demands for independence from England, the British police were suspicious of me, and followed me everywhere. They wanted to make sure I didn't add to the general unrest by fanning revolutionary fervor.

"When I visited the Maharaja of Mysore, the police there tried to entrap me. They paid an English woman to create a public scene. Their plan was for her to approach me, throw her arms around me, then kiss me ardently. Press photographers were to be standing nearby, ready to snap that photograph. The picture would then be published in the newspapers—locally, and perhaps nationally—as a means of slandering me. God showed me their plan, however.

"At a public gathering, a young white woman came up to me in view of everyone, and was about to embrace me when I grabbed her by the waist, lifted her high above my head, and turned to the photographers. 'Now,' I called out smiling, 'take your photograph!'

"Of course, they did nothing of the kind. To have published such a picture would only have embarrassed the authorities!"

117

"While I was in India in 1935, I met a wonderful saint; the two of us became great friends. Together we sat under a tree, discoursing to many people. Someone placed rupees 200 in my lap, then fled so that I wouldn't be able to thank him. Everyone pleaded with me, 'Please don't leave us. Remain here. If you'll agree to stay, we will build you a hermitage.'

"I could have remained in that setting very happily. But I thought of you all—the 'potential saints' in America—and I knew I had to come back.

"The next time I am born in a human body, however, I will spend many years wandering blissfully by the Ganges."

The Master told us he would in fact be reborn after another 200 years. He would live for a time the life of a wandering sadhu. Then he would gather his disciples around him, and withdraw, like Babaji, to the Himalayas.

118

"There was a little girl living with her mother here at Mount Washington. She decided to make me a little 'surprise.' One day, before she could spring her surprise on me, I thanked her for it.

"'You peeked!' she cried, miserably.

"'I didn't peek,' I said to her lovingly. 'God told me about it. I wanted you, too, to know He'd done so, and to thank you.'"

119

"The other day I was looking at the picture of my mother. I saw Divine Mother in her face: She was looking a little stern. I said, 'Divine Mother, why don't You smile?' And the photograph itself smiled! All of you know that picture. It shows my mother, in fact, looking fairly serious.

"I then said to Divine Mother, 'There are so many wonderful souls around me, Mother. Please bless them. Deepen their desire to feel Your love in their hearts.'"

The Divine Mother blessed a gathering at which I (Walter) was present, by appearing to the Master's inner gaze. After a time She left, giving as Her reason for doing so the fact that in the hearts of some of those present there were too many desires lurking.

120

"I remember a young pair who attended a class series I gave in Phoenix, Arizona. They were the most beautiful couple I have ever seen; that is saying a lot! Of course, attraction to beauty is measured more or less by a person's own blindness! A mother had a very ugly son, and tried to enter him in a beauty contest. The judge laughed at her, whereupon she answered, 'You fool, this is the most beautiful child in the world. If I were judging this contest, I would give him the prize without even bothering to look at another!' Still, by the standards of modern 'blindness' those two young people *were* beautiful. The whole class enjoyed seeing them; they seemed so perfect—as if blown together by the breeze of their love.

"One day after class, I called them to me. I'd known they had very little money, but I had just learned that they'd sold their little car so they could take the classes. My practice in those days was to charge a little money for classes. The money went to the work. But now that I'd heard about their sacrifice, I told them I wanted to return their money. It took me a whole hour to persuade them to accept it.

"The boy then said to me, 'May I ask you for a favor? Please bless me that I find a job.' I told him he would find one right away, and he did. But then I said something else to them both.

"'Everybody in the class,' I said, 'envies you your love. I don't envy you, for the love in my heart is a hundred times greater than what I see expressed in your eyes. I'd like to see you develop toward the experience of ever deeper, divine love. In a year's time, I plan to return to Phoenix. I would like to see if your love is still as strong then as it is now.'

"I did come back the next year, and tried to look them up. It wasn't easy, but I managed at last to locate the boy. He was working in a store. When he saw me, he came out with me to the car and stood beside it. He looked worn out. It saddened me to see him like that.

His back was bent instead of straight like a yogi's. In a weak voice he said, 'I still believe in God.'

"'What is the matter with you?' I cried. 'I expected to find you communing with God daily!'

"He answered, 'I'm working so hard, I hardly have time for anything else.'

"He took me to his home. They'd had a child, and his wife was expecting another one. I said, 'I miss the luster that I used to see in your eyes.' I felt sorry for them, and gave them a mental and spiritual 'shaking'! As I was leaving, I saw in their eyes again a glimmer of their former love and happiness. They promised me to start meditating again.

"But just see how easy it is to let the world creep in and steal your happiness. Tread the spiritual path very carefully. Delusion awaits you around every corner, hoping to seize you!"

121

Sananda Ghosh told me, "Paramhansaji used, as a boy, to worship images of [the Divine Mother] Kali with great devotion. After our mother died, however, I never saw him do so again. I think grief must have driven his devotion inside. He sought the Divine Mother in ever-deeper meditation."

122

When I (Walter) went to India in 1958, some people who had known the Master during his earlier visit told me, "The Master led a kirtan one evening in a private home in Calcutta. The house was full, and so also was the street outside, and the roof of a building across the street was covered with people. They sang and danced in God all night, uplifted in their love for Him. Such was the Master's magnetism!"

123

Henry Schaufelberger (who later became known as Brother Anandamoy) said to the Master, "Sir, would you bless me that, when I meditate, I be able to sit in the lotus pose? I've tried and tried, but I just can't seem to get it."

"Do not be concerned over such little things," the Master responded. "Ask God for His love. That is much more important!"

124

Norman told me, after the first time he'd performed the yoga postures for the Master in front of guests: "I was doing the postures kind of blindly. Every time I'd start getting into a pose, however, Master would point a finger at me. Some of the postures weren't easy for me, and I'd never been able to do them well. As Master pointed at me, however, I suddenly found I could do each one to perfection."

The Master liked having Norman demonstrate the postures, because of his strong and well-formed body. He wanted to correct a widespread impression people had of yogis, that they are thin and emaciated!

125

To the nuns he once said, "Ladies, don't devote too much time to dressing or caring for your appearance, lest you fall into temptation." He didn't mean they should be indifferent to the normal standards of neatness and good taste, but only that they should not be oversolicitous in these matters.

❧ 126 ❧

The Master told us this story: "I had a vision when I was young in which I saw myself married. My wife was sleeping beside me. I was appalled. 'How dare you!' I cried indignantly. 'This body belongs to God!'

"Sitting up, I took a sword in my hand and began to cut off my arm, piece by piece. I was determined to destroy my whole body.

"Just then I woke up and found that I was striking my arm with the side of my palm. Oh, what a relief it was to find I wasn't married after all! Joyfully I exclaimed again, 'This body belongs to God!'"

❧ 127 ❧

During the last months of the Master's life, someone gave him an expensive Cadillac car. He referred to it several times as his "hangman's dinner."

"You know," he explained, "when someone is about to be executed by hanging, it is traditional to give him the best dinner possible. Divine Mother wanted, as a send-off, to give me something special because my work in this lifetime is finished."

128

The Master assumed whatever attitude was appropriate to the situations before him. When he was doing business, he was conscientiously businesslike. (It must have been affecting to watch! Giving, rather than taking, was so intrinsic to his whole nature.)

He returned one evening to Mount Washington after an outing, during which he had been to an antique shop and purchased a few umbrellas. Interestingly, the Master did have one or two little hobbies of this sort. It was as if to hold his interest in this world. Teaching and writing took him to a higher, more abstract consciousness, and left him with the need to ground himself in something more mundane. I've learned that this is, in fact, a common feature in the lives of many people whose activities are largely mental or, above all, spiritual. Another "hobby" of the Master's was collecting opals, which reminded him, he said, of the opalescent light of the astral world.

On the above-mentioned occasion, he had bargained carefully, trying always to get a good price. After completing his transactions, however, he ceased to be the conscientious buyer. Gazing about him now, he told us with sympathy afterward:

"I saw what a poor shop that man had, and gave him more money than I'd saved while bargaining with him. He said to me, 'You are a gentleman, Sir!' He gave me, in return, an especially fine umbrella."

The Master paused a moment in reflection, then commented, "What a poor-looking floor that man had in his shop! I think I will buy him a new linoleum floor covering."

Always, his first emphasis was on human and spiritual, rather than "practical," material values. To him, every stranger was a dear friend in God.

129

There is a story in *The Path* which was told me by Debi Mukherjee, from Bengal, of a time he went out with Master in his car. The Master had suddenly said to the driver, "Stop the car!" He got out and walked back several doors to a small, rather dingy-looking variety shop. There, to Debi's astonishment, the Master had selected a number of items that couldn't possibly have been of any use to him. He then went up to the counter. The owner, an older woman, added up his bill, which the Master paid. At that moment, the woman burst into tears.

"I very badly needed just this sum of money today!" she told him. "It is near closing time, and I had given up all hope of getting what I needed. Bless you,

Sir. It was God Himself, surely, who sent you to me in my time of need!"

The Master said nothing of this episode to anyone. It was clear, however, that he'd sensed the woman's difficulty while driving by in the car, and had responded to it with divine sympathy.

Throughout his life, he actively demonstrated the biblical teaching, "Love thy neighbor as thyself." Indeed, he gave that teaching a new and deeper meaning, for he saw everybody as, literally, his own Self in the great oneness of God.

130

The Master could, if he so chose, withdraw his mind completely from any pain his body suffered. One day, long before I came to him, he demonstrated this inner freedom. It was when the concrete "wishing well" was being installed at Mount Washington.

The well slipped from the grasp of the men lifting it, and dropped onto the Master's foot, which was crushed under the weight of a thousand pounds. His automatic reaction wrote itself eloquently on his face: Physical pain made him wince involuntarily.

"I will show you something," he said to those present. "I will focus my concentration on the point between the eyebrows." As he did so, instantly every trace of pain vanished from his face. He could walk back and forth easily.

"Now," he said, "I will lower my mind from the spiritual eye." Instantly, his physical expression again displayed the body's automatic reaction to the pain.

Several times he repeated this demonstration. Years later he told us, regarding another pain his body was enduring: "Last night I wanted to feel pain as others do, so I brought my mind down to the body and held it there for a time."

I (Walter) realized then that, just as it takes effort for most people to rise above body-consciousness, so it takes a master an effort of will to bring his mind down to the body.

He would say, "Tell yourselves constantly, 'I am not the body: I am not this form which changes and passes away! I am eternal bliss!'"

ᚾ 131 ᚾ

In a lecture one day he said: "Someone once asked me, 'Is it possible to be inspired at will?' I replied, 'Not if you let inspiration control you, but if you are in control, you can call on it at will.'

"One time," he continued, "I was in my upstairs

room at Mount Washington, preparing to attend a large banquet downstairs. Two hundred people were there, waiting. Someone asked me just then, 'Would you give us a poem?' [Probably the thought was for the Master to read that poem at the banquet.]

"'At once!' I replied. 'Take down these words.' Sitting for a moment, I focused my mind at the point between the eyebrows, then dictated:

"'O Father, when I was blind I found not a door which led to Thee, but now that Thou hast opened my eyes I find doors everywhere: through the hearts of flowers, through the voice of friendship, through sweet memories of all lovely experiences. Every gust of my prayer opens an unentered door in the vast temple of Thy presence.'

"This poem, as it happened, was the first one I included in what later became the book of prayers and poems named, *Whispers from Eternity*. When that book was published, a London newspaper review stated, 'There is one poem in this book that we cannot refrain from quoting.' And this was the one they quoted.

"Inspiration, you see," the Master concluded, "can be called upon at will. To receive it, concentrate deeply at the spiritual eye in the forehead. At that point, then, demand to be given the inspiration you seek."

ᓚᘓᕉ 132 ᕈᘐᕽ

The Master favored calm, determined renunciation over emotional world-rejection. When one feels emotional rejection, there usually lingers inside him also a subconscious attraction.

During a discussion with me at his desert retreat, he told me the following story: "I met a young woman years ago in Mexico City. She taught yoga, and was very committed to this path. One day I asked her, 'How do you feel about marriage?' Her answer quite surprised me.

"'I have given my life to God,' she fairly shouted with intense vehemence, 'and I will continue to serve Him alone, without a mate, faithfully, devotedly, every year of my life, forever, *UNTIL I DIE!!!*'

"'My goodness!' I exclaimed. 'Why that emotion? One must renounce feelings, also. I was going to compliment you on your spiritual commitment. Seek God lovingly and one-pointedly, but seek Him also with deep *calmness.*'"

ᓚᘓᕉ 133 ᕈᘐᕽ

"There was a man lying unconscious in a hospital room," the Master told us. "He was near death; a blood clot had formed in his heart. A friend of his asked me to intercede, so I prayed for him in a superconscious state. All at once, a great power went out of me. At that very moment, the man sat up in bed, completely healed.

"The nurse, who had been attending him in that room, testified later that, a moment before the man had sat up, she had heard an explosion, and had seen a great flash of light."

134

Doctor Lewis told us this story: "I was called away from the Master's presence one Sunday evening to the telephone. To my serious concern, I learned that my daughter Brenda had just been stricken with convulsions.

"When the Master heard this, he stepped briefly behind a screen. A few moments later he emerged, smiling.

"'Don't worry, Doctor,' he told me. 'She will be all right.' Confidently he added, 'And she will never have another one.' Brenda was completely cured. Moreover, she has never had another seizure."

135

There was an old man, a disciple of the Master's, who wanted to visit his Guru at Mount Washington. The Master instructed him, "Go by streetcar to the bottom of the hill. When you get there, phone up, and I'll have someone drive down and pick you up."

The man, however, when he reached the bottom of the hill, decided to walk up to the ashram. He had no idea that the way was so long, and so steep. Apart from his age, he was handicapped by a severe pain in his back. He had been walking only a short distance when the pain grew excruciating. He was also exhausted, from fatigue. He simply wasn't able to proceed any further. He also, however, couldn't retrace his steps. He sat down by the roadside, helpless.

Just then, a car that was coming up the hill stopped beside him, and the driver called to him, "Get in!" Gladly the man accepted. As they continued up the hill, the driver commented, "I don't know what made me come this way. I usually come by another route."

When the Master greeted his elderly disciple, he remarked, "I had to work a bit to get that man to come your way!" He then placed his hand caressingly on the man's back, and the pain vanished instantly.

❦ 136 ❧

There was a certain man in Encinitas who sold real estate. His wife had been seriously ill for ninety days. When the man heard of the Master, who lived locally and who had healing powers, he went and asked him to pray for her. The Master prayed, but was told, for then, not to go to the woman's bedside. Shortly thereafter, to the husband's despair, the wife died.

Then only was the Master told in meditation to go to their home. On entering, he found some thirty people assembled, all of them grieving. The husband was by the woman's side, weeping and shaking her desperately. The Master calmly motioned him away, then placed one hand over the dead woman's forehead, the other one on her back, and began to invoke the Divine Power.

Five or ten minutes later, her body began to shake— "like a motor," as the Master described it later. Presently, a deep calmness stole upon her. Her heartbeat and breathing returned. She slowly opened her eyes. In them was a far-away expression, as though she had just returned from a long journey.

She was completely healed.

ᕈ 137 ᕽ

"During my 1935 visit to India," the Master told us, "I was walking down a street in Serampore, where my Guru lived, when I heard loud lamentations coming from a house. As it happened, this home belonged to the relative of a friend of mine. I went inside, and was told this relative had just died. His family were all weeping. I went to the body and prayed deeply over it. By God's grace, the man was restored to life."

Doctor Lewis told me many years later, "I once asked the Master, 'Did you enter that home because of your personal connection with the man? or was it because God told you to?'

"The Master at once replied, 'Oh, because God told me to. Otherwise, I would not have gone in.'"

ᕈ 138 ᕽ

"There was a woman," the Master said, "who had been told by her doctor that one of her kidneys needed removal. She came to me for advice. After asking God, I said to her, 'Why not check with several other doctors also? Don't base this important decision on the opinion

The Master at his boys' school in Ranchi, India, meditating
on a leopard skin.

of one man alone.' She went to two or three others, all of whom gave it as their opinion that the kidney might be saved.

"I then suggested she stop eating any form of meat and eggs, and drink lots of grapefruit juice. Within a month, she was feeling well. She then went to her doctor, who found that her kidney problem had completely vanished."

Whenever possible, the Master's cures were based on simple common sense. His "common sense," however, had in it also the ingredient of intuitive insight. Thus, depending on the circumstances, he would recommend various approaches to good health. In his practical way, he endorsed the dictum, "God helps those who help themselves."

139

On another occasion, a man complained to the Master of a "tricky heart." He was alarmed, however, to see the Master pick up a pair of scissors!

"Don't be afraid," the Master reassured him. "I am not going to operate on you!" What he did then was snip off a button from the man's waistcoat. "Leave it that way," he said to him. "Don't sew it back on."

A few days later the man returned. He reported almost incredulously, "I am perfectly well again!"

162

The Master then explained to him, "I saw you fiddling with that button, which was right over the heart. That was why you felt an irritation there! When you were no longer able to fiddle with the button, the irritation disappeared."

A simple cure indeed! Who, however, before that man came to the Master, had even thought of that solution?

🙠 140 🙢

The Master generally recommended a vegetarian diet. Doctor Lewis said to us, "When I met the Master, I gave up eating all meat and fish. Some time later, however, I began to suffer mysterious aches and pains in my body. The doctors could find no reason for them. Finally I asked the Master what I might do.

"'Your body had grown accustomed to eating meat,' he said. 'Its cells have been missing that diet. Once a week, therefore, eat a little lamb or chicken. No red meat; just lamb or chicken—or a little fish.'

"I followed his advice, and in a very short time all the pains went away."

ࣷࣵ 141 ࣹࣶ

The Master remarked during his later years, "To my first generation of students, I didn't say much about a vegetarian diet; it was too unusual, then, for the people in this country. Diet was secondary in importance, anyway, to the teachings of yoga.

"For the next generation, I recommended that they eat less meat. Most of them, on an average, became healthier.

"For this third generation, I've recommended a completely vegetarian diet, and find that, of the three groups, the present one is the most healthy.

"I don't care much, however, for that word, 'vegetarian.' Too many people are fanatics on the subject. I've coined what I consider a better word: 'propereatarian.'"

ࣷࣵ 142 ࣹࣶ

"Lahiri Mahasaya was a vegetarian," the Master told me, "although, where others' sensibilities were concerned, he wasn't rigidly so. One evening, he attended a dinner that happened to be attended also by my uncle Sarada. Fish was the main course.

"Many Bengalis, you know, consider fish almost part of a vegetarian diet. My uncle, knowing that Lahiri

Mahasaya was usually very careful of his diet, wondered what he would do on this occasion. As they were eating, Lahiri Mahasaya leaned forward so that my uncle could see him in the line of guests, and called out, 'You see, Sarada? I am eating the fish.'"

ༀ 143 ༀ

"There were two ladies," the Master related to us one day, "who used to leave their car unlocked even when parking it on the street. I said to them, 'You should be practical. In public places especially, there may be thieves about.'

"'Where is your faith in God?' they demanded airily.

"'I have faith in God,' I replied, 'but I don't expect Him to do everything for me: That would be presumptuous! You should rely also on your own common sense.'

"Well, they wouldn't listen, but continued to leave their car door unlocked. One day, they purchased several expensive paintings, and left them, unprotected, on the back seat of their car. When they returned, they found that the paintings had been stolen. It upset them terribly. The next time they saw me, they related their 'tragedy' to me.

"I said, 'Perhaps you'll understand, now, the importance of cooperating with God's grace. Remember what

Jesus said in the wilderness, after Satan tempted him to throw himself off a mountain just to prove that God would protect him. He said, "It is written, Thou shalt not tempt the Lord thy God." In future, be more careful, and don't "tempt" God: that is, don't ask Him to do favors for you that you can do perfectly easily for yourselves.'"

There is an interesting sidelight to this story. It concerns the emotional upset of those ladies over the loss of their paintings. Their distress suggests, obviously, an emotional attachment. For faith to be true, however, one must place *everything* in God's hands—not only the safety of his possessions. One should be sensible, but at the same time he should be non-attached. True faith in God is unconditional. Its consequences never distress the mind. The Master taught always, therefore, the importance of combining common sense with equanimity.

⟐ 144 ⟐

Referring back to that last "conversation," it must be understood that divine principles need to be applied variously also, according to one's own level of consciousness. On another occasion, the Master told us a story about Tulsidas, a great devotee of Rama (the hero of the *Ramayana*). Many people in India look upon Rama as the Lord Himself in human form.

"Tulsidas," said the Master, "was the priest in a temple that housed several priceless gold objects. Often, when he meditated, he would become so immersed in ecstasy that he became oblivious to everything else. Yet he harbored still a slight concern for the safety of those gold objects, for which he was responsible.

"One day a stranger, dressed like a gentleman, approached Tulsidas and said, 'Sir, I am a humble devotee desirous of worshiping in your temple. Every time I try to enter it, however, I find the way blocked by that fellow standing guard at the entrance. He won't let me pass through.'

"Tulsidas, knowing that there was no such guard, inquired, 'What does this man look like?'

"'Well, he is dressed somewhat picturesquely, in an antique style, and holds a large bow.'

"Tulsidas, when he heard this description, was overwhelmed with joy and devotion, for he understood that Lord Rama himself, for his devotee's sake, had been posting himself at the temple entrance to protect it while Tulsidas meditated.

"'I will ask him in future,' said Tulsidas, 'to let you pass through.'

"The thief—which of course is what he really was—came the next day, and entered freely. He snatched up every gold object in sight, then took to his heels. Tulsidas saw him running away, and went inside to see what had been stolen. There he saw one gold object left, which the man had overlooked. Picking it up, he ran after the thief. 'Wait!' he cried. 'Wait!' Finally he caught up with him and said, 'Here, Friend: you forgot this item.'

"The thief, confronted with such extraordinary forgiveness, recognized in this example of perfect non-attachment a quality so inspiring that he was over-whelmed. He returned to Tulsidas everything he had taken."

❧ 145 ❧

"A woman once informed me, a trifle smugly, that in a former incarnation she had been Mary, Queen of Scots. 'That's interesting,' I replied. 'Tell me, how did you receive this information?' Well, it seemed a certain 'psychic' had told her so.

"Soon afterward, another woman told me the same thing. When I asked her about it, she said she'd re-ceived this 'news' from the same source. I called the two women together, and repeated their stories to them. I then asked them, 'Now, how can *both* of you have been Mary, Queen of Scots?' They realized, of course, that they'd been fooled.

"What I want to say in relating this story is, Don't listen to every claim by people who say they have special knowledge about you. As to your own past incarnations, moreover, be guided above all by self-knowledge, and by your own intuition. What does it really matter, after all, who you were in the past? Whoever that was, you are still yourself and have only one challenge before you that is worth considering: how to get out of delusion and find God. Be guided above all by that need, which is eternal."

146

"Desire and anger are the two greatest barriers to wisdom. They destroy a person's peace of mind, and obstruct the flow of his understanding. When anger seizes you, you may think, 'Oh, this feels *wonderful!*' In exhilaration, you may do something terrible, not even counting the cost. That is how murders often get committed. Later, however, comes retribution: The murderer in turn finds his own life completely ruined.

"Desire, again, confuses the mind. Its frustration is what produces anger. It is important that you always remain inwardly calm and non-attached. Accept with unruffled mind whatever comes. I often say, 'What comes of itself, let it come.' This is just as true for the bad things in life as for the good. Only calmness will give you a sense of correct proportion. It will inspire you to behave with unfailing good sense."

⋘ 147 ⋙

During the last days of Master's life, Binay R. Sen, the ambassador from India, visited him at Mount Washington. A certain man, prominent in the Indian community of Los Angeles, arrived with the ambassador's entourage. For many years, this man had spoken against the Master.

When the Master saw him among the guests, he made it a point of saying to him quietly, when out of earshot of the others, "Remember, I will always love you. Why don't we work together?" A disciple of the Master's happened to be standing close by, and overheard those words. It turned out also that this moment was captured on film by a photographer. One wonders whether this wasn't, for that man, a very poignant moment. He is shown gazing at the Master. In his eyes are a mixture of surprise and wonder.

⋘ 148 ⋙

Henry Schaufelberger (Brother Anandamoy), a disciple of the Master's, endured a series of physical inconveniences. First, he broke a rib. Then a rash plagued him and made his life miserable. Then he broke another rib. He seemed to be getting a steady stream of such petty annoyances.

The Master said to him one day, "Always more troubles, isn't it? But that's good. You have lots of work to do, that's why. God wants to make you strong. We don't produce D.D.'s here. [D.D. is short for 'Doctor of Divinity.'] Our ministers don't receive their authority to teach with diplomas that declare they've completed a course of intellectual study. They win their right in the fire of divine testing."

৯ 149 ৯

The following words were among the last advice he gave to the monks:

"No one can give you the desire for God. You must cultivate that desire in yourselves. God Himself couldn't give it to you. For when He created human beings, He didn't make them puppets. You must desire Him, *yourselves*.

"Be wary of developing too keen an intelligence. Many people use their powers of reasoning cleverly to justify their delusions. Concentrate more, instead, on developing heart quality. Devote as much time as you can, daily, to meditation: to actually experiencing God.

"Don't sleep too much. Sleep is the unconscious way of contacting God. Sleep is counterfeit ecstasy.

"Don't joke too much. I myself, as you know, like a

good laugh, but if I make up my mind to be serious, no one can make me even smile. Be happy and cheerful—above all inwardly. Be outwardly grave, but inwardly cheerful.

"Don't waste the perception of God's presence, acquired in meditation, by useless chatting. Idle words are like bullets: they riddle the milk pail of peace. In devoting time unnecessarily to conversation and exuberant laughter, you'll find you have nothing left inside. Fill the pail of your consciousness with the milk of meditative peace, then keep it filled. Joking is false happiness. Too much laughter riddles the mind and lets the peace in the bucket flow out, wasting it.

"Wine, sex, and money: These are the three great delusions. Don't be trapped by them. Some of you are weak, I know, but don't be discouraged. Meditate regularly, and you will find a joy inside that is real. You will then have something you can compare to sense pleasures. That comparison will automatically make you want to forsake your sorrow-producing bad habits. The best way to overcome temptation is to have something more fulfilling to compare it with.

"Sex seems pleasant to you now, but when you discover the joy of real inner union, you will see how much more wonderful that is. This union can be achieved physically also, by what is known in yoga as *kechari mudra*—touching the tip of the tongue to nerves in the nasal passage, or to the uvula at the back of the mouth.*

"Don't waste time on distractions: reading too much, and so on. Reading can be good if it is instructive or inspiring, but if you let it interfere with meditation it becomes an evil. Read only a little bit, to find inspiration, but spend most of your time in meditative silence.

"Consider this: Every day one hundred books, more or less, are published. You couldn't read them all if you wanted to! No one, no matter how brilliant, could absorb more than a tiny fraction of the knowledge available. Scientists often pride themselves on their knowledge, but can they explain how even a simple leaf was created? Why stuff your head with other people's discoveries, anyway? That is all one accomplishes, by reading all the time! I always say, 'If you read one hour, then write two hours, think three hours, and meditate all the time!'

"No matter how much the organization keeps me busy, I never forgo my daily tryst with God. Faithfully I practice Kriya Yoga, and meditate.

"Some of those who come here, and later return to the world, go out with a spirit of rejection. After a life of renunciation, they 'renounce' any further spiritual effort! They don't know what they had here. Please, all

---

*It isn't possible, unfortunately, to explain this esoteric technique here. I hope it will suffice simply to allude to it.

of you, realize your good fortune. How easy the spiritual path is, if you give even a little time each day to meditation. Meditate intensely, morning and evening.

"Even fifteen minutes of meditation is better than no time at all. Better still, make it half an hour, or even one hour. Do 108 Kriyas; chant *AUM* at the spinal centers, then listen inwardly to the sounds. If you like, resume your practice of Hong-Sau. Or do *Bhakti Yoga* [devotional self-offering to God].

"Practice watching the breath with Hong-Sau in the spine, if you like. Go up and down the spine with it, instead of watching its flow in the nostrils. Tell your body: 'If you don't meditate regularly, I will give you a whipping!' Meditate even one and a half hours at a time, if you can. Everything you do—even if it is only picking up a straw off the ground, like Brother Lawrence—offer it mentally to God. If only you will do that, He will reach down and help you.

"Another thing I urge all of you: Give to one another the respect you have always shown me. Be kind to one another, just as you have been kind to me. If you see evil in one another, you desecrate the image of God that is in both of you. God is in everyone. To see good in all is to see Him everywhere."

With Luther Burbank, the "American saint," to whom Yogananda dedicated his Autobiography of a Yogi. He gave the Master a cutting of his spineless cactus, which now thrives on the grounds at Mt. Washington.

❦ 150 ❧

The Master often reminisced about his early years as he approached the end of his life.

"There was a temple in Benares," he told us, "which I enjoyed visiting. I found there an opening inside; it led into another world—how different from the busy street outdoors! The opening was just wide enough for me to squeeze through if I went in sideways. And remember, I was only a boy then, and thin for my age. Within that opening, I found a flight of stairs leading down. I descended three storeys. I couldn't take a candle with me, as there was no fresh air. It was completely dark, down below, and *completely* silent. The sound of *AUM* boomed loudly. I discovered a little niche there, just big enough for me to sit in, and there I sat, did a few Kriyas, and went into breathless ecstasy."

❦ 151 ❧

Another time he told us, again reminiscing, "When I was a boy I liked to play football. In one of the neighborhoods we moved to, the boys cursed and used vulgar language. I didn't care for it, so I said, 'As long as you talk like that, I won't come and play with you.' That led them to decide that we were enemies.

"One day they hatched a plot to punish me. There was a crazy fellow who lived in our neighborhood; people called him 'Jotin, the mad fellow.' He would pick a fight with anyone, even without any reason. Those boys threatened to set him on me if I refused to play with them. Still I said, 'I won't come so long as you go on using foul language.'

"Well, the following evening this man was waiting for me in the park through which I passed every day. I saw him even before entering the park. He was carrying a big stick in his hand. There were two friends of mine walking with me; they said, 'Don't go in there. He means to give you a big beating.' I answered, 'Don't be afraid. We can go in.'

"First, however, I returned to my room and meditated. There I prayed to Shiva, Lord of Destruction. 'Let my love and blessings destroy Jotin's anger!'

"I then returned to the park. My friends wouldn't join me. Jotin blocked the path, menacingly brandishing his stick. I walked up to him slowly, and looked him straight in the eye, calmly and steadily. There ensued a pause. Then he dropped his gaze, smiled a little sheepishly, and left the scene.

"That next night, in meditation, I asked Shiva to change Jotin. In the afternoon of the following day, I went back to the park. Jotin was standing there; this time, however, there was no stick in his hand. Evening was falling, and Jotin began to follow me. My friends, who had come with me, whispered fearfully, 'He is coming this way. He intends to beat you up.' They hurried away. When Jotin caught up with me, however, he prostrated on the ground before me and cried, 'What have you done to me? Shiva appeared before me in a vision last night, and said to me, "You are being unjust."' He added, 'I want to follow you.' Thus, he became my student.

"A few months later, he said to me one day, 'You have helped me in so many ways—God, through you. Can you help me in my present predicament? Every time my boss scolds me, I become angry and slap him. Owing to this weakness of mine, I can't hold a job. But I just can't help myself. I lose my temper too easily.'

"I said to him, 'I have taught you meditation. Tonight, while meditating, keep these words in mind: Whatever thought you hold strongly, surround it with energy, and let it wash away the habit you wish to destroy.'

"Jotin did as I'd suggested. He practiced this simple technique daily for weeks. One day, he came and told me gratefully, 'Mukunda, I have overcome my anger.'

"I decided he needed to be tested. He too, after all, had to be sure in himself that the change was firmly established in him. Recalling the many enemies he'd made, I told a few of them to do everything they could to make him angry. They gave it a good try! However, they failed. Jotin never faltered for a moment. He had, indeed, overcome his anger."

✺ 152 ✺

The Master told us this beautiful story about Durbasha, a saint in ancient India:

"Durbasha was called 'the angry one.' Well," remarked the Master with a chuckle, "his anger may have been a bluff to protect himself from curiosity seekers. He was, however, a great yogi, and a deep lover of God. One day, in ecstasy, Durbasha danced in the Spirit with Lord Krishna. In his exaltation he suddenly beheld his body lying on the ground, lifeless. His body now was that of a young man. From then on, others saw him rejuvenated. And Durbasha cried out with joy, 'I was dancing in the Spirit with Lord Krishna, and I saw my old body lying there in a heap. Krishna has given me a new suit of clothes!'"

153

"Women are more influenced by feeling," the Master used to say, "and men, more by reason. You can see it in the very shape of their bodies. Women's breasts are in the heart region, where the feelings reside. Men's foreheads, on the other hand—the area covering the brain, where the intellect is centered—are square, and often have a slight projection above the eyebrows.

"One day I was talking with a successful woman author. All her life she had been competing in what was primarily a masculine arena, and she prided herself on her intellectual outlook on everything. 'In everything I do,' she told me, 'I am guided entirely by reason.'

"I said nothing. Gradually, however, I steered the conversation around to another woman author—this woman's 'competitor.' When it came to discussing this 'trade rival,' the woman had nothing good to say.

"'Aha,' I said teasingly, 'you go only by reason, do you?' She saw immediately what I meant, and we had a good laugh over it."

154

An astonishing aspect of Paramhansa Yogananda's life was his extraordinary mental fluidity. It revealed his utter freedom, inwardly. Sometimes he compared his own thought processes to writing on water. He didn't mean he was forgetful: far from it! Indeed, his memory was utterly clear. In the freedom of his consciousness, however, he responded suitably to every circumstance he faced. He could be stern, loving, good-humored, aloof—always depending on the need, and never on his own personal feelings. Even his facial expressions would change subtly with every shift in people's attitudes around him. His sensitivity to their consciousness never ceased to amaze me.

In the years that I got to live with him, I never saw him in quite the same aspect twice. It may seem strange, but I found it difficult—in contrast to the clarity with which I remembered his spoken words—to remember clearly what he looked like. I loved to meditate on him, but always I had to look, first, at a photograph. I couldn't instantly recall his facial features to mind.

He was a flawless mirror. Constantly he reflected back to people what they were. It wasn't that he reflected back their flaws. If they were angry, for instance, he wouldn't show anger. What he reflected back was the reactions of their own higher Self to anything they were feeling. No one could fool him. Before his calm gaze, a person's inner life was stripped bare. Some people, for that very reason, feared to be around him.

I've often reflected on two extreme examples of this extraordinary manifestation of an altogether superconscious nature. He was *triguna rahitam*—beyond the three *gunas,* or basic qualities of Nature.

One example is a photograph of him standing beside Emilio Portes Gil, who at that time was the president of Mexico. Señor Portes Gil was a large, rather heavy-set man. The Master, next to him, looked somewhat large and heavy set also. Both even wore similar expressions.

"Well," one might say, "so the Master was large and heavy set." But he wasn't. In the first place, he was rather short, being only about five feet six. For another, though strong, he wasn't heavy set. The impression conveyed by that photograph was due more to his consciousness.

The other example was also a photograph. He is shown standing beside Amelita Galli-Curci, the famous Italian opera singer. Madame Galli-Curci was small. She seemed, moreover, in the photo at least, rather frail. Strange to say, the Master also looked somewhat small and frail. In his expression, too, there seemed to be a rather old-world outlook.

And yet, looking at him face to face, one saw that he was, simply, himself: not tall, though robust and strongly built, his features completely pleasing to the eye.

The Master greatly appreciated the natural wonders of America.
Shown here with a "friend" at Yellowstone, 1925.

155

On the subject of the Master's clear memory, I remember an episode involving Oliver Rogers, a disciple about fifty-five years old—well past the age of most of us—who came as a disciple about a year after I did. "Rogers," as the Master called him, said to him one day, "I heard you many years ago, Master, in Boston's Symphony Hall. Something impressed me particularly that day: In that full auditorium, you kept your gaze fixed on me."

"I remember," answered the Master quietly. It had taken his disciple all these years to come. Rogers added, "During all that time, I never forgot you. I kept wondering where you were, and asking about you. How wonderful it is, to have found you at last!"

156

On another occasion, the Master said to Rogers, "You have clear sailing."

Several of those present wondered, naturally, "What about me?" "What about me?" The Master caught their thought. Not wanting to leave them "hanging," he added, "and—you will all have clear sailing, if you keep on to the end."

Two or three of them exulted afterward, "Did you hear that? Master said we'd *all* have clear sailing!"

I decided not to remind them that he'd added that one little word, "if." Their deliberate oversight of it, however, revealed a tendency I've often observed in disciples, when recollecting the things he said and did: to let their memory be colored by their desires.

❧ 157 ❧

That last reflection naturally raises a question: How reliable are you, Walter, when you quote him?

Fortunately, my interest has always been in what he actually said, not in what I wanted him to say. I've been blessed in this life, too, with a very clear memory. It serves me best when it comes to words and speech patterns. Perhaps that was why I aspired, as a young man, to be a playwright. It may also be why I've always had a certain facility for languages. In my mind I can "hear" people speaking, after hearing them speak a little. From that recollection, I am able to phrase my own sentences.

Rod Brown, a friend of mine in college, told me after reading my autobiography, *The Path,* "I have only one objection to your book: You have total recall!"

In 1950, the Master decided to return to India, if

possible. He planned to take me, as well as several others, along with him. One day at his desert retreat I said to him, "I believe I could learn Bengali easily."

"*Very* easily," he replied. Then, pointing to his mouth, he said, "*Mukh*"; to his nose, "*Nak*"; to his eyes: "*Chok*"; to an ear: "*Kan*"; to his hand: "*Hath.*" Eight years later, when finally I got to go to India, I verified that this memory was accurate.

I remember reading a note someone had scribbled in the margin of a letter that I had once written. I'd written the letter over forty years earlier. Beside my quote of what that person had said to me, she had scribbled, "Not in those words!" But yes, *exactly* in those words! I'm quite certain, for even today I can hear in my mind the very tone of her voice as she spoke them.

It may be that the Master gave me a special blessing in this respect, for though he told me to write down his words, I knew no shorthand. Yet even years later, I found that I could recall clearly, word for word, what he'd said, and just how he'd said it. Nothing I've ever experienced has caused me to question this ability.

I say these things not to boast, but only to reassure the reader that what I recorded in those notebooks was accurate.

Probably it was also owing to the Master's extraordinary magnetism that his words, especially, lingered clearly in my mind. Whatever he uttered penetrated deeply, and remains with me to this day. Once, at a gathering of the monks and nuns, he sang a song in Bengali:

"Mukti dete pari,
Mukti dete pari,
Mukti dete pari—
Bhakti dete pari koi?"

As I mentioned earlier, I knew no Bengali at that time, and have never heard the song again, yet the words have remained with me. Next, he sang the song in English. It was a song to the devotee as if sung by the Divine Mother:

"O devotee, I can give you salvation,
But not my love and devotion.
Ask of me salvation,
But not my love and devotion,
For in thee, then, when I give those away,
I become poor—walking on your heart's way!"

Such was the Master's magnetism that not only his words, but the melody as well, have remained with me ever since, though he sang it once only. Years later I learned Bengali, and found that I'd remembered also the Bengali words accurately. Both versions, Bengali and English, and also the melody, remain with me to the present day.*

*I wasn't aware that this speech was recorded. I'm told there was a slight error in my memory. Curiously, it concerns a slip of the tongue of Master's, which I kept wanting to repeat but knew was a mistake.

158

The song I've just quoted was so heart-meltingly sweet, it brought tears of longing to the eyes. Ah! one thought, for Divine Mother's love! Obviously, what the words meant was, "*Don't* seek Me merely for salvation: Seek Me for My love."

It is easy to see that many women, especially, encountering such tenderness and sweetness in the Master's nature, must have looked upon him with motherly eyes. Yet his nature was, at the same time, extraordinarily powerful. For men, it was often quite different. They felt challenged—even intimidated—by the power he emanated. Their masculine nature found it difficult to accept, and adapt to, such strength in another human being. Few men—perhaps especially in America, where independence of spirit commands respect and admiration—found it easy to be his followers. This, probably, was the reason he also attracted enemies—though their enmity, in every case, was self-generated; he, himself, sincerely loved everyone.

Of course, the truth is, his strength challenged them to become *real* men: not proud and aggressive, but noble, fair-minded, generous whether in victory or defeat, and above all strong *in themselves.*

As it turns out, therefore, the mistake was both of ours!

One thinks, in this respect, of Jesus Christ, whom the Pharisees opposed from the beginning because, even without speaking, he emanated so much spiritual power. It was a power incalculably greater than their own.

The image many people have of the Master—one that has been projected, perhaps, by an overbalance in the number of women disciples—is of someone so sweet as to be almost cuddly! I smile when I think of his other side. He *was* lovable, certainly—utterly so. Yet he was also the very personification of power!

❧ 159 ❧

The subject of that power deserves a commentary of its own. For he told us that, in a former incarnation, he had been William the Conqueror.

What an irony for me, personally! I'd been raised until the age of thirteen within the English school system, where little good was said about William. Indeed, I considered him one of the great villains of history. And here suddenly, to my self-admitted dismay, I found that this "villain" was my own guru!

Naturally, on first receiving this news I made it a point to read up on William's life. From that reading I learned that what people had found "villainous" about him was above all—apart from the obvious fact that he frustrated many people's selfish ambitions—his aura of enormous power. Baron after baron pitted himself futilely against him. Even while William was a boy, he had to fight for his birthright. Later in life, his own oldest son Robert (nicknamed "Curthose") fought against him, motivated by fierce envy.

William had an important role to play in history. His vigor was not due, as historians generally suppose, to personal ambition. He acted in obedience to God's command, inwardly.

His was a hard life. So also were the times he lived in. He had no alternative but to respond appropriately to the countless challenges he faced. Had he been more acquiescing, he would have failed in his task. It must be remembered that God sends not only nourishing rain upon the earth, but also lightning, drought, and raging floods. William was a divine instrument in an important destiny. He forged into a single nation a patchwork of loosely knit, warring fiefdoms. England, too, had a divine destiny: to unite East and West, and thereby gradually to help mankind in its struggle to enter a new and higher age: *Dwapara Yuga.*

William was, in fact, a deeply spiritual man. It is said of him that he never for a day missed receiving the Eucharist. He built and strengthened monasteries. His closest friends were saintly men: Archbishop Lanfranc (who in the present life, Yogananda told us, was his guru, Swami Sri Yukteswar), and also Anselm. In an age notorious for its promiscuity, it is said of William that he was completely faithful to his wife.

The purpose of this book, obviously, is not to analyze the life of William the Conqueror. I mention it here to underscore an important aspect of Yogananda's character: his extraordinary power. This was evident to all who knew him personally. It was an aspect of his nature that many people have overlooked, or else have known little about. Again, as I said, that widespread lack of awareness may be due to the fact that, apart from Dr. Lewis, hardly any man seems ever to have spoken or written much about the Master. Even Dr. Lewis, though a deeply devoted disciple, saw his Guru only in terms of his own personal love for him. He never showed a deep understanding of the universality of the Master's mission, nor of the universal love he bore *everyone.* Sananda Lal Ghosh, a brother of the Master's, years later wrote a book about the Master's early life called *Mejda,* but Sananda wasn't a disciple, and never did anything actually to serve the Master's mission. His book is completely personal, though also fascinating.

Many people have commented, in fact, how surprised (not to say shocked) they were when they first heard the Master's voice on a recording. Resounding clearly in that voice is no ba-a-a of a gentle lamb, but the mighty roar of a spiritual warrior.

☙ 160 ☙

I asked the Master once, after I'd pondered his life as William, "Is it possible, Sir, for a liberated master not to live in a state of *samadhi* [the highest state of ecstasy]?" He replied: "One never loses the awareness that he is inwardly free."

Indeed, when I reflect on *avatars* like Lahiri Mahasaya, I see that, in order to fulfill their earthly roles—in Lahiri Mahasaya's case it was to marry, to work like other householders, and to raise a family, and at the same time to be, inwardly, an exalted yogi—they had to accept a certain veil of delusion. It was only when Lahiri Mahasaya met Babaji in the Himalayas that he fully recalled his true spiritual stature.

A liberated master, however, though assigned even the task of walking among worldly people as a worldly person himself, never loses his awareness that nothing in this world can touch him, inwardly.

☙ 161 ☙

"History," Napoleon Bonaparte is reputed to have said, "is a lie agreed upon." Among such lies, certainly, are many of the legends surrounding William the Conqueror. A disciple of the Master's was reading William's

192

life once, and came upon a passage where William was described as courting Matilda by knocking her down and dragging her about the room by the hair. Amused, the disciple read this section aloud to the Master. He replied in amazement, "How they distort history! What happened wasn't like that *at all.*"

ஜை 162 ஜை

Patterns repeat themselves in the lives of individuals, no less than in the history of nations. The Master told us that his oldest son in that life, Duke Robert, was Swami Dhirananda in this life. Dhirananda once again betrayed him, and for the same reasons as before: envy and jealousy.

In *Autobiography of a Yogi,* there is an episode where Yogananda's guru, Sri Yukteswar, expressed displeasure with Yogananda to the Master's father. The book states, "The only cause of Sri Yukteswar's displeasure at the time was that I had been trying, against his gentle hint, to convert a certain man to the spiritual path." That "certain man" was Swami Dhirananda.

It was the Master's responsibility in this life, as it had been in former lives, to help this disciple. Sri Yukteswar, for his part, saw it as his own responsibility to spare his disciple the great problems he foresaw in his future. In fact, as Tulsi Bose (a boyhood friend of Yogananda's) told a close disciple of the Master's years later, "Paramhansaji once said to me when we were still boys together, 'Someday Bagchi [which was at that time still Swami Dhirananda's name] will betray me and marry a white woman.'" The Master had known what would occur, in other words, from the very beginning.

Why were Sri Yukteswar and Yogananda at odds on this matter? Such, the Master himself told me, is the divine "play" in the lives of masters. To us, that play can seem very mysterious!

I (Walter) got to meet William's second son of that lifetime, William Rufus. In the present life, Master told us, he was a New York businessman named Vickerman. Mr. Vickerman was a sincere spiritual aspirant, and the Master's disciple. At our meeting, he remarked that he felt toward me "like a brother"—a feeling that was based, I believe, on an old memory.

During that meeting, he related to me the following story:

"I began to meditate many years ago. After I'd been practicing for some time, however, I encountered an insurmountable obstacle: the breath. I couldn't go deeper in meditation so long as my breath kept on pumping away, distracting my concentration. I had to learn how to go breathless. In fact, I needed help. The problem was, I didn't know where to go for it.

"One day I saw in the newspapers that a certain

Swami Yogananda was scheduled to give a lecture in Philadelphia. I dismissed the thought of listening to him, and told myself impatiently, 'I've heard too many swamis! I'm not interested in what they have to say. But if this man can help me to go breathless, I must go and meet him.'

"I didn't attend the lecture, but waited for him in the hotel. On his return, I went up to his room and knocked on the door, which he opened. Determined to waste no time, I asked him bluntly, 'Can you help me to go breathless?'

"'Yes,' he said, equally briefly. 'Come inside.'

"I entered, and he touched me. All at once, my breath stopped: I entered the breathless state of superconsciousness. Since then, I have been his devoted follower."

William Rufus, too—King William II, as he became—is said to have had a brusque personality. A diamond in the rough is how he might be described. He was, however, in his own, somewhat heavy-handed way, completely loyal to his father, as Mr. Vickerman remained to Paramhansa Yogananda.

✺ 163 ✺

"Someone once said to me," Yogananda said, "'You are a good salesman.'

"'That,' I replied, 'is because I have sold myself on the merits of what I teach!'"

◦❧ 164 ❧◦

"Most people," the Master said, "lose all interest in this world at the time of death. That is natural and right: After all, they are soon going to have to leave it! Besides, this world isn't ours: It is God's. That mental disinvolvement at the approach of death should remind everyone of the need for being inwardly non-attached all through life, even while busily engaged in worldly activities.

"I recall, in amusing contrast," the Master added, "the story of a man who, as he lay dying, saw that the oil lamp in his room was burning too high. He called out to his son, 'Hey, Ramu, turn down that light: It is wasting oil!' There the man was, on the point of leaving his body; the 'oil' in his own 'lamp' was nearly exhausted. And still he worried about wasting the oil in that lamp! Such is worldly attachment. Even at death, people cling to what they call life.

"Don't be like that," the Master concluded, with a blissful smile. That smile was a reminder in itself of the eternal bliss that awaits all of us, if we will remain ever non-attached to this world, and "attached" only to God.

❦ 165 ❦

To the monks, the Master would sometimes quote something a saint had once said to him:

"Woman leads a twofold existence. During the day, she is very sweet and pleasing to look at. Thus, she lures men into her trap. At night, however, she becomes a tigress and drinks man's blood!

"Did you know that one seminal emission is equal to losing a quart of blood? It saps your power. There *is* power in that fluid, naturally; there has to be. It was given you to create new life."

❦ 166 ❦

The Master summoned Clifford Frederick, a disciple at Mount Washington, to his desert retreat. Clifford came, but was privately worried about the duties he was neglecting by his absence.

The Master said to him, "I know you are worried, but this, now, is your responsibility. I go by the orders of the 'Supreme Boss' up there. It is to Him you are answerable. Don't bother with anything else. Be free, inside.

"If God told me at this very moment, 'Come home,' I would gladly drop everything—organization, buildings, work, books, people—everything, to do His will. This world is His business. He is the Doer, not you or I."

ᥣᥱ 167 ᥱᥩ

Television appeared on the market only late in the Master's life. He cautioned us against watching it too much. "Television has a satanic influence," he said. "Don't let yourselves be too fascinated by it. Seek, instead, the 'television' of superconscious visions in the spiritual eye."

ᥣᥱ 168 ᥱᥩ

I once asked the Master if, during classes that I was giving for new monks, it would be all right to include a few stories from the life of Krishna. To my surprise, he replied cautiously.

"It's all right to tell them a few of those stories," he said, "but be careful to choose only those with a clear message. The stories of Krishna—especially those of his boyhood in Brindaban—are allegorical. They have been greatly misunderstood by Westerners, and by many Indians as well. Westerners, especially, when reading them, think the gopis were ordinary young women

The Master at Mt. Washington, 1925.

enjoying the emotion of human love. Actually, the gopis were incarnated *rishis* [sages]. They took birth to show, allegorically, the soul's relationship with the divine Beloved. There was nothing sensual or impure in that relationship. Worldly people, when they hear those stories, project onto them their own sensual or selfish tendencies. The reality wasn't like that at all.

"Those stories were intended to win people *away from* lust and desire. Therefore I say, Be careful how you present them to your classes."

༃ 169 ༂

Showing the transcendent nature of Krishna's relationship with the gopis (cowherd girls; Krishna's disciples), the Master told us the following story:

"Krishna and Radha, his closest gopi disciple, were walking together in the forest. She felt drawn down, briefly, to the delusion of being a woman, whose own dear beloved was Krishna. With sagging shoulders she said to him, 'I am feeling very tired!'

"Krishna, well aware of what she was feeling, asked her, 'Would you like me to carry you?' Oh, she was so pleased! 'Yes!' she cried happily. '*Would* you?'

"He bent down to let her jump onto his back. The moment she jumped, however, he disappeared! She landed flat on the ground. At once she realized her mistake, and cried tearfully, 'O Krishna, Lord, please forgive me. I know that in your true nature you are infinite, and that your love is given equally to all. Please, come back to me!'

"Krishna appeared again, quite unconcerned at what had occurred. Peacefully they continued their walk through the forest."

❧ 170 ❧

Arthur Smith, a minister in the Master's work, left it after my arrival there. The Master told me later, "Smith announced to me one day, proudly, 'Do you know, I never take any of the collection money from the church. It all goes to the work.' The moment he said that, I knew he was not for this path."

What the Master meant was that such an act, in a true devotee, would have been only natural; it would not have been a cause for pride.

❧ 171 ❧

"God watches the heart," the Master said. "Seek to please Him above all. Don't act with the prime motive of pleasing others."

I was struck especially by his next words, which showed how balanced he was in everything he taught. "It is even good," he added, "to do good for the sake of praise. That is better than not to do good at all! Still, when you do good to please God alone, that is true *Karma Yoga*. It is almost as good as meditation. Indeed, it is 'half meditation.' Even if others misunderstand you, God will never misunderstand. Live to feel His smile in your heart."

172

To those who grieve over the death of a loved one, the following words of the Master's should offer deep consolation.

"Departed relatives and friends sometimes come to one in dreams. Be open to that possibility, especially if you deeply miss your loved ones, for such dreams can be true experiences.

"When Woody's mother died of breast cancer,* I became very withdrawn for a time.

"'Don't be moody,' someone said to me.

"'This is no mood!' I exclaimed. (How can genuine

*Woody was a close woman disciple of the Master's.

sorrow over the loss of a friend be called a mood!) I prayed deeply. Then at last I saw her in the astral world.

"An angel was leading her away from me. I saw her pause briefly and smile at the beauty of the flowers in a meadow. I called to her, and she turned. At first she didn't recognize me. But then I touched her on the forehead, and she cried, 'I remember!' She parted the gown she was wearing and said, 'See: no more cancer!' She was free, and wonderfully happy."

❦ 173 ❦

Rogers, before coming to Mount Washington, had been a professional house painter. The Master once said to him, "I see you, in the astral world, creating flowers by thought alone." Rogers's love of visual beauty, the Master was saying, would be fulfilled on that plane. Indeed, though worldly desires can only be satisfied on the physical plane, pure desires can be fulfilled better in the astral world.

"Many great works of art, poetry, and music," the Master said, "are inspired by astral memories. The desire to do noble, beautiful things here on earth is also often a carryover of astral experiences between a person's earth lives."

❧ 174 ☙

"Sir," a student asked him, "is everyone conscious in the astral world?"

"Not everyone," he replied. "People of worldly consciousness enter a sort of gray mist. Some of them are vaguely conscious, depending on the sensitivity of their perception, but for many of them it is like a dream. They aren't quite sure what is going on. If your intuition is even slightly developed, however—especially if you've meditated and prayed some in this life, but also if you've served others, even as a soldier who fought heroically in battle—you will find, after you leave this world, that that other world is far more beautiful than this one, and extremely enjoyable!"

❧ 175 ☙

"A couple expressed to me their desire for a spiritual child. I prayed for them, then showed them a photograph. This soul, I told them, would be suitable for them, and was also, I felt, ready to be reborn on earth.

"'Meditate on this soul,' I said. 'Concentrate especially on the eyes. Invite him to come dwell in your home. In addition, have no sexual contact for six months; abstinence will increase your magnetism.

"'When, at the end of that time, you come together physically, think of that person, and think also of God. If you follow my advice in all these respects, that soul will be born to you.'

"They followed what I'd told them, and, some time later, that was the very soul which was drawn into their home."

❧ 176 ❧

"I knew the following case personally," the Master told us.

"A certain man went to a great master and requested initiation for himself and his wife. The master agreed, and said to him, 'Go fetch your wife.'

"'Oh, no,' the man answered. '*You* have to bring her! She is no longer in this world.'

"Well, what could the master do? He had given his word! He meditated, and summoned the man's wife from the astral world. She appeared before them in her physical form.

"'Be careful,' the master warned, 'not to touch her!' He then initiated the two of them together. After the initiation, the wife disappeared."

༄ 177 ༄

It is a common belief these days that until a child is actually born, it is not yet a consciously developing human being. This belief is fallacious.

"When does the soul enter the body?" someone asked the Master.

"At the moment of conception," he replied. "When the sperm and ovum unite, there is a flash of light in the astral world. Souls there that are ready to be reborn, if their vibration matches that of the flash of light, rush to get in. Sometimes two or more get in at the same time, and the woman has twins, triplets, or even—well!

"It is important, therefore, to come together physically with an uplifted consciousness. That flash generated in the astral world reflects the couple's state of consciousness, especially as they felt during the moment of physical union."

༄ 178 ༄

The Master was reminiscing one day. "There was a woman in our Ranchi school in India," he told me. "She was a disciple of this path, and was very humble. She served me devotedly—hand and foot, as they say— obeying strictly everything I asked of her. Everything, that is to say, except one: She insisted on going about barefoot. I warned her not to, but she didn't consider this piece of advice serious enough to heed, though I was as insistent on it as she was. She continued to go barefoot everywhere.

"When I left for America in 1920, I made her responsible for initiating those into Kriya Yoga who asked humbly for it. Upon my return there in 1935, I asked her, 'How many people have you initiated?' Almost with embarrassment she answered, 'Oh, not many, Guruji. Only five thousand.' Five thousand: what a *huge* number! Still, wherever she went, it was barefoot, and still I insisted she mustn't.

"Some time later, she absorbed a disease through the soles of her feet, and died. She needn't have died that way, had she listened. It is important, you see, to be faithful in *everything* Guru tells you."

There is much food for thought in this story. A few readers may imagine, on hearing it, that the spiritual path resembles a game of musical chairs, where the ability to continue in the game depends on sheer accident. It must be remembered, however, that the Master wasn't advising that woman casually, merely, to wear shoes. He insisted on it, repeatedly. People do often die, moreover, of apparently quite trivial causes. She had a karma to die that way. He wanted to prevent that karma from bearing fruit.

Saint Lynn, the Master's chief disciple, died at a

Yogananda sails for a visit to Alaska.

relatively young age. Doctor Lewis insisted to me, later, that it was because Saint Lynn had not considered it necessary to heed the Master's caution to be less particular about his diet. Who knows? I remember how often the Master warned us, "You *must* listen to what I tell you, even in the little things." I think we may take his words to mean, "*especially* in the little things." For these, particularly, though they seem unimportant, may be vitally important for one, especially if he emphasized them repeatedly. He was thinking of our benefit. It was not the Master's way to insist strongly. If he spoke earnestly about anything, however, one did well to listen to him carefully.

Few people, of course, have the benefit of a living guru. They should at least watch, therefore, for tendencies in themselves that they tend to "push out of sight": things their conscience tells them they ought, or ought not, to do, that seem to them unimportant. They should look carefully, especially, at anything in themselves that they'd rather ignore, for in that very wish to ignore it there might be a danger signal.

❧ 179 ❧

The Master sometimes reminisced with us, as I said, about his boyhood days.

"I remember going to the Ganges for a bath one day," he told us. "My practice was to stand in the water up to my neck, singing to God. I would visualize the water's flow as God's flow of grace.

"That day, as I was returning from the river, I met an aunt of mine. On seeing me she cried out, 'Disgraceful child! Look at you!'

"I looked down, and saw that my body was completely naked. I'd left my clothing on the riverbank.

"I looked at her calmly and said, 'The sin is in you.'

"'Impertinent brat!' Angrily she slapped my face. Nothing could upset me that day, however. Quietly I turned away, and, singing to Divine Mother, retraced my steps to the riverbank where I retrieved my clothes."

❦ 180 ❦

Laurie Pratt—who, as I've said earlier, and as readers of my book *A Place Called Ananda* will recall, was to become, in later years, my severest test—was for some time one of my dearest friends. She once told me the following story:

"You know, in the early days, in the 1920s, Master didn't talk about creating a monastery. One day I entered his study to find him smiling broadly.

"'Would you like to be married?' he asked.

"I hadn't thought about this possibility, and wasn't particularly interested in it. As things turned out, however, I did get married later on. Maybe he was seeing marriage in my karma. At any rate, he certainly didn't indicate to me that he was opposed to my marrying."

Laurie returned, several years after her marriage, to Mount Washington. To me (Walter) the Master said regarding her, "She was never touched, inwardly, by that experience."

Most of his highly advanced disciples either were, or had been, married, including Saint Lynn, Mr. Black, and Doctor Lewis. He once said, "If one marries out of necessity, he will have to reincarnate to reach the point where he wants to live only for God."

The key to that last sentence lies, of course, in those three words, "out of necessity." What did the Master mean by them? As I understand them, he meant that if a person marries to fulfill an actual emotional need, and a desire for an earthly companion, he must return to find fulfillment in God alone. "Out of necessity" doesn't apply, in other words, to social or family pressure, or to some outward convenience.

⁂ 181 ⁂

The Master, soon after my arrival at Mount Washington, was planning to send Harvey Allen, a brother monk, to India. Harvey went later to visit his parents, and by the time he returned he'd "caught the bug" of delusion, losing his attunement with our way of life. Not long afterward, he returned to "the world."

The Master said to me, "After Harvey Allen returned here, I passed him one day as he was working the garden. As I went by, I felt a hot wave coming from him, and said to him, 'Things aren't going so well, are they?' He didn't answer. I knew, then, that our way of life was no longer for him."

⁂ 182 ⁂

Two young men applied for resident discipleship. They had had printing experience, and we were all glad to see their interest in living with us, for the print shop was in need of workers. Those two men, however, left "for just a few days," never to return. Afterward, the Master commented, "I knew as soon as I met them that they were not suited to our way of life. I felt a hot wave coming from them, and knew from that feeling that they belonged in the world."

🕉 183 🕉

"Too many men," the Master said, "come here impure. Their problem is lack of a proper upbringing. They come after they've had too much experience of the world. Sex washouts, I call them. They come here seeking relief. After some time, however, the memory of their old bad habits reawakens in them, and they grow lonely for that past evil.

"Then too, boys are fickle. They change girls; they change wives; they think in the same way they can change gurus any time they want to. They don't have loyalty. It is the upbringing that is at fault. In India there are just as many men devotees as there are women, because there they receive character training. Here in America, they get spoiled."

I (Walter) have often reflected since then that the Master, at that time, was addressing the men disciples. He also told us, "In men, sex temptation is stronger." Reassuringly, however, he added, "Well, women have their troubles, too. They have greater attachment to *maya*." In conclusion he said, "When men do get there, they become very great."

Lest any woman think women are "more spiritual than men"—as a senior nun once told me smugly—she would do well to remember the saying, "It takes two hands to clap." Many men disciples, moreover,

213

remained deeply loyal to the Master to the end of their lives.

After the above words, the Master spoke of Andy, a middle-aged, kind-natured man who had come to the ashram for training. "Andy was a good man," the Master said after Andy had left. "However, he'd had too much experience of the world. There was no inner strength left. After the age of forty, a person must be very determined to change; otherwise, it will be difficult for him to adjust to a new way of life.

"Once," the Master continued, "when I introduced Andy to a guest, I said, 'This is my baby.' I glanced at Andy to see how he had taken it, and then added, 'I call him that because I am babying him.' The problem was, I hadn't been able to inject any strength into him. I then said to Andy, 'I hope you don't mind my calling you that?'

"'Oh, no Sir,' he replied with a gentle smile.

"Don't think you can reach God with only a *gentle* attitude! As I have often told you all, You must be 'tough!'"

❧ 184 ☙

After the Master finished writing his Bhagavad Gita commentaries, I often walked with him around his desert compound in the evenings. On one such evening, Boone, who had just arrived, also walked with us. Boone at first walked beside the Master, who took his arm for support. A moment later, however, the Master released his arm with the word, "Hot." He then asked me to walk with him so that he might use my arm to lean on.

The Master needed a degree of physical support on those walks—not because he was ill or infirm, but because his state of consciousness was remote from this world.

Boone began to pester him with questions. Finally the Master said to him, "You shouldn't talk so much when I am in this state." He paused a moment, swaying slightly as if about to fall. After a few moments, he began walking slowly again, remarking softly, "I am in so many bodies, it is difficult to remember which one I am supposed to be moving!"

❧ 185 ☙

One of the questions Boone asked that day was following our walk. We were doing the energization exercises together, in the Master's company, by the garage. Boone's question concerned a saint who had appeared to the Master in a vision at the Encinitas hermitage.

"I don't know to whom you're referring," the Master said.

"It was on the bluff overlooking the ocean, Sir," Boone explained, "behind the hermitage."

"Well, so many come to me there. I often see them."

Both of us were surprised. "Is that so?" I exclaimed.

"Why be surprised?" the Master demanded. "Wherever God is, there his saints come."

He paused in his practice, then went on, "Yesterday, I wanted to know about the life of Sri Ramakrishna. I was sitting on my bed, meditating. Sri Ramakrishna materialized on the bed beside me, and we sat together a long time, holding hands."

I was thrilled to hear this account. "Did he tell you about his life?" I asked.

"Well," replied the Master, "in the interchange of vibrations I got the whole picture."

At the end of this brief conversation, he went back to exercising.

I submitted this interchange to the editorial department years later, after the Master's *mahasamadhi*. We had all been invited to send in material for a new book, which was published months later with the name, *The Master Said*. The editor was certain, evidently, that the Master would never have spoken so openly about his spiritual state as to say, "Wherever God is." She amended those words, therefore, to read, "Wherever *a devotee of God* is. . . ." (Aren't all of us, however, devotees? That editorial change reduced his statement to virtual insignificance.)

I feel I owe it to him to state that yes, he *did* say on that occasion, "Wherever God is." During his last years, at least, and particularly when speaking with the monks, he often referred with a perfectly natural air to his inner oneness with God. Several times during this period he said to me, "Write my words down, Walter. I don't often speak from this level of impersonal wisdom."

♦ 186 ♦

In his last years, the Master became much less reticent in referring to his true state of consciousness. One day at the Lake Shrine in Pacific Palisades, we were moving a large statue of the Buddha. Someone asked him, "Where would you like the Buddha to sit, Sir?"

"The Buddha," he replied with a slightly mischievous smile, "prefers to remain standing."

♦ 187 ♦

The Master expressed his need for masculine power in his work. Only thus, he must have felt, would his mission generate the power it needed to exert a broad influence on society. At his desert retreat in 1950, he said something to me when we were alone that I have quoted elsewhere, but never so clearly as here:

"Apart from Saint Lynn, every man has disappointed me." He paused a moment, as if to impress on me the urgency of his meaning, then added with great emphasis, *"And you mustn't disappoint me!"*

I knew that his disappointment wasn't over the spiritual zeal of his men disciples, even though fewer came to him than women. I understood, therefore, that his words referred to the men's understanding of the broader needs of his mission. Though many of them were deeply dedicated spiritually, more than zeal for their own attainment was needed if the work was to expand and change the world. No man, apparently, had ever grasped the vital importance of his mission *to the world.* Masculine energy was needed, for it to be spread and understood in its broadest context.

Inwardly I vowed that day never to disappoint him. To the best of my ability, I have remained faithful to my vow.

⋆⌇ 188 ⌇⋆

I asked the Master once, during our days together at the desert retreat, a question that others must sometimes have asked at least mentally. "Sir," I said, "were you Jesus Christ?"

"What difference would it make?" he replied indifferently. "The ocean of Spirit is the Reality. If one wave, or another one, becomes aware of its oneness with the ocean, both have attained the same awareness. The issue isn't how high the wave is. In that case, any tall wave might prove, in comparison to some other wave, to be the shorter or the taller. In the case of masters, however, it is the *lowness* of their wave of manifestation that determines their greatness in God. A little wave knows, more than the high waves can, that the goal—the 'perfection' of which Jesus spoke—is to become one with the ocean of Spirit."

The Master accepted, however, that outward differences do exist, even among great masters. Those differences are not a question of their spiritual realization, but rather of the outward roles they've played. Comparisons, in this world, are inevitable. Some masters have important—that is to say, public—roles to play. These, however, are mere outward considerations. They have no bearing on a master's true greatness, which must be determined by his closeness to God.

In the case of a true master, closeness to God means remoteness from the little ego. Perfect closeness to Him is the same for all masters. A wave may be higher or lower than other waves, but where the criterion is the elimination of the wave altogether, there can be only oneness; there cannot be competition. Perfection lies in how fully merged a master's consciousness is in the infinite ocean.

⁓ 189 ⁓

"Are you an avatar, Sir?" I asked him once.

"It would take such a one," was his quiet reply, "to bring a mission of this importance."

During this last period of his life, he was very much withdrawn from outward consciousness. He hardly seemed even to have a personality. Truly, as he often told us, "I killed Yogananda long ago. No one dwells in this temple now but God."

⁓ 190 ⁓

To the monks, during this late period of his life, he said, "When I see that God wants me to be born again in another body to help others, and when I see that I am to re-assume a personality, it seems at first a bit like donning an overcoat on a summer day: hot, and a bit itchy. Then," he concluded casually, "I get used to it."

~ 191 ~

My understanding is that, on this planet, Paramhansa Yogananda was—and has been for many incarnations—a special instrument of God who keeps returning in different forms to render special assistance according to God's requirements for the world's evolution. Many are the roles he has played.

"I have been, among other things," he told us, "a ruler, a poet, a warrior, a hermit (many times). My role as a ruler explains a natural interest I have in national and international affairs, and a certain aptitude I have for them. I have been a poet: That is why poetry has come to me easily in this life. I have been a warrior." (To me, Walter, that explains the fiery aspect of his personality.) In Spain, his mission seems to have been to fulfill God's will for Christendom, to save its tradition (today we would call it the Judeo-Christian tradition). He had told us also that he had been Arjuna, the great hero of the *Mahabharata*.

Always his role seems to have been to uplift humanity, and not only to save a few spiritually seeking souls. He has been sent to launch great movements, those which were destined to affect the course of history. Thus, the theologians are not wrong in countering the claim of mystics that God cares only for man's inner life. The claim of theologians has been that God is concerned also with larger, historical developments. And, meditating on Paramhansa Yogananda's life and on those of others like him, one sees such indeed to have been the case.

Someone once asked Ananda Moyi Ma, a great woman saint in India whom I used often to visit, "What will be the future of this planet, in view of the violent nature of our times?" She replied, "Don't you think that He who created this world knows how to take care of it?"

My deep belief is that Paramhansa Yogananda is one of God's channels for "taking care of" this world. Someday, I believe, he will be seen as the *avatar* of Dwapara Yuga. Indeed, his entire life seems to have been designed with that purpose in mind: to point toward a higher age that would include a greater awareness of energy.

❦ 192 ❦

Another way that God is "taking care of" the world is by what might be called "cross-incarnation." Souls are being born, the Master said, in such a way as to help bring about a greater balance on earth.

"Many souls are being brought from India to America and Europe, and many others are being brought from America and Europe to India. Thus, many Americans today have Indian *samskars* [tendencies], and many modern Indians feel comfortable with American and Western values. Thus, too, the world is being united in a more Dwapara Yuga consciousness."

ᘓᕽ 193 ᘔᕽ

"It wasn't easy, during the early days at Mount Washington," the Master told us, "to get this work started. Few people understood, and few even cared about, what I was trying to accomplish. Once I actually had to move away from Mount Washington. I rented a house elsewhere. 'Divine Mother,' I prayed, 'chop off all their heads!' After a few days the place was empty; the troublemakers had gone, and I was able to return once again to an atmosphere of peace.

"In the vision I had in 1948,* Divine Mother said to me, 'In the early years I sent you a few bad ones to test your love for Me. Now I am sending you angels, and whoever smites them, *I* will smite!'"

*I wrote about this vision in *The Path.*

The following story appears in my book *The Path*. It concerns Durga's (Florina Darling's) brother, who was extremely hostile to the Master for having drawn his sister to Mount Washington. This brother was physically strong; he decided to give the Master a good beating so that he could boast later in public how he'd bested this "charlatan."

"I was seated on my bed one morning, meditating," the Master told us, "when God warned me that this man was coming up the stairs, intending to beat me up. When he arrived at my door, he paused briefly on the threshold. I opened my eyes and said, 'I know why you've come. I want you to know that I am very strong; I could easily best you, physically. I won't do that, however. I won't lift a finger against you. Nevertheless, I warn you: Don't cross that threshold.'

"'Go on, prophet!' he sneered. He stepped across the threshold, and fell suddenly, screaming, to the floor. 'I'm on fire!' he cried, 'I'm on fire!' He leapt to his feet and rushed down the stairs, running out of doors. There he rolled on the lawn in hope of finding relief on the cool grass. I hurried after him, stooped down, and, reaching out my hand, relieved him of his pain.

"'Don't come near me!' he shouted, terror-stricken. He sent for his sister, had her fetch his belongings, and fled."

195

"Why," someone once asked me, "did Yogananda display such particular love for Rajarsi (Saint Lynn, his chief disciple)?"

"It was never particular," I answered. "He felt the same love for everyone. He couldn't express that love to all of us, however, for we wouldn't have been able to understand it. It would have given most people a big ego. Few sincere disciples, even, were pure-hearted enough to understand the divinely impersonal level of his love for everyone. The Master couldn't show deep feeling except to those who themselves knew what it is to love impersonally."

He once told me, "When I met Yogi Ramiah,* in Ramana Maharshi's ashram, it was a true meeting of souls. We walked hand in hand around the ashram together. Oh! if I'd remained in his company another half hour, I could never have brought myself to leave India again! He represented everything that is, to me, the true India. It is why I love that country so much.

*When I met Yogi Ramiah in 1962, in his native village of Buchireddypalayam in Andhra Pradesh, he was known as Sri Rama Yogi. Paul Brunton, however, in *A Search in Secret India,* calls him Yogi Ramiah. That also was how the Master knew him.

"Paul Brunton, whom I met there, was another disciple of Ramana Maharshi's. Brunton once told me that, during meditation one day, Yogi Ramiah had materialized before him and asked him to send him my photograph. He wanted to put it in his room. It is sitting there still."

I asked Master, "If Yogi Ramiah was fully liberated, did he have disciples also?"

"He must have had," the Master replied. "One must free others, to become completely freed oneself."

"How many does one have to free?" I asked.

"Six," was his reply.*

ꙮ 196 ꙮ

I asked the Master why he hadn't included Ramana Maharshi among the saints in *Autobiography of a Yogi*. He replied, "I didn't include him because Paul Brunton had already written about him in his book, *A Search in Secret India*."

Though I didn't say so, I wondered whether there might not have been another reason also. For these two

---

*I have a memo to myself in my notebook to check this figure. I never did so, and must therefore offer it as it is. In fact, however, I do believe that I've quoted that figure correctly.

great masters, Paramhansa Yogananda and Ramana Maharshi, had very different roles to play. There is a book about Ramana Maharshi in which is described a visit Yogananda paid to that ashram. Few books about the masters show real understanding of their lives. That book, too, suggested no inwardness in the encounter. Yogananda told a brother disciple of mine, Debi Mukherjee, "Ramana Maharshi's brother [who was known, among the 'ashramites,' as something of a martinet], tried to engage me in argument. Ramana Maharshi saw him and shook his head a little sternly, saying, 'Come away from there.'"

I recall also the Master's comment to us on his visit to the *Kumbha Mela* (religious fair) in Allahabad in 1936. He said, of his meeting with Kara Patri, a famous religious figure, "I hid from him." In other words, he didn't let Kara Patri perceive his spiritual stature so that he might express himself as he normally did. One wonders, Did the Master do the same thing with Ramana Maharshi? He might very understandably have held back, out of courtesy, not wishing to appear a teacher in that great master's own ashram.

ᢞᢇ 197 ᢞᢇ

The following story isn't a conversation with the Master. Yet it relates to his teachings; I therefore include it here:

Sri Rama Yogi, whom I (Walter) met in 1960 in India, said to me, "Always ask yourself, 'Who am I?'" This was the fundamental teaching of his great guru, Ramana Maharshi.

"That wasn't what my own Guru taught us," I replied.

Sri Rama Yogi smiled wryly. "If all the disciples of the great masters really understood what their gurus taught, there would not be the bickering one finds everywhere in religion!"

I reflected, then, that of course the Master had said repeatedly, "Know who you really are. You are not this little ego: You are the infinite Self."

ᢞᢇ 198 ᢞᢇ

"I once met a very successful and wealthy man, who said to me, 'I'm disgustingly healthy, and disgustingly wealthy.'

"'However,' I replied, 'you are not "disgustingly

happy," are you?' He admitted he was not. Soon afterward, he became a student of this path."

༄ 199 ༅

"A wealthy man came here [to Mount Washington] and stayed for a time. Our work at that time was in dire financial straits, and he might easily have saved the situation for us. But he wanted concessions from me that, on my conscience, I would not make, for they were unprincipled. He left, and when he did so he said to me, 'You'll starve because you didn't listen!'—'Listen' meant, to him, my consent to his disgraceful proposal. Well, we survived. God alone, always, is our 'stocks and bonds.'"

༄ 200 ༅

"When I was new in America, I used to walk about Boston in my orange robe, with my long hair flowing out behind me. Many people thought it strange. One day a group of factory girls followed me, giggling. One of them finally summoned up the courage to tweak my hair, and they all laughed. I turned around, then, and addressed them earnestly.

"'I am a foreigner in your country,' I said. 'Is this how you welcome strangers? How would it be if one of you were to visit my country, dressed in short skirts, as I see you here? You would not be accepted, I can tell you. Every country has its own customs. You should respect the customs of others.' The girls were very ashamed, and apologized to me earnestly."

⚘ 201 ⚘

"After some time in America, I took to dressing more 'normally' in public. Someone offered to buy me an overcoat, and I accepted with thanks. When I saw what he wanted to buy me, however, I exclaimed, 'Oh, that's *much* too good for me!' He insisted on buying it, and also bought me a beautiful hat to go with it.

"I always felt uncomfortable, however, decked out in all that splendor! 'Divine Mother,' I prayed, 'this coat is too good for me. Please take it away.'

"Some time later, I entered a restaurant and left the coat hanging in the entranceway with the other coats. I placed the hat on a shelf above. As I left afterward, I found that the coat had been stolen. What a relief! And then I saw the hat still sitting there. 'Divine Mother,' I prayed, 'You forgot the hat!'"

Yogananda and Sri Yukteswar at a religious festival during his
return to India in 1935.

Doctor Lewis told us the following story:

"When the Master was new in this country, I'd had no experience with anyone of his spiritual stature. Who had, after all, in America? At our first meeting, he looked into my eyes with deep love and asked me, 'Will you always love me as I love you?' I was deeply moved; something inside me responded. I answered, 'Yes. Yes, I will.' I have always been true to that pledge. I admit, however, that my faith has sometimes been tested.

"Once, back in those days, someone told me false tales against the Master. I didn't believe them, but still I was a little shaken. I was working in my dental office that day, and the Master was riding a streetcar. All at once he got off, walked several blocks to my office, and entered the door. Walking straight up to me, he looked deep into my eyes and asked, 'Do you still love me, Doctor?' What could I do? Of course, I melted! My faith was completely restored.

"He then told me, 'Someone borrowed a sum of money from you awhile ago, isn't that so? You haven't been able to get it back.'

"'That's true!' I marveled. 'I've been really needing that money.'

"'If you go there now,' he said, 'you will get it.' I went, and, indeed—though I'd been waiting a long time—the man gave me what he owed me."

❧ 203 ❧

Doctor Lewis told us many fascinating stories from his long years of association with the Master.

"There was a man," he said, "who had been wrongly condemned to death. The case was widely reported in the papers; almost everyone thought it an obvious case of miscarriage of justice. I told the Master about it with some indignation.

"He paused, and looked very serious. Then he withdrew into himself. When he resumed normal consciousness, he was smiling. Soon thereafter, the condemned man was pardoned.

"Was the Master responsible for his reprieve? He himself said nothing about it. I had known him already long enough, however, to have my private suspicion!"

❧ 204 ❧

The Master, when I (Walter) met him, told me a strange story. "There was a young woman I met in Chicago," he said. "She asked if she might see me alone. I always keep a door open when giving interviews, and have someone sit outside where I can be seen. This young woman, however, was insistent on seeing me alone, so I told her she could speak softly.

She then looked at me alluringly and said, 'You are very nice!'

"I looked her straight in the eye and said, with an expression of great distaste, 'Sin and disease!' At that, she burst into tears. After I'd probed a little, she admitted to me that a man had once betrayed her, and had infected her with syphilis. 'Since then,' she said, 'I have tried to revenge myself on all men by giving syphilis to everyone I can.' Imagine such despicable behavior! I gave her a blessing, and she was healed. But I made her promise never again to behave so contemptibly."

✧ 205 ✧

Food is many people's religion. They are fanatics on the subject.

"I was once invited," the Master told me, "to a place where they served 'unfired foods,' as they called it. Everything in their diet was in a raw state. With great pride they served me an utterly tasteless meal. The food was dreadful, and not at all scientific.

"Afterward they asked me to give a speech. I declined. When they pleaded with me, I replied, 'You won't like what I have to say.' Still, they kept insisting.

"You know, I can't be untruthful no matter what the cost. I prefer to be polite, but if I must speak I have to say what I really think. They were begging for a specific opinion, and I couldn't equivocate. After they'd persisted for some time, I finally answered them frankly.

"'Well,' I told them, 'in the first place, I have never in my life eaten worse food. Not only was it tasteless, but your diet is unbalanced and completely unscientific.'

"As you can imagine, they were in an uproar. 'You don't know what you are saying!' they shouted.

"'You will see that I am right,' I replied firmly. 'If you don't listen to me, fifteen days from now someone in this place will die because of this diet.' That, in fact, was what actually happened. Fifteen days later, one of them died, and the place had to be closed down."

❧ 206 ☙

"I was invited by a famous choir to hear them perform. Afterward, they asked me to say something. I told them truthfully, 'As far as technique was concerned, your singing was flawless. But to whom was the music addressed? Wasn't it supposed to be to God? Were you trying to please Him? Or were you trying to impress me? Next time, keep your hearts focused on Him for Whom the music was written.'"

᎒᙮ 207 ᘓᎈ

From Bernard I heard this story:

"The Master," he said, "was once invited to a dinner at a wealthy home in New York City. Everyone there belonged to the 'upper crust' social set. They asked him afterward to give a speech. He politely declined. They insisted, however. At last he said, 'You won't like what I have to say.'

"I imagine they couldn't believe he would say very much—at most, a few platitudes. Their own lives, after all, were superficial; they couldn't imagine the Master's perception being very deep. After they'd kept on insisting, the Master finally rose to address them. He spoke at length about the shallowness of their lives, and the emptiness of their ambitions. Many of those in the room were reduced to tears.

"His hosts weren't happy, of course, but he himself had not had any other choice but to speak as he felt. His commitment was to the truth. Many people were changed that evening, I suspect, by thoughts he'd awakened in them."

᎒᙮ 208 ᘓᎈ

The Master told us during his last years, "I used to

go to saints as a boy. I wanted to learn from them. They, however, kept asking *me* questions. I went to them in the hope of gaining from them, but they were hoping to gain from me!"

🙖 209 🙖

"When I was a boy I went to a man who, so I'd been told, was a great saint. I went with humility, as I approach every manifestation of the Divine, and bowed reverently before him. He, when he saw my devotion, decided to impress me further. He declared, 'I am God!'

"'You don't say so!' I cried, leaping to my feet. I had a little pocket mirror with me, which I used as an aid to introspection. Facing this mirror toward him, I demanded, 'Is that God? It is not the God I am seeking!' Turning, I strode out of the room.

"That man was truly sincere, however. He'd made the common mistake of thinking that the scriptures, in declaring, *'Aham Brahmasmi'* ('I and Infinite Brahman are one'), mean one may also say of oneself, 'I am God.' This is an error. How can the little ego be infinite? The man, rising hastily from his seat, ran after me. Bowing before me, he said, 'You have awakened me from a great delusion. I want to thank you!'

"I accepted his apology, then said, 'The ocean is all

of its waves. The wave, however, should never say, "I am the ocean," even after it has realized its own oneness with the ocean.'

"The man understood, and thanked me sincerely. He then prostrated before me, in the full gaze of his students. 'You have wakened me,' he repeated, 'from a great delusion!'

"'You are a great soul, indeed,' I said to him. 'Otherwise you would not have admitted your error so quickly, especially before your own students, and when shown to you by a mere boy. You have proved your true greatness.'"

❧ 210 ❧

"When I was a schoolboy, I felt guided to write a note to the boy sitting next to me in the classroom. The note read, 'I am your guru.'

"'Bad boy,' he answered, shaking his head in disapproval. That night, however, he was shown a vision in which he saw me as indeed his guru. The following day, he tried to find me. This time, however, I hid from him! I was being playful. I also felt, however, that he must work a little, now, to *earn* that blessing. When at last we met, we accepted each other lovingly."

211

"When I was young, a certain student of mine wanted me to lead a revolution to free India from foreign domination. 'That is your job,' I told him. I added, however, 'India will be freed during my lifetime by peaceful means.'

"He was determined to follow the way of armed revolution, however, though I tried to dissuade him from it. The British caught him, and he was executed. Divine Mother punished him for trying to use force."

"Master," I asked, "if Divine Mother didn't want it, and you knew in advance it wouldn't happen anyway, why did you let him go ahead with his plans?"

"That was his determination in this life, according to his karma," was the Master's answer.

To the soul, as he often told us, death means nothing. People, in their true Self, see "their exits and their entrances" (to quote Shakespeare) as fleeting appearances, merely, on the stage of earthly existence. Such is life's endless drama.

212

"There was a woman disciple of Swami Shankaracharya's," the Master once told me—perhaps as a warning, for during that time I suffered intensely from self-doubt—"who doubted all the time. She kept expressing her doubts and fears to her guru, and would ask him, 'But what if this happens?' or, 'What if I do that?' One day she said to him, 'But what if I—die?'

"Calmly her guru looked at her and said, 'Very well, then: Die!' In that instant she fell over, dead."

My first thought, on hearing this story from the Master was, "What a drastic lesson!" It didn't even have the usual miraculous follow-up! a revival afterward, for example, or the discovery that she wasn't really dead after all. On further reflection, I realized that life teaches many lessons, some of them drastic. To grow spiritually is not easy. To give birth is not easy. To be born is not easy. On the soul's long journey through endless-seeming incarnations, the death of one body is no more appalling than birth into another, and into a completely new environment.

That woman in her soul, however, would not easily have forgotten the lesson her guru had given her. Evidently it was not one he could have administered more gently. Surely she learned at least that whatever a person invites to himself, by expecting it, he must eventually receive. Desire is one way that man extends that invitation. Fear and doubt are two others.

"Be careful always," the Master said, "to hold positive expectations, for you will attract to yourself anything you project into the universe."

A true guru like Swami Shankaracharya always acts from the desire to *help* his disciples. Never is it his wish merely to get them "out of his hair." Thus, Shankaracharya's drastic-seeming treatment of his disciple was, in fact, a demonstration of divine love and friendship.

ༀ 213 ༀ

"I was supposed," the Master told us, "according to my horoscope, 'to marry three times, being twice a widower.' It is interesting to note that my father tried three times to get me married. On two of those occasions, I simply refused. The third time, he tried to spring the event on me unexpectedly so that I wouldn't be able to back out.

"I met the girl. As a woman, she truly was beautiful. For an instant, satanic delusion tugged at my mind. I heard the voice saying inwardly, 'Isn't she beautiful? Go ahead: why not marry her?'

"'Never!' I replied with great force. I looked at the girl through the spiritual eye and saw, beneath the skin, her muscles and internal organs: all red with blood! Her bones looked like any skeleton. No one, under the skin, is beautiful!

"People were very disappointed when I refused to

go along with the plan. I told them, 'I know you feel let down because you were looking forward to a feast! Well, I won't disappoint you.'

"I asked Prabhas Ghose, a dear cousin of mine, if he would marry her. He was delighted to get such a beautiful bride. And so the wedding came off.

"In 1935, when I returned to India, I visited Prabhas's home. His wife had become a terrible nag. Prabhas would go tiptoeing about the home like a mouse, scarcely daring to open his mouth. Seeing that situation, I took the wife aside and said to her, 'I have some right to speak to you on these matters, for you were intended to be mine. I just want to tell you, if you had treated me as I see you treating him—one week: that's all I'd have given that marriage. Then I'd have been off for the Himalayas!'

"From then on, she was softer in her behavior toward my cousin."

❧ 214 ☙

The subject of the Master's horoscope bears a little contemplation. He used to say, "Don't let the karmic tendencies described in your horoscope, no matter how valid the prediction, enslave you to anything that your will rejects. The prediction made by our family

242

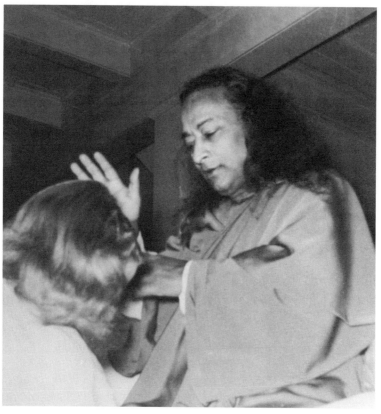

The Master at a large Kriya initiation ceremony.
He bestowed love equally on each initiate.

astrologer was accurate according to the stellar positions, but that didn't mean I had to accept it as a cosmic dictate."

A further question is likely to arise in the mind about that prediction: Why would the horoscope of a master predict anything so different from his actual destiny? The answer, I can't help thinking, is that one must be born at *some* time, simply to be born at all. No timing, probably, will ever be perfect. The planets move as they move, without paying any particular intention to anyone. Our actions, however, can be determined by our own will, despite what our horoscope says. The will, especially when it arises from deep within, is our real "writ of destiny." *That* is the destiny we should follow, seeking ever to attune our own human will to God's infinite will.

Another explanation, certainly, is valid also. For a liberated master is reborn not to expiate karmas of his own, but to take on, and to free others of, their own karmic burdens. It may be that in his very horoscope are written some of the burdens of others.

❦ 215 ❦

The Master told this little-known story of the meeting between Swami Shankaracharya and Babaji, whom Shankaracharya eventually accepted as his guru.

"Babaji was living in a home in Benares, when Shankaracharya visited that city. Shankara was at that time a famous astrologer. Babaji's manservant went therefore to see him. He received from Shankara the shocking news that, that very night, it was his destiny to die! In fear and trembling, on his return, he approached Babaji with the news.

"'Go back,' said Babaji, 'and say to him that you will not die tonight.'

"The servant carried this reply back to Swami Shankara, who affirmed, 'This karma is so fixed that, should you survive it, I shall go to your master and ask him to accept me as his disciple.'

"That night, a terrible thunderstorm lashed the city. Lightning struck everywhere. It felled trees all around the house where Babaji lived. The great master stretched himself out over the servant's body, to protect him. When morning came, the servant was still alive. He then went and presented himself to Shankara. The Swami was amazed. Realizing that he had encountered a power much greater than his own, he went to Babaji and took initiation into Kriya Yoga."

216

The Master told us that when he first came to Sri Yukteswar's ashram, he would keep his mind and gaze focused at the point between the eyebrows as much as possible. "If you want to make very rapid progress on the spiritual path," he used to tell us, "keep your mind always centered there."

This practice must be joined to, however, and supported by the heart's devotion. For concentration at the spiritual eye, which is known as the *ajna chakra,* develops great will power, but it can also make one *ruthless* if it isn't combined with the heart's love. When will power is combined with love, great joy is the consequence.

217

"During my boyhood," the Master told us, "my family moved for a time to a rough neighborhood.

"One day, about fifty boys ganged up on me.* 'We will kill you!' they cried, emboldened by their own numbers. I backed up against a tree, facing them, and cried

---

*This number was lessened to fifteen in the account that appeared in my book, *Stories of Mukunda.* Laurie Pratt, the editor, told me, "Fifty is unrealistic." (This little volume was first

out with great ferocity, 'Yes, cowards! In such numbers, you can surely succeed! Woe betide the first of you, however, who dares to approach me!' I spoke with so much power that they all hesitated. The ringleader then said, 'It's all right, Mukunda, we were only testing you. Let us be friends.'

"'If friendship is what you want,' I said, 'you have it already.' And so the crisis passed."

❧ 218 ❧

"I used as a boy to meditate in many places: in that underground chamber of the Benares temple I told you about; in graveyards; on the hot sand in full sunlight on the beach at Puri; in water up to my neck, chanting; and finally, of course, in my little attic room at 4 Gurpar Road. I didn't go to many temples after my mother's death. From then on, my devotion turned more inward.

"One day, a group of friends came and said they'd found a Kali temple we hadn't known about, not far from where I lived. Knowing of my devotion to Kali, they were certain I'd be eager to go there with them.

---

published by Self-Realization Fellowship. I had written it as a Christmas present for the monks.) She may have been right. Fifty, however, is the number I heard the Master state. I've no wish to argue the point. It's possible that I heard incorrectly.

But I replied, 'You all go. I'll stay home this evening.' They went and offered formal worship to the image of Kali. Meanwhile, I called to Her in my little attic room. And She appeared to me, smiling radiantly, with infinite love!"

219

"I underwent many disciplines as a boy, so as to get a feeling for different spiritual disciplines. For a while I even went about with a begging bowl—not actually begging from people, but holding out my bowl to them to give them a chance to share with others in God's name, if they so desired. Anything I received from them, I gave away to the needy."

220

"Once, I and a few friends went about and raised money for a great feast we planned to give to the poor. Many contributed to this cause. Later, crowds of the poor were fed. That whole day I cooked, served, and was active constantly. At the day's end, my body was exhausted. The thought came to me, 'Surely this is one time God won't mind if I don't meditate!'

"At that moment, I heard Satan's voice speaking in tones of honeyed sympathy: 'Poor boy! He has worked *so very hard*. Let him rest. Surely he deserves a good sleep.' I leapt up in outrage from my bed, sat firmly in meditation posture, and did a few Kriyas. All of a sudden, I became filled with energy. For the rest of that night, I remained wide awake in ecstasy."

๑๑ 221 ๑๑

"Once as a boy, during meditation, I entered a state of ecstasy. My breathing and heartbeat were stilled. Then I decided to play a little prank. Well, after all, I was only a boy! When people came in they saw me lying there, apparently lifeless. What a commotion! What wails! What lamentation! All the family stood around saying how highly they'd thought of me.

"And then an old, faithful servant of the family, whom we used to call Maid Ma, cried loudly, 'Ah! Ah! Now I won't have anyone to fight with anymore!' That was too much for me! I couldn't contain myself any longer.

"'Oh yes you will!' I cried.

"'You!' she shouted angrily. 'I *knew* you were only fooling!' She picked up a broom and flung it at me.

"Was it naughty of me? Well, I must say, it was great fun!"

I (Walter) have since thought of a piece of advice the woman saint, Ananda Moyi Ma, once gave to a visitor: "Tell your child to be good, but not *too* good!" The image of solemnly pious child-saints is a bit cloying, surely. After all, it takes great energy to find God. The popular description of the Master of Galilee as "gentle Jesus, meek and mild," could not possibly be applied to anyone of true spiritual fervor. Certainly, from the legends one reads about the child Jesus, the first words that spring to mind to describe him are neither "gentle," nor "mild." The word one thinks of is, "powerful."

222

The Master spent many hours reminiscing with me at his desert retreat in May of 1950.

"Once," he told me, "I visited a saint who lived in a jungle. This *sadhu* [holy man] wore no clothes. I was touched to see that his genitals were the size of a baby's. Such was his purity that his sexual organs had not even matured.

"He asked me, 'What if you were going to sit down and eat, and just then a stranger came who hadn't had anything to eat. What would you do?'

"'I would give him my meal,' I replied.

"'And what if,' the sadhu continued, 'after feeding him and preparing another meal for yourself, another person came who also hadn't eaten? What would you do, then?'

"'I would give him, too, what I'd been about to eat.'

"'And what if this happened a third time? What would you do then?'

"'I would give him half my food, and eat the other half myself.'

"'Off with you!' he cried. 'You are no renunciate.' What he meant by that dismissive expression was, simply, 'For shame!'"

It was impressive to me that the Master in telling me this story had made not the slightest attempt to justify his hypothetical third decision, nor to answer the sadhu's scolding with a perfectly reasonable justification. Often, I found, where only he was concerned, he would graciously leave to others the last word.

I do feel I owe it to him, however, as my Guru, to add that every answer he gave that sadhu seems to me to have been exactly correct, both morally and spiritually. Indeed, the sadhu might have extended his hypothetical questioning to the point where the Master was dying from hunger, while continuing to feed others! By contrast, what the Master always demonstrated was common sense.

That sadhu's counsel might be taken as spiritually valid only in the case of someone who was directing his every effort toward feeding others. Otherwise, that counsel contradicted the principle of sensible moderation. The Master's solution, surely, even from the loftiest spiritual point of view, was not only sensible, but right. I was impressed, however, that he made no effort to justify himself, even to me. His silent acceptance of that man's rebuke was an inspiring teaching in itself.

223

"My older brother Ananta," the Master said, "when he saw my determination to go to the Himalayas and dedicate myself to a life of solitary meditation, said to me, 'Your life will become like dry leaves, of use to no one.'

"'You may be right, Brother,' I replied with a smile, 'but dry leaves, don't forget, make very good manure!'"

224

It may not be easy for people outside of monasteries to understand and sympathize with the Master's uncompromising attitude on certain issues. As a monk himself, he naturally hoped to establish a monastic way of life at his headquarters on Mount Washington. Few of those who came to him, however, were ready for that way of life. He once said to me, "In the early days, many of those who came, especially the men, saw no reason why they shouldn't go out dancing whenever they felt like it."

Perhaps it was on beholding my eagerness, after he'd placed me in charge of the monks, to develop a more monastic way of life that he decided it was time they were organized properly. As far as I know, little or nothing had been done, before that, to systematize things. Certainly, any seeds that had been planted had not survived. I didn't like *telling* others what to do, but I realized also that if I didn't take seriously the responsibility the Master had given me, and if our way of life continued to be treated as casually as it had been, we would never have a truly monastic way of life, and men would keep leaving any time the thought arose in their minds.

The only rules in existence when I came there were two in number: "No mixing of the sexes," and, "Silence at mealtimes and, as much as possible, during any gatherings." These rules were posted in the Master's handwriting, but were honored mostly in the breach.

Silence at mealtimes was itself given the silent treatment. At table, everyone chatted away freely. The Master, of course, could not be there to enforce the rule. It seemed obvious to me that, if we were ever to have a true monastery, someone would have to sacrifice some of his own convenience. For example, I decided

I'd no longer set food aside at lunchtime and go off to meditate, eating afterward. *Someone* had to sit there throughout the meal, to remind everyone that there was a rule. That "someone," obviously, had to be me.

Until that time, the position of "monk in charge" had never really meant anything. The Master himself couldn't give the time to stay with us and help us to develop our way of life. His counseling work and his writings kept him more distant from the daily scene.

Seeing my willingness to take seriously the responsibility that he'd given me, he responded with greater firmness in his talks with the monks. As nearly as I can tell, it was at this time that he began to insist earnestly on such "hardships" as not going downtown on a mere whim, and living in other ways a more truly monastic way of life.

I had seen too many men leave the ashram during that year of testing, 1950, and grieved deeply over the fact. I determined to do all, therefore, that was in my power to ensure a more coherent way of life for those who remained, and for those who would come in the future. I instituted daily group meditations, weekly classes, and set in motion other rules, always insisting that I was doing so only on Master's behalf. The Master supported me in my efforts. Even so, the task proved somewhat difficult, and not wholly popular. It meant developing a way of life that was entirely different from the way everybody had been brought up. I'll never forget the months it took simply to get everyone to follow that basic rule: "Silence at mealtimes."

It was possible, now, for the Master also to be more severe in the attitudes he was trying to implant in us.

"Never discuss those who leave," he told us. "Don't even think about them. Think about the stronger ones, rather, who faithfully follow our way of life. Don't discuss the weak ones who have abandoned it. Even if you look upon some of them as your personal friends, never forget that God is your greatest Friend. Be loyal, above all, to Him.

"When Kumar—the young man you've read about in my autobiography—had to leave Sri Yukteswar's ashram, my guru became very withdrawn toward him. He had shown him special fondness, but when Kumar opted for worldly ways, he wouldn't even look at him anymore."

I (Walter) realized from this statement that Sri Yukteswar had been exemplifying an important principle: firmness in choosing what is right. The Master wanted us not to be wishy-washy in our choice of God. He didn't mean we should be harsh toward anyone, for that was not his way, and is not his teaching. He did want us, however, not to be specially sympathetic toward worldly attitudes, or toward those who embraced those attitudes, for in that sympathy we might expose ourselves to delusion.

"Why be open to negativity?" he asked, rhetorically.

255

"Those who left came here for the glamour of the spiritual life. They were attracted by what I call 'the romance of religion.' When tests came, however, they fled. They refused to follow our few, simple rules while living here. There were many reasons why they fell. If you could see into their hearts, you would understand."

Some of these things the Master may have said for my sake, for it had caused me great suffering to see so many leave a way of life that, to me, seemed in every way right. I could envision only unhappiness ahead for those who had turned away, and I sorrowed for their sake. I was reminded of the last part of Christ's life when, the Bible says, many left and walked with him no more. From a higher point of view, this sifting process was necessary, for, as we all knew, the Master expected soon to leave his physical body. The ranks, therefore, needed to stand firm. My own sorrow was not so much directed toward those who left as for our way of life. I was concerned above all with how to make it more magnetic.

These are a few of the bleaker realities of the spiritual life. As Jesus said, "Many are called, but few are chosen." We must, as our Guru told us, be "tough" in our decision to seek God alone.

The Master discussed this subject again after Boone's departure. He told me, "When Boone went to Phoenix, he started living a dissolute life—sexually, especially. If only he had married!"

"That," I exclaimed, "would have been a hundred times better."

"Well," the Master mused, "I consider everything evil that keeps one away from God. I don't mean that marriage itself is an evil; if it helps the spiritual seeker, it is a good thing. But if it takes one away from God, it is evil.

"Evil is the absence of true joy. In Boone's case, the advantage to marrying would have been that it might have kept him from sinking deeper into delusion. That would have been, at least, a relative good. I told him before he left that he should get married."

❦ 225 ❧

"Evil," I have just quoted him as saying, "is the absence of true joy." These words seemed obscure to a certain disciple, when I quoted them to her years later. I've therefore pondered the words more deeply, and I see that in fact they do hint, however obscurely, at a deep truth.

Evil is delusion. It is the veil over the bliss-nature of the soul. One who turns away from the spiritual path fails to realize that, by so doing, he spurns the joy of his own being. The choice before the spiritual aspirant must be taken very seriously. It is no light matter. It does not concern relative stages of fulfillment: lesser versus greater joys, for example. It is far more drastic. It is quite simply a choice between joy and suffering.

The choices offered by the world are not so extreme. People in delusion face varying degrees of fulfillment and pain. They find themselves happier, for example, when they serve others than when they seize everything they can for themselves. The choice, however, between seeking God or turning away from Him is absolute. *Not* to seek Him, or, worse still, to turn away from Him or— God forbid!—against Him, is to opt blatantly for delusion. This is, whether or not one realizes it, a choice for evil. For what else can the rejection of God be, if not evil? Evil obscures one's true nature of inner bliss.

"I have kept track of all those who left," the Master told me. "God has smashed their lives. Not a one is happy. They remember the spiritual peace and perception they developed here, and in that memory only suffer all the more. Such is the penalty for turning away from God.

"The only solution," he added, "once one knows deeply the true meaning of life, even if, afterward, he abandoned his calling to it, is to turn back to it again: to resume a life of meditation and divine devotion. God won't turn those away who turn back to Him. Most of those who leave, unfortunately, condemn themselves to a 'life sentence.' It is only they, really, who mete out their punishment. It isn't God who punishes them. Happiness is what He wants for them, eternally. The thing is, He won't give it to anyone who seeks an alternative."

226

Jerry Torgerson said to the Master, "I'm sorry I'm so stubborn, Master."

"That's all right," the Master answered him reassuringly. "I attract stubborn people."

It wasn't stubbornness he minded. What he warned against was stubbornness in rejecting wise guidance. Otherwise, he actually approved of stubbornness, especially if it meant steadfastness in one's quest for God. He didn't want "goody-goody" disciples: "yes-men" who answered with a limp smile and said, "Yeth, Master, I underthtand"—then did nothing! He preferred people who questioned, who even held back until they'd really taken a teaching to heart—as long as, eventually, they *took* it to heart!

227

At the same time, he said, "Some people, when you call them, mutter groggily, 'Don't bother me; I'm sleeping.' Others, if you shake them, stretch their arms a lit-

At his last birthday party, January, 5, 1952. I, on behalf of the monks, placed one of these garlands around his neck.

tle and even sit up, but the moment you turn your back on them they fall back to sleep again. The kind I like are those who, as soon as you call them, leap up, fully awake and ready.

"That is why I challenge my audiences: 'How is everybody?' 'Awake and ready!' they reply. God won't reveal Himself to spiritual 'sleepyheads.'"

❧ 228 ❧

"It is bad karma, of course, that takes people back to the world. God gives everybody a chance, however, to snap the karmic bonds. You can do it. Everybody can. The problem is, so few make the effort."

❧ 229 ❧

"If a man wants to be a concert pianist," the Master told us, "he must practice playing for twelve hours a day. One who pecks halfheartedly at the keyboard a few minutes at a time, then gets up and eats something, will never become a true musician. That isn't the way to seek God. You can't expect to find Him by only half trying!

"Ram Gopal—the 'Sleepless Saint' in *Autobiography of a Yogi*—meditated eighteen hours a day for twenty years, then twenty hours a day for another twenty-two years. And even he said, 'I don't know if I have yet found favor in God's eyes.'

"It is very hard to find God. Those who make the effort, however, *will* find Him. And out of the small minority who seek Him that way, we are blessed with quite a few here. Just look at Saint Lynn."* The Master went on to praise him, speaking of how this disciple would spend hours at a time in *samadhi* on the lawn of the Encinitas hermitage.

≈ 230 ≈

"Don't gossip about others. And don't be inquisitive about them. As soon as you become inquisitive about them, they will be inquisitive about you. You've no idea

*The Master later gave him the name, Rajarsi Janakananda. "Rajarsi" is a title; it means "royal rishi (sage)," or "king among rishis." Durga Mata argues in her book about the Master that the title should be, "Rajasi"—that is, it should be without the *r*. She was, though understandably, mistaken. She was no linguist. Nor did that *r*, as I clearly heard the Master utter it, come across to American ears like a separate letter. Americans are used to pronouncing their *r*'s very differently. I was able to catch Master's way of saying it, for I'd been brought up on several languages. It

how quickly a rumor can fly! Give a lie a twenty-four hour start, I often say, and it becomes immortal.

"We had a man here once who started a false rumor about someone. When the rumor reached me, I started a false rumor about him! It reached him soon enough, and he came to me protesting indignantly, 'Do you know what people are saying about me?' I said, 'You don't like it, do you?'

"'You bet I don't like it,' he exclaimed.

"'Now you know,' I told him, 'what that other person felt when you started a false rumor against him.'

"He was so astonished. 'I want you to know,' I continued, 'that I was the one who started that rumor about you. I did it to teach you a lesson. Now then, don't ever gossip about anyone again.'

"Oh, boy! Six months' silence! Reflect, though, if ever you feel like gossiping: How would you like to have others gossip about you? God has given people the privacy of their own thoughts so that they may correct themselves. He watches the heart, not one's actions.

"All of you who live here are brothers, moreover. Why not help and encourage one another? What are you here for if not harmony? Cling staunchly to the thought that you want peace, outwardly as well as inwardly."

---

took friends in India, finally, to persuade the SRF president that the title *had* to be "Rajarsi." Readers have been confused on this point, especially since Durga Mata's book appeared. Therefore I have tried in this footnote to clarify the matter.

❧ 231 ❧

The Master gave me the following advice for when I lectured:

"First, meditate deeply. Then, holding on to your inner calmness, reflect on what you might say. Write down your ideas. Add a few illustrative examples, including a funny story or two because, when people laugh, they relax and become more receptive. End your talk with a story from the Praecepta lessons. Then put your notes away and forget about them.

"When you lecture, later, ask the Spirit to flow through you. Remember a few salient points from your outline, but otherwise let the words flow from the inner source of Spirit. Finally, never speak from ego-consciousness, or you won't feel inspired."

❧ 232 ❧

"Do not be anxious if you don't have meditative experiences. The path to God is not a circus! Don't even be anxious about such fruits of meditation as inner joy and peace. Everything will come in God's time. Meanwhile, consider meditation, too, as a form of *Karma*

Yoga: action without desire for the fruits of action. Meditate above all to please God, not yourself.

"Every sincere effort is registered in the divine consciousness. Your duty as a devotee is to accept whatever He sends you—and, for that matter, whatever He doesn't send. God alone knows what past karma keeps you from perceiving Him right now. He may want you to finish up your karma in this life, before He gives you eternal bliss in Him."

❧ 233 ❧

I (Walter) tended perhaps toward overenthusiasm in my meditations. The Master once said to me, "Do not get excited or impatient. Go with slow speed. You will get there sooner if you go that way."

I'm sure that expression, "Go with slow speed," was his creative adaptation of the common American expression, "Make haste slowly."

234

The Master had to face innumerable financial difficulties in establishing his work in America. He never compromised, however. Never, for example, did he seek to attract a wealthy following by charging more for his classes, thereby excluding persons who couldn't afford them. Certain famous teachers had become wealthy by charging high prices for their lessons and attracting a wealthy clientele. The Master wasn't interested in wealth: He was interested in serving. He wanted everyone to benefit from what he had to give. Unfortunately, what this meant, as I said, was that his financial worries were both constant and considerable.

One time he exclaimed with a sigh of regret, "I've had many people say to me, 'If ever I get money, I'll give most of it to you.' If ever they had a sudden 'windfall,' however—an inheritance, perhaps, or a soaring return on a stock market investment—it was only rarely that they fulfilled their promise. Instead, what I find is that they actually became stingy! Money is a trap. The more one has of it, the more he depends on it for his security."

235

A certain disciple often suffered from moods. "Why do I have them?" she asked the Master.

"Moods are caused," he replied, "by past overindulgence in sense pleasures. They are the consequence of over-satiety and disgust. Don't give in to them." Frequently he advised people, "If you indulge in moods, they will reawaken your past desire for their opposite pleasures. Thus, they will pull you down into delusion again."

One might ask, "Why would indulging in moods reawaken the very desires that caused one to suffer in the first place?" The answer, the Master explained, is that life manifests the principle of duality. It is like a pendulum—"swinging unceasingly," as he put it, "back and forth between opposite states of awareness. The farther the pendulum swings in one direction, the farther it must swing back in the other. Indulgence in moods returns a person, with or without his consent, to their opposite pleasures."

To stop that unending to and fro movement, the secret is to resist it, as a child does who wants to get off a swing. "In this case," the Master said, "the solution is to preserve a mental non-attachment. When a child wants to get off a swing, he stops it by resisting *both* the forward *and* the backward movements. The same is true for the pendulum-swing of life: Resist, inwardly, the pleasure you feel in anything, and resist also the sadness life brings you in consequence. Strive to be even-minded in all that happens, so that nothing touches you inwardly. This doesn't mean to allow nothing to please you—to become apathetic. Simply realize that whatever pleasures you enjoy are *in yourself,* not in outward sensations. Your pleasure, that way, will actually be all the greater."

ᕼᘺ 236 ᘺᕼ

The Master found amusement, if anything, in pedantry. He would sometimes joke about its pretensions. A story he liked to tell, laughingly, was the following:

"The wife of a certain philosopher asked him to go out and buy her a bottle of oil. He was returning, later, with the bottle when he began to muse, 'Now, is the oil *really* in the bottle? Or do my senses deceive me? Could it be, rather, that the bottle is in the oil?'

"His wife met him at the door and demanded, 'Where is the oil?'

"'My wife,' the philosopher declared grandly, 'I have just made an important discovery!'

"'Where is the oil?' she repeated.

"'I am coming to that,' he assured her. 'Listen: I purchased the oil. Then, looking at it, I thought, "Yes, this is oil, and it appears to be inside the bottle. My apperceptive perception, however, doubts whether the oil *really is* in the bottle, or whether the bottle might not, possibly, be inside the oil."'

"'Where is the oil?' demanded his wife.

"'Yes, yes, I'm just coming to that,' he assured her hastily. 'So then I upturned the bottle. And now, I think that *maybe* the oil was in the bottle!'

"'You fool!' cried his wife. Picking up a broom, she beat him over his 'apperceptively perceptive' head with it.

"'Now I *know*,' the philosopher concluded in triumph, 'that the oil was in the bottle!'"

The Master commented, "With real intellectuals, you don't have any trouble. They want the truth, not mere definitions of the truth. With these half-breeds, however, the moment you open your mouth they are already convinced you are a charlatan."

I myself (Walter) remember hearing a scholar in India expatiate at length, with vast pride in his learning, on the subtle differences between *samprajnata samadhi* and *asamprajnata samadhi*. The problem was, he obviously had never experienced either of those states.

And I remember two men from South America who visited Mount Washington some fifty years ago. They owned a bookstore in their country. When they discovered that I didn't know the Sanskrit names for the spinal *chakras,* they wrote me off as a nincompoop. Yet the Master taught us only the Western medical equivalents for those terms: "coccyx, sacral, lumbar," etc. I don't remember him even calling them *chakras,* though he may have done so. To us, they were simply "centers."

Seeing those visitors look down their noses at me with such scorn, however, I decided to learn the Sanskrit terms lest I scandalize some of the people I was supposed to teach yoga. Really it didn't matter, however. The inner *experience* of truth is what counts.

Rajarsi Janakananda, a fully enlightened yogi, spoke the name of his Guru's Guru, Sri Yukteswarji, almost comically: "Seer Ooktetraji." What did it matter? He saw Sri Yukteswar in visions. Once he was actually touched by that master, physically, as he meditated with our Master. He had attained the same level of enlightenment as Swami Sri Yukteswar.

Someone asked Master the meaning of *Yukteswar.* He said, "It means one who is united (*yukta*) to Iswara, or God."

The Master knew perfectly well the correct terms for the *chakras!* He knew everything he ever needed, or wanted, to know—not only Sanskrit, but in everything.

There was an amazing story that Eugene Benvau, a devout disciple living in Encinitas, told me: "I was sometimes present when Master conversed with medical doctors. He'd had no medical training, but I observed he could rattle off complex medical terms as though he himself were a doctor! The others there obviously accepted him as one of their own. As for the Master, he was quite natural about it, and gave no outward indication of knowing that he was displaying exceptional knowledge."

Señora Cuaron, the wife of the SRF center leader in Mexico City, told me in Spanish during my visit there in 1954, "I once had an interview with the Master. I don't know any English, and he didn't know any Spanish, but somehow—I still don't know how—we managed to communicate perfectly!"

"You don't need to seek understanding outside yourself," the Master said. "Everything you want to know exists already within yourself."

One time, in writing a poem, he used the word, "noil." Others pointed out to him that there was no such word in the English language. "It exists," the Master insisted. He made them search through several dictionaries. At last somebody found it in an old Elizabethan dictionary. I myself have looked the word up in a recent edition of Webster's International. It appears there with the definition, "a short fiber." I somehow doubt that the Master used it in that sense. Often, however, I found that he demonstrated knowledge that he couldn't possibly have received by ordinary means.

271

ᶒ 237 ᶒ

The Master was never narrow in his application of spiritual principles. If a disciple committed a minor infraction, he might say nothing, or refer to it only in passing.

A story about James Coller illustrates this practice beautifully. James was a very devout disciple who, despite his sincerity, might be described as rather less than ardent when it came to adhering to the rules.

He was driving back one evening from Phoenix, Arizona, where he served as the minister of SRF's church there. James was hungry. It was late at night, however, and every restaurant he saw on the highway was closed. At last he came upon one that was open, and entered it. All they had to serve him, unfortunately, were hamburgers—meat, in other words, and therefore forbidden to the monks. "Oh," he thought, "*he* won't know!" (thinking, of course, of the Master). James ate a hamburger—and possibly two of them.

When he reached Mount Washington, he spoke with the Master on the telephone. At the end of their conversation, the Master added, "Oh by the way, James, when you are out on the highway late at night, and you come to a restaurant that serves only hamburgers, better not eat at all." He didn't make an issue of it, but simply let James know that he hadn't gotten away with this little secret he'd hoped to keep from the Master!

Where something really important was concerned, on the other hand, the Master was rock firm where others might have been lenient. Once he was upbraiding some of the monks who were falling out of tune with his ideals.

"If ever I find the ladies and the men mixing together in this place," he said with great emphasis, "then, no matter where I am in space, I shall return and blast this organization out of existence!"

He once said to us, "The reason Buddhism failed in India was because of laxity in the rule of non-communication between monks and nuns. Evils arose from that freedom, and Buddhism lost its power."

Where individuals were concerned, however, he could be endlessly forgiving. "God will never let you down," he assured his disciples, "so long as you make the effort. If ever you tell yourself, 'I am lost,' it will be so—at least for this incarnation. But if you keep on trying, the Lord will never stop trying on His part to help you."

I recalled the example of Sadhu Haridas, who had left the spiritual life and his disciples to go live with a woman. Later on, he realized his mistake and returned to the disciples. The Master said, of Sadhu Haridas (as I stated earlier), "He left his body, at death, a free soul."

ॐ 238 ॐ

"There was a disciple of Sri Ramakrishna's," the Master told me, "who was so deep spiritually that Ramakrishna would say of him, 'He was born, and I was born'—raising, thereby, the question, 'Who came because of whom?'

"This young devotee once told his Guru that he'd been meditating with a woman devotee, and was helping her.

"'Sadhu, beware!' warned the Master.

"'Oh, I will be all right,' said the young man, who knew nothing of the delusive magnetism that exists between the sexes.

"Well, delusion caught him. A little bad karma came out, and he went to her, abandoning his dedicated life.

"Even saints, you see, can fall until they reach *nirbikalpa samadhi*. Never tell yourself you are safe from temptation until you have reached that highest state."

ॐ 239 ॐ

Because harmful gossip poses a major problem even among those who strive sincerely, in good company, to rise out of delusion, the Master said, "You will always encounter people who will try to pull you down. Don't let them affect you by their words and thoughts. Know in your own heart what you *really* want. Above all, be guided by your own aspiration. Remember, God watches the heart. He will never let you down, so long as you cling to Him with love."

❦ 240 ❧

The Master, like every great master, viewed sex as one of the three great delusions. The other two, he said, are money and alcohol. (Along with alcohol he would certainly have included hallucinogenic drugs, had they been as popular in his day as they became later.) Sex, he said, is a delusion because of its power to draw people into the hope of fulfillment outside themselves. Where devotees are concerned, many are taken away from the spiritual path by sexual desire.

To the Master, however, everything, including every spiritual precept, is relative, in the sense of *directional*. Nothing except God is absolute. Like Saint Paul, he would have liked to see all live a life of dedication to God alone, but he was realistic, and worked with the world as it is, and with people as they are. He had not been sent to serve a society of monks or hermits. The world he served included people at every stage of life. His mission, in fact, was to uplift *society as a whole,* and not only a handful of disciples. Obviously, even sincere seekers could not all be realistically expected to withdraw into monasteries. He was supportive toward all who sought God. Like Lahiri Mahasaya, he saw it as his mission to help all who humbly asked for help in their divine quest.

He himself loved the monastic life, but he did not approve of monastic arrogance. He wrote scathingly, in fact, of *sadhus* (India's holy men) who despised as materialists those very people who gave them the food they ate.

As it happened, most of the Master's highly advanced disciples either were, or had been, married. First in importance, as he saw it, were the qualities of *inner* non-attachment and *inner* dedication.

Moreover, he did not condemn the natural attraction that exists between men and women. Rather, he strove to purify it, so that each might learn to see God in the other. Neither is better than the other, he insisted: They are simply different. Physical attraction between the sexes should be purified, eventually, to the desire for union with God alone. Even in marriage, then, provided it is a truly spiritual union, the ultimate goal should be divine union. Meanwhile, he urged everyone to see in all the one Infinite Beloved.

He once described Sister Gyanamata, his most advanced woman disciple, in these words: "I have searched her life, and found in it not a single sin, even of thought." "Sister," as he called her, had been married before she

276

came to him, and had borne a child. (Her name, then, was Edith Bissett.) Once, the Master told us, when Mrs. Bissett and her husband were both old, the husband had wanted to go on a journey. He hesitated to do so, however, because he thought "We are both growing old. What if during my absence she were to . . . ?" His wife spoke firmly on the matter: "What is death? Make your journey now, if you want to." Our union, she was implying, is eternal; what do momentary partings signify?

At her funeral, the Master said, "I saw her sink into that watchful state: final liberation." (The image, here, was of a wave sinking back into the divine ocean.) "She attained her freedom through wisdom," he added. "My way has been through joy."

ᰨ 241 ᰨ

"Sir," the thought came to me (Walter) when he'd uttered those last words, "if she attained liberation, how is it that she didn't have disciples?" He'd once told me (as I mentioned earlier) that it is necessary to free six others before one can, oneself, attain liberation.

The Master, reading my mind, replied. "She *had* disciples." He didn't elaborate further. It would be well for all devotees to remember, however, that God doesn't want us to find Him only for ourselves. The following story, which the Master told us, conveys this truth dramatically.

❧ 242 ❧

"The following story," said the Master, "happened before my time, but my father was personally acquainted with it. A maharaja had been excavating a lake on his property, and beneath the mud at the bottom, three yogis were discovered in good condition, seated in the lotus pose. An engineer working on the project estimated that they must have been there at least three hundred years.

"They were in *samadhi*. To reawaken them to outward consciousness, the maharaja had someone apply hot pokers to their feet. Finally they succeeded in bringing them back.

"'You should not have done this,' they told him severely. 'We were very near liberation. Now we shall have to be reborn, and to continue working toward that goal in new bodies.' It was not possible for them to keep their bodies any longer, having been out of them for so long.

"Before dying, they said to the maharaja, 'You have committed a serious transgression by disturbing our deep state of communion. You will have to pay the price.' In fact, soon after these yogis left their bodies in death, the ruler and his whole family died. That was his punishment for disturbing the harmony of those yogis' inner communion.

"On the other hand, the yogis themselves, by being so rudely forced out of their inner state, were paying a price for seeking liberation for themselves alone. Divine Mother didn't want them to merge in the Infinite without first helping others, too."

One hears many strange things in India. I've encountered a number of them, myself. During my four years there, a friend in Delhi related to me an account that had come out recently concerning an excavation that was just being conducted in Subzi Mundi, across the river from where he lived. The workers had come upon the body of a yogi seated in meditation. They were able somehow—I hope the means used were kinder than in the foregoing story—to revive him to outward consciousness. When he spoke to them, however, they couldn't understand him. A pundit (Sanskrit scholar) was summoned, who said the man was speaking an old form of Sanskrit. The man asked, "What *yuga* is this?" They told him it was *Kali Yuga*. He wasn't interested in remaining. He couldn't retain his body, after his revival. Before leaving it, however, he said to them, "If you dig over there [he indicated a spot near the place where they'd found him], you will find the *murti* (the sacred image) I used to worship." He then left his body. They dug where he'd indicated, and found there a sacred *murti*.

₰ 243 ₰

A Hollywood actress, who—so I learned afterward—
had starred in several well-known movies, came to visit
the Master. I was present during the interview, which
was private otherwise. This visitor, as things developed,
was someone who might be described as a devotee of
D.H. Lawrence, or of Sigmund Freud, both of whom
considered sexual repression to be the chief source of
all present-day unhappiness.

"I *love* sex!" she proclaimed enthusiastically. "Isn't it
wonderful?"

"Certain things," the Master replied calmly, "are infi-
nitely more so."

She continued her theme with exuberance, however.
After a few minutes, the Master pleaded with her, "You
shouldn't dwell on such things in the presence of a
young monk."

"Oh!" she exclaimed in surprise, "do *they* know
about sex?"

"Well, they are not dumb," the Master replied.

Later, happening to find me alone, she smiled at me
in what I supposed was meant to be a dazzling way. I
had a good chuckle over it. The Master, however, when
we spoke about her afterward, called her a "demon."

244

A certain woman was an early editor of the Master's. He never liked her work, for she had her own opinions as to what was and was not spiritually true, and she never hesitated to intrude her own views into her editing.

"She was," the Master told me, "a convert to the modern 'gospel' of sex. Once she showed me a book of poems she had written. They were filthy! I said to her, 'I could write a poem about a bowel movement that would make you think I was describing the most beautiful thing in the world. But why concentrate on such unworthy subjects? Leave them to others. As for your erotic— *neurotic*—friends, have nothing more to do with them.'

"Sometimes I would try to give her advice. Whenever I did so, back, several days later, would come a letter pages in length, explaining how greatly I had misjudged her. I wonder sometimes why she ever came here. Instead of accepting my teachings, she tries to impose her own 'wisdom' on what I write. She is good at English, but of what use is knowledge if it isn't backed with understanding?"

~ 245 ~

"Remember," he told us, "It is Divine Mother who tests you through sex. And it is She also who blesses, when you pass Her test.

"As soon as the first thought of sex enters the mind, that is the time to catch it. However tempting it seems now, once you are out of it you will see that it is the greatest delusion."

Those words, "the first thought of sex," mean more than when that thought assails the mind pleasurably. Even the idle thought, the Master would have added, when there is no desire, is best avoided.

~ 246 ~

Peggy Deitz, whom I'd known at Mount Washington as Peggy Bowman, was a sincere devotee. After some years in the monastery, however, in obedience to the Master's instructions, she left our way of life. After her departure, she kept in close contact with him.

"He instructed me," Peggy informed me years later, "to give Kriya initiation to anyone I met, if that person seemed to me ready to receive it. When he told me that, I protested, 'But Master, what will the organization say?'

"'Are you following them?' he asked. 'Or are you following me?'"

Yogananda with Luther Burbank and his wife, Elizabeth.
About Burbank the Master wrote,
"Behold a man in whom there is no guile."
(Autobiography of a Yogi, 1946 edition)

❧ 247 ❧

"When you work for God, not self," the Master told us, "that is just as good as meditation. Then work helps your meditation, and meditation helps your work. You need the balance. With only meditation, one becomes lazy, and the senses become strong. With only work, the mind becomes restless, and one forgets God."

He told us he'd seen hermits in the Himalayas fighting over blankets. "Such non-attachment!" he commented ironically.

❧ 248 ❧

I (Walter) had to work hard in the beginning to develop devotion. I'd become overbalanced in the direction of intellectuality, thinking it to be the way to find truth. "Keep on with your devotion," he said to me lovingly one day. "Think how dry your life was, when you depended on intellect!"

I had been thinking that the inner change was due primarily to the long hours I'd been spending in chanting, praying, and meditating. Then someone said to me that the Master had told a few disciples in Encinitas, "Look how I have changed Walter!" I then realized that, whereas my own efforts had been important, it is ultimately God's power alone, through the Guru, that makes any real change in the disciple. The disciple's part is determinedly to open his heart to the inner flow of divine grace.

⇦ 249 ⇨

"Sir," I began once, "my father. . . ."

"You have no father!" he replied, interrupting what I had been about to say.

"I'm sorry, Sir," I said. "I meant, my earthly father."

"That's better," he replied. "God alone is your true Father."

I rarely heard him offer others this correction. In fact, it may have been the only time I heard him give it at all. Some people may think those words were too strong, but often he had a particular, if hidden, reason for what he said. Perhaps he sensed my father's opposition, which later became apparent, to my choice of a spiritual way of life.

It was an interesting feature of my first two years as a disciple that, every time I tried in meditation to visualize my Guru, my earthly father appeared first in my mind. Only by sustained effort was I able to substitute for that image the features of my Guru.

285

↢ 250 ↣

The Master once said to me, along these same lines, "My father remarked to me one day, 'I heard someone say he'd seen your guru give a flower to a woman.'"

"'Of all things!' I replied indignantly. 'Physical birth is something, but if ever I hear one more word from you against my Guru, I shall disown you as my father forever!'"

I (Walter) was obliged, a few years later, to express very much the same words in a letter to my own father. Though I didn't offer him that drastic choice, I pleaded with him not to force me to it.

↢ 251 ↣

The Master said to me one day, "Keep on becoming good. You are doing better now."

I answered him: "I've had a few things to work on, haven't I?"

"Yes," replied the Master. "There was too much intellectual aloofness."

"I know," I said. "It has been a strong habit with me. I'm still working on it."

"Habits," the Master replied, "can be changed in a day. They are nothing but concentration of the mind. You've been concentrating one way: Simply concentrate another way, and you'll completely overcome the habit."

This was basically the same advice he had given to his early student, Jotin.

252

"Men think to 'possess' their women," said the Master with a chuckle, "but women tend to view their husbands, no matter how prominent or powerful, as their own children!"

253

Master had given all his time to others. At last the Divine Mother gave him a period of respite in the desert. Speaking of the peace and solitude there, he remarked to me one day, "Wherever there is a well, thirsty people gather. Sometimes, however, the well likes to be quiet for a while."

I was slow in catching what he meant. Then I understood it, and the Master said with a quiet smile, "I was speaking of myself."

Vance Milligan was not yet legally of age when he came to Mount Washington. He left, later, in obedience to his mother's wishes. When he grew older he returned, but this time it was with his mother's sanction.

"It is good you have her permission," the Master remarked to him. "Without it, you should still have come, but with it is even better. Remember, you are God's child for eternity, not for this one lifetime only.

"When Swami Shankara was only a child, he felt inspired to leave home for God. His mother tried to dissuade him. Shankara, instead of pleading with her, jumped into a nearby river and let a crocodile catch him. 'See, Mother,' he cried out, 'I will let the crocodile pull me under if you don't agree to my leaving home!' Even at that young age, you see, he had spiritual power. Well, what could she do? Hastily she gave her consent. Shankara then made the crocodile release him. He swam to shore, and straightway began his historic mission.

"Years later," the Master continued, "he cried out suddenly, 'I taste my mother's milk. She is dying.' Contrary to the brahminical code regarding renunciates, he went to his mother, and helped her in her final moments. Then, with a divine fire emanating from the palm of his hand, he cremated her body."

༼༄ 255 ༄༽

"Don't go into the city," he used to tell the new monks. "This ashram is your 'city.' It has everything you need."

༼༄ 256 ༄༽

At a Christmas banquet, looking around, he remarked, "Divine Mother sent me all these souls that I might drink Her love in all these forms."

༼༄ 257 ༄༽

"Those who are with me," he once told me at his desert retreat, "I never have any trouble with. Just a glance with the eyes is enough. It is much better when I can talk with the eyes. I just wilt when I have to scold, outwardly. All those who are with me—most of them, anyway—are saints from before." (What he meant, I think, was, "all those who are in tune with me.")

"Sir," I said, "what about those who don't seem all that saintly?"

"Well, some of them are fallen saints."

"I was thinking of myself, Sir," I explained.

"It is better to have neither a superiority nor an inferiority complex," he replied. "Whatever you are, give it to God."

ᕯᕓᕔ 258 ᕕᕗᕖ

"Loyalty," the Master often said, "is the greatest law of God, and treachery is, before God, the greatest sin."

ᕯᕓᕔ 259 ᕕᕗᕖ

During my early days with the Master, he constantly urged me, "Get devotion. Get devotion. Remember the words of Jesus, 'Lord, Thou hast hid these things from the prudent and the wise, and hast revealed them unto babes.'"

One day he bought a few toys. I wonder, in retrospect, if it wasn't for my benefit. I never saw him with them again. We were seated around the little kitchen table at his desert retreat. He lifted a paper bag from the floor, set it on the table, and asked that the light be turned off.

All of a sudden I heard a sound: 'bzzz, bzzz.' Tiny sparks flew into the darkness from some mechanical gadget. The light was turned on, and I saw him holding in his hand a little toy pistol. It emitted sparks when the trigger was pulled.

Next, he took out of the same bag another toy. This one, when he pulled the trigger, sent a folded piece of cloth or paper into the air. As it came down, it unfolded to become a parachute. We watched gravely as it descended slowly to the floor.

"How do you like them, Walter?" He looked at me as if with special meaning. I was still endeavoring to get over my surprise. Laughingly I affirmed, "They're *fine,* Sir!"

He looked at me keenly then, and, quoting from the Bible, said, "Suffer little children to come unto me, for of such is the kingdom of heaven."

260

"It's awfully hard to change, Master," Jerry said one day. He was that "stubborn" disciple to whom I alluded earlier. "But," he continued, "I'll go on to the end of life."

"That's the spirit," the Master replied approvingly, adding, "The wave cannot separate itself from the ocean anyway. All it can do is protrude further from the ocean bosom. Its connection to the ocean, however, is eternal. Eventually, it *has to* go back."

Jerry stubbornly resisted my every effort to get the monks organized. He left the ashram later, stating, "Now that things are getting organized, it's ridiculous for me to remain any longer." It is a pleasure for me to be able to report, however, that, despite having departed, Jerry remained loyal to the end of life.

He kept his promise to the Master.

ᘓᕲ 261 ᕲᕪ

Master was having trouble with a certain disciple. He remarked, marveling, one day, "People are so skillful in their ignorance!" Later he said, "What a job you take on your hands when you try to help people! You have to go inside their minds and see what they are thinking. A rose looks beautiful when we see it standing in its vase. We tend to forget all the work that went into making it that way. And if it takes so much work to produce a beautiful rose, think how much more work it takes to produce a beautiful human being."

ᘓᕲ 262 ᕲᕪ

An older woman who had read a great number of metaphysical writings once said to me (Walter), "The soul may be destroyed, if, after it fails repeatedly to attain enlightenment, God decides that its case is hopeless. In such a case, the soul simply ceases to exist."

During my early years on the path it was my karmic burden to be plagued by self-doubt. I had done no metaphysical reading, having come to the Master in utter ignorance of this field. The first book I read, *Autobiography of a Yogi,* led me straight to him. I was, therefore, unarmed against that woman's bleak announcement, which I confess festered in my heart for nearly a year. One day, finally, I summoned up the courage to ask the Master, "Is it possible for a soul to be lost forever?"

"Impossible!" he declared with absolute certainty. "The soul is a part of God. How could any part of Him be destroyed?"

Absurd as it may appear, that reply brought me deep relief.

❧ 263 ❧

"For 500 million years," the Master said, "creation rests in the Night of Brahma. Then for another 500 million years it is manifested again as the Day of Brahma."

"Sir," I interposed, "science has found that the earth is already well over two billion years old."

"Well," he replied, "it's quite possible that the scriptures, in writing 'years,' were referring to a much longer time period. In the Book of Genesis, too, God is described as taking only seven days for the Creation."

I (Walter) have found that, where scripture and spiritual teachings are concerned, it is wise not to be too exacting in one's analysis of them unless the teachings themselves ask one to be so. The date 1700 A.D., for example, as the beginning of Dwapara Yuga, is an exact date, not a symbolic one. The days and nights of Brahma, however, and the "days" referred to in Genesis, are symbolic.

How can one know the difference? Basically it may be said that spiritual truths—as opposed to literal facts—are *directional.* Intuition is not achieved by analysis. It flows with the river of time; it is not a frozen sheet of ice. Vast time periods cannot be measured specifically even in science. Swami Sri Yukteswar, though he showed the yugas to be directional, placed them also in specific periods of time. In many spiritual teachings, however, the *direction* is one of consciousness, not of historic fact. A Day of Brahma itself is the projection of an *idea.* It cannot be cut and spliced like a movie film, nor measured out exactly for correlation with other discoveries. It simply *is:* a thing in itself, appearing out of timelessness rather than being a function of time. Indeed, it is itself the *creator* of time!

The Master sometimes said to us, therefore, "There are many teachings which it is wiser to accept on faith. You can't know everything, so how can you expect to be able to judge everything? Judgment can only be formed on a basis of actual knowledge. Don't depend too much on reason, for that is where Satan catches you. Intelligence is a tricky guide. To seek the guidance of devotion is much surer and more trustworthy."

ᚷ 264 ᚷ

"Sir," I asked him, "is it all right to kill flies, mosquitoes, and other such pests?"

"It is always better to kill harmful creatures," he replied, "than to allow human life to be endangered." He had taught that, if one's choice lies between the life of a human being and that of a less evolved animal, karmic law dictates that the human life is the more important.

I carried the point further: "One can't really say that those insects are necessarily a danger to human life. Flies, for instance, are more of a nuisance than a threat."

"Even so," he replied, "in countries where such insects are allowed to thrive, the mortality rate is higher owing to the diseases they carry, and because of the filth they spread. In countries where they are kept under control, there is less filth and disease, and people, on an average, live much longer. It is best, therefore, to keep those pests under control, especially in populated areas.

"Besides," he added, "such insects are instruments of evil. As such, their proliferation should be discouraged."

⚜ 265 ⚜

He once said that disease germs come like clouds into this world from *tamasic* universes. Their sole purpose is to wreak havoc. And the punishment they receive from man, in his constant war against disease, is their destiny. The Master then added something very strange:

"Those germ clouds are fallen souls. It *is* possible for the soul to fall even that low, if it has become completely steeped in evil. Ordinarily, once a soul evolves to the human level, it doesn't fall back again to a lower level. If ever it does so, as happens occasionally, it descends for one lifetime only, to the level of the higher animals. One may have to be sent back repeatedly, but it is always for only one lifetime. If a person continues for too long in his error, however, he may be thrown back very far down the ladder of evolution. When one descends so low, he doesn't completely lose his awareness that there is something amiss. This very knowledge is a great punishment. There are whole galaxies, as I've sometimes mentioned, where evil predominates. From those galaxies it is that epidemics come."

❧ 266 ❧

"Did Mahatma Gandhi keep up his Kriya Yoga practice, after his initiation by you?" I asked the Master.

"Gandhi was a man of his word," the Master replied. "He was a great man, and a man of truth. Yes, he kept up his practice."

"Was he a master?"

"Great as he was," answered the Guru, "he was not *that* great. Rather, he was a great moralist, but for all that far below the spiritual level of a master like Sri Yukteswar. I would say, of Gandhi, that he was certainly fit to 'untie the latchet of my Master's shoes,' but not greater.* He was great, but he created no saints, as a master would have done."

267

"When I was in India," the Master said, "I knew that I must return to America. Yet I felt a strong affinity with India, where the very soil breathes love for God. And then I saw all of you, waiting for me—those, especially, whom I had yet to meet in this life. You were my real family, much more so than my blood relatives in India. Those relatives were, except for a handful, spiritual strangers to me. You were my own. And this was my true home: my family in God."

268

He always placed great emphasis on the importance of practicing Kriya Yoga. I recorded his comments one evening:

"Practice Kriya night and day. It is the greatest key to salvation. Other people go by books and lesser practices, but it will take them incarnations to reach God. Kriya is not only, as I've often said, the airplane route to Him, but also the greatest way of destroying present temptation.

*The Master was paraphrasing the words of John the Baptist about Jesus: "There cometh one mightier than I after me, the latchet of whose shoes I am not worthy to stoop down and un-loose." (Mark 1:7)

When you feel that joy within, no evil will be able to touch you. To you, sense pleasures will then seem like stale cheese compared to the nectar of God's joy.

"While others are talking or idly wasting time, *you* go out into the garden and do a few Kriyas. Whenever you have a free moment, stop, sit down, and do a few Kriyas. What else do you need? You could read countless books, and what would they give you? You could seek perfection by adhering to spiritual rules, but rules can be broken. A rule is a fragile stick; if you lean on it too hard, it will break. When you know divine joy, however, nothing will be able, ever again, to take it from you.

"When you clean your room, it looks tidy, afterward, for a few days. But after those few days, the dust settles again. So is it with outer spiritual practices. The aid they give is only temporary. Once you've tasted inner bliss, however, and immersed yourself in it, you know there isn't anything else that matters.

"I know all those who don't practice Kriya," he added. Looking penetratingly at Clifford, he said, "You do not practice it much, do you?"

"That's true, Sir," Clifford confessed.

"You see, just a flash I got. You *must* practice it. Instead of talking so much, and listening to flattering words, sit down every chance you get, and do a few Kriyas."

To all of us then, he said, "Kriya contains everything you need. Practice it faithfully, night and day."

299

I (Walter), who was always seeking clarification for a broader audience, asked him, "Is it safe for people to practice Kriya a great deal?" (He had told us that one ought, in the beginning, to practice only a few Kriyas at a time.)

"Of course it is safe!" he replied forcefully. "You must get out of your mind that thought that it is not. The thing is, however, that one shouldn't do so many that his concentration wanes. It is better to do even a few Kriyas, concentratedly, than many Kriyas automatically."

✿ 269 ✿

Bernard told me he'd asked the Master the following question once: "You've said people shouldn't increase the number of Kriyas they practice daily, without first obtaining official permission. What if someone lives far away, or for some other reason can't get his Kriyas checked, and can't even write to Mount Washington for permission to increase them?"

The Master, Bernard said, gave this response: "If they are sincere, and feel the need, they will do more Kriyas anyway!"

~ 270 ~

Of the Kundalini force (the energy that is locked at the base of the spine), the Master said one day, "When one thinks good thoughts, the Kundalini automatically starts moving upward. When one thinks evil thoughts, it moves downward. When one hates others, or has wrong thoughts about them, it moves down. And when one loves others, or thinks kindly about them, it moves up.

"Kundalini is not awakened by yoga techniques alone."

~ 271 ~

The "serpent power," as it is called in many books, is the Kundalini. This "serpent," the Master said, was the one described in the Book of Genesis of the Bible. That description is meant in an allegorical sense.

A fundamentalist Christian once insisted to the Master that every statement in the Bible should be taken literally, and not considered a mere allegory. "What about the Garden of Eden?" Master inquired. "We read in the Bible," he continued, "that the serpent spoke to Eve. Would you say, of that story, that it was meant to be taken literally?"

"In those days," this true believer replied, "serpents could speak."

What more was there to say? As the Master often reminded us, "Fools argue; wise men discuss." He respected the fundamentalist as a child of God, but how could he respect his obstinacy? Removing his hat, and matching gesture to words, he replied ceremoniously, "I bow to the colossal temple of ignorance that I behold before me!"

❧ 272 ☙

"Was Moses a master?" I asked him one day.

"Indeed, yes!" he replied with assurance. "That is what the Bible means in saying that Moses lifted up the serpent in the wilderness. 'Wilderness' means the meditative silence, where no shrubs of human thought grow.

"Jesus said also," the Master continued, "'As Moses lifted up the serpent in the wilderness, even so must the son of man be lifted up.' This was not, as the New Testament implies, a reference to his coming crucifixion. It was a reference to human beings, or 'sons of man.' He was saying that, to know God, one must raise the kundalini power—which locks him in identity with his body—and unify it with the Spirit centered at the top of the head."

❧ 273 ❧

"When sex temptation comes," the Master said, "say to yourself, 'Lord, Your power is manifesting in me. I will use it to grow stronger in myself, and to create through proper channels.' Then inhale, tense; exhale and relax. Repeat that several times.

"Don't let the frogs of weakness kick you around! (That is how my Master put it.) The more you control sex, the more powerful you will become in every way, but if you declare weakly, 'Oh, I have to spill it,' you will enslave yourself for life. The more you give in, the less you will be able to free yourself from the meshes of delusion."

❧ 274 ❧

"Kamala Silva is the only one I have told to leave here and marry. Others have left for that purpose, but they haven't soared in God as she has. One man told me he was leaving to marry. 'Wherever I am,' he solemnly assured me, 'I will always follow you, and meditate daily.'

"'You won't,' I told him. 'Your place is here. If you give in to delusion, you will lose the inner clarity you've gained.' Well, he did leave, and in time he forgot his resolution to be loyal and to meditate regularly.

"Never forget this: Evil has power. If one sides with it, he will find himself imprisoned by it."

Again I (Walter) want to emphasize that the Master was not against marriage as such. He even saw it as spiritually wholesome, provided two people live together in the right spirit. People who abandon their spiritual calling to get married, however, are leaving a life of dedication to high ideals to pursue their own personal desires. To do that is to move in the wrong direction. It isn't the fact of being married or living a normal life "in the world" that pulls one down. It is that one who is lukewarm in his devotion, and *chooses* the world, has made a choice that will pull him down. As the Master put it, "It isn't where your body is that determines how spiritual you are: It's where you are *in consciousness.*"

I have noticed over years that the first thing most renunciates do who leave their monastic calling is get married. What that almost invariably means is voluntary reinvestment in self-interest, with the endless desires and attachments that such interest entails.

275

The Master once repeated for us a story he'd written in his autobiography about a man who was dying of diabetes.

"The doctors," he told us, "had given him three months to live. He determined, in the time remaining to him, to find God. He sat in meditation, gradually extending to longer and longer periods the time he could sit. At first, it was only fifteen minutes at a time, after which he needed to get up and relieve himself. Slowly, however, he sat longer until finally he was meditating several hours at a stretch. Constantly he prayed, 'Lord, come into my broken temple!'

"The allotted three months passed. Still he lived, and was sitting for steadily longer periods. Three years passed: *still* he was alive. At last one day God appeared to him. The man, emerging from his ecstasy, discovered that his body was completely healed.

"'Lord,' he cried, 'I didn't ask You to heal me. All I asked was that You come into my broken temple.' And the Lord answered, 'Where My light is, there no darkness can come.' The saint—for he'd become one—then wrote in the sand, 'And on this day the Lord came into my broken temple, and made it whole!'

"What will power!" the Master cried as he finished this story. "If you tried that hard, how fast you would go! You all have strong will power. I urge you, *Use* it!"

276

"When Smith left," the Master told me, "he went to his wife and said, 'Come on, we're leaving this place.'

"'Oh, no,' she replied. 'You leave if you want to. I am staying with my Guru.'

"I always said the reason God brought that family here was for her sake. I remember during the depression years, when they had little money for food and often went hungry, Smith would sometimes go alone to his parents' home to have a good meal."

Someone asked the Master, "When will he return?"

"Never," was the reply. "He was never in."

Of Norman, on the other hand, the Master said, "He hasn't left. His heart is always with me."

277

The Master was under no illusion that his, or that any other, organization was perfect, for mankind itself is not perfect. "Don't speak of the bad side of the organization," he told us. "If I wanted to list all its faults, I could start now and never stop! By concentrating on that side, however, one loses sight of the good. And there is also much good here.

Amelita Galli-Curci, the famous Italian prima donna,
was a devoted student of the Master.

"Doctors say that millions of terrible germs pass constantly through our bodies. Most of them don't affect us, partly because we aren't even aware of them. Knowledge of their presence might make us more susceptible, by causing us to concentrate on them. That is what one should do here: Do not concentrate on the negative side. When you look at that side long enough, you take on its qualities. But when you look at the good, you take on goodness."

❧ 278 ❧

"Don't mix with people too closely," he counseled us. "The desire for outward companionship is a reflection of the soul's desire for companionship with God. The more you seek to satisfy that desire outwardly, however, the more you will lose His inner company, and the more restless and dissatisfied, in consequence, you will become."

❦ 279 ❧

"The senses of sight, hearing, smell, taste, and touch are all separate suggestions of God. I can disconnect them one by one. I used to do that as a boy. I came to realize that this is all God's movie: true not only to the senses of sight and sound as movies are, but also to the senses of smell, taste, and touch.

"For hours I practiced disconnecting the senses, one by one, by withdrawing the energy from them and bringing it back again, until I'd gained full control over the suggestions they gave to the mind."

❦ 280 ❧

Someone had asked the Master to pose for a photograph. He obliged, then commented with a gay laugh, "Everyone likes to see his own picture. The Lord made it so that we couldn't see our own faces. Only others get to see them. In that way we wouldn't find out too soon! But now, with photography, we can see ourselves finally as others see us!"

That expression, *"Find out too soon"*: How often I heard him use it! It would be wise, in trying to understand the great movie that is life, to realize that its pluses and minuses are carefully balanced. It is no simple nursery tale or B-grade movie, where the heroes all wear white hats and the villains are all dressed in black ones.

In Paramhansa Yogananda's book, *The Rubaiyat of Omar Khayyam Explained,* in his explanation of Stanza 73, we read: "Is life so difficult to understand? Well, of course it is! If it were easy to grasp the drift and purpose of this spectacle, how well would that speak for the skill of the Dramatist? The Divine Playwright has concealed the direction of His plot—which is, in itself, straight-forward—behind endless subplots and complexities. He has cloaked the wonderful ending of the play behind a network of confusing hints and plausible-seeming, but false, explanations for the events taking place. It is a story wrought with incalculable skill, its true purpose concealed with sublimest artistry behind myriads of tragic and comic secondary plots."

God does want us to "find out"—the sooner the better. However, He doesn't want to "clobber" us with miracles! To become worthy of knowing Him, we must develop our own discrimination.

281

The Master had several recordings of Indian devotional songs. One was a song recorded by the famous singer of Bengal, Mrinalkanti Ghosh. I and several others were listening to it one day with the Master. The song describes the devotee praying to the Divine Mother, Kali, asking Her to appear before him dancing all over creation. Afterward the Master exclaimed, "As I listened, I was dancing with Kali all over creation. I could hear the music in my soul."

282

The Master was in the process of healing me of headaches I'd been having. I referred, in the presence of others, to my progress in following his advice. To my surprise, he responded rather sternly. "You must not talk about these things before others," he said. "The Divine doesn't work that way." He had been helping me from within, in other words, and not only through the outer suggestions he'd given me. To speak of it before others invited their consciousness into the process, and might have diluted his subtle vibrations.

Later he told me privately: "You will get well, provided you don't talk about it. It is in silence that God comes."

༄ 283 ༄

In September, 1951, looking at the young monks as he reminisced about the old days, he said regretfully, "I wish you all had been with me then. So many years had to pass before you came!"

༄ 284 ༄

"There was a devotee," the Master said, "who sat before the image of his guru, casting flowers onto it. All of a sudden his concentration became interiorized, and he beheld within himself the whole universe. His body was motionless, but his consciousness had expanded to infinity. Later he cried, 'Ah! I was putting flowers on the image of someone else, and now I see that I, untouched by the body, am the sustainer of the universe! I bow to myself!' And he began casting flowers onto his own head.

"My Master it was who first told me that story," he continued. "Oh! when I heard it, I was so thrilled I went into *samadhi*."

285

The Master, gazing jocularly at Leo Cocks, remarked,
"Look at Leo, how fat he is becoming—like a real Bengali
babu! Pretty soon he will be like Trailanga Swami, with a
belly in three steps." I suspect he wasn't merely teasing
Leo, but hinting at his need to lose weight, and not eat
so much. There was no deep teaching here, of course, but
it sparked another thought in me.

"Sir," I said, thinking back to an earlier conversation
we'd had, and remembering from his autobiography
that he'd said that Hindus held Trailanga Swami in great
reverence, "was Trailanga Swami an *avatar?*"

"He was a great master," he replied, "though not an
avatar. An *avatar* comes with a special mission. Trailanga
was a '*jivan mukta,*' which means, 'freed while living.' In
that state, one is fully Self-realized, but not yet completely free from all past karma."

One day, during a Kriya Yoga initiation, he told us,
"Through the practice of Kriya, you should hope to become at least *jivan muktas* in this lifetime."

During another Kriya Yoga initiation—I believe it
was in 1949—he said also, "Of those present, there
will be a few *siddhas,* and quite a few *jivan muktas.*" A
siddha, or "perfected being," has attained full liberation.

286

Boone had caused someone considerable inconvenience by revealing, in answer to a question, something that hadn't needed to be said. He was scolded for doing so, and tried to justify himself by saying, "I only wanted to be honest. That's why I told the truth."

This matter was later reported to the Master, who commented indignantly, "Supposing someone came to me with the Holy Bible, the Bhagavad Gita, and every great scripture in the world and said to me, 'If I tell you something, will you swear on these sacred books never to repeat to anyone what I've said?' And supposing I replied in good faith, 'Yes, yes, I promise.' And then, supposing further, he told me, 'I have put a rattlesnake in M——'s bed!' What would I do? It would have been wrong on my part to promise, but should I then compound that mistake by saying, 'Oh dear, I have promised; now I must say nothing'? Which is worse, to break a promise? or to let someone be killed when I am in a position to save him? *Of course* I would speak out! Imagine that boy causing serious trouble, then trying to justify himself by saying he only wanted to tell the truth!

"Truth is always beneficial. Boone wasn't telling the truth, for what he did resulted in harm. What he stated was a fact only, not a truth. He need not have an-swered at all! It would have been far better for him to say nothing. If he needed to speak, however, it would have been better at least to equivocate than to let someone be hurt as a consequence."

֍ 287 ֍

A few of us were working on the grounds at Master's desert retreat. One afternoon, the Master came out and shoveled alongside us. It was a hot day, and, seeing him pant a little, I commented pleasantly, "Hot work!" He looked at me a little sternly, and said, "It is *good* work!"

֍ 288 ֍

The Master remarked once to Doctor Lewis, "For everyone who has crossed my path in this life, there has been a reason."

289

During the Korean war, someone asked the Master, "Do the American soldiers fighting there get bad karma for killing?"

"They are fulfilling their duty as soldiers," the Master answered. "No, they don't get bad karma for that. This is a holy war. The villain must be defeated, otherwise the whole world might become enslaved."

There was more to this story. The Master told a few of us, after that war began: "When South Korea was invaded from the north, I myself put the thought in President Truman's mind to go to its defense. That situation was a threat to the whole world. Had South Korea fallen, the communists would have gone on to take Japan, and would then have come up and taken the Aleutian Islands, from where they would have invaded Alaska and North America. The whole world, ultimately, could have been swept up into the material-istic philosophy of communism. For these reasons it was very necessary that South Korea be defended. That is why I have called this a holy war."

I was fascinated to hear this intimation that the masters sometimes play an active role in world affairs. That means they are concerned not only with the salva-tion of individuals, but with the spiritual upliftment of humanity as a whole.

When Hitler first rose to power, Paramhansa Yogananda, for several reasons, saw some hope in that accession. One of those reasons was the unfairness of the Versailles Treaty, which had forced Germany into virtual destitution. He also saw, as he told a few people, that Hitler had been, in a former lifetime, Alexander "the great" of Greece, who had shown an interest in the yogis of India. When Hitler allowed himself to be seized by ambition for power, however, that ambition distorted his potentially spiritual leanings. At that point, several masters began to work against him. The masters always work *within* the karmic law. Thus, they don't try to change the destiny of the world, but work *within* the karmas of the individuals concerned. They worked, therefore, *with* Hitler's consciousness as it was. They were at liberty, however, to put the thought in Hitler's mind to make the mistakes that led to his eventual destruction. They suggested to him from within, for example, to divide his forces and fight both in the east and in the west, and also in Africa. This they did by feeding the confidence he felt in his own ability to win "everywhere." Militarily, there was no need for Germany to divide its fronts. That self-division proved, for it, a fatal error.

On the subject of the former incarnations of a few world leaders, it is interesting to note that the Master said Mussolini was Marc Anthony, of ancient Rome; that Stalin was Genghis Khan, the scourge of Asia; and that

Winston Churchill was Napoleon. (I once asked him, "Who was Roosevelt?" He answered, "I've never told anybody." After a brief pause he added, "I was afraid I might get into trouble!")

Of Napoleon he said, "He wanted to destroy England. As Churchill, he has had to preside over the dissolution of the British empire. The divine purpose behind the Second World War was to liberate the 'third world' countries, most of which were British colonies. Again, Napoleon was sent into temporary exile on the island of Elba. Later he returned to power. Churchill, similarly, was sent out of politics: now he is back again in power."

❧ 290 ☙

The Master was sitting on the stage at the Hollywood Church one Sunday. The stage curtains were closed, as he gave lunch to a few guests. I, as a minister of the church, was present. A lady asked, "Master, wasn't Doctor Lewis your first disciple in this country?"

"That's what they say." He sounded almost offhanded. Then, noticing her surprise, he added, "I never call people my disciples. God is the Guru. They are *His* disciples."

≈ 291 ≈

"You have to individually make love to God," he insisted to us. "Keep your mind at the Christ Center in the forehead. As you work, remember also that you are working for God and Guru. Always chant mentally: God and Guru; God, Christ, and Guru.

"Many come here, then pass their time in idle gossip and joking: Well, they won't get God! There are many rats and mice living in the canyon on this property also, but they aren't advancing spiritually; they aren't finding God. It isn't just being here that will get you to Him. You have to make your own effort. Each one of you, in the end, stands alone before God."

≈ 292 ≈

Norman told me of a vision he'd had in which he saw himself with the Master in Lemuria eighty thousand years ago. Was the vision true? I of course had no way of knowing, and was only mildly interested in the actual existence of Lemuria. What that vision did do for me was raise another, to me more pressing issue:

"Master," I said, "have I been your disciple for *thousands of years?*" The very thought that it could take so long to find God appalled me.

"It has been a long time," he replied; "that's all I will say."

"Does it always take so long?" (I hoped to learn that at least I wasn't the only laggard!)

"Oh, yes," the Master replied offhandedly. "Desires for name, fame, and the rest of them take people away again and again."

And what, I thought, have all those desires accomplished? Life ends so very soon—and then?

༄ 293 ༄

Debi Mukherjee joked and laughed continuously. Life to him was one long succession of pranks and hilarity. He identified mentally, I suspected, with the pranks played by the boy Krishna. One day, the Master said to him, "You have devotion, but you waste too much time joking and keeping the others rollicking. You must learn to be more serious."

"I know it, Master," Debi said remorsefully. "But my habit is so strong. How can I change it without your blessing?" (How common it is for devotees to try to shift the responsibility for changing themselves onto God's shoulders.)

"Well, my blessings are there," replied the Master. "God's blessings are there. It is *your* 'blessings' that are needed!"

294

"In God," the Master said, "everything goes on in the present tense. It is like a movie, which can be turned backwards or forwards. The action on the screen may cover centuries, but all the while up in the projection booth, it happens now.

"The secret of life is to learn to live fully aware of present bliss. When you can learn to be happy in the present, you have God."

I remarked, "Very few live in the present, isn't that so?"

"That's true," he replied. "Most people live in the past, with nostalgia or regrets, or in the future, with hopes and fears born of desire."

295

The Master remarked to me, "I have been just like a watchdog here, keeping the men and women separate. Even so, as soon as I am out of things a little bit I find the mixing begins. When I leave this body, the men and women *must* live in separate colonies." He often commented, further: "That is why Buddhism failed in India. Corruption entered because the monks and nuns lived in too close association with one another."

296

"I was spending so much of my time," the Master said, "giving interviews and lecturing that I began to worry that I might be forgetting God. And then I realized that in that very thought I was remembering Him."

297

Master saw people differently from the way most of us do. He didn't see merely their present bodies, outward expressions, age, and sex. To the Master, human life is a fleeting manifestation of an unending succession of lifetimes.

Sometimes, when he looked at Jan Savage, a boy of nine who had come with his mother to Mount Washington, he would ruffle the child's hair playfully and comment, "Jan is not a little boy: He is an old man!"

Occasionally we would mention to him something that we'd been experiencing—it might be anything at all—and he would say casually, "That is because, . . ." then give us some (perhaps trivial) piece of information about what we'd done, or wanted, or experienced in a former life.

I'd been enjoying the calmness of the desert. One day I remarked to him, "I've always wanted to live alone like this." His reply was matter-of-fact: "That is because you've done it before. Most of those who are with me have lived alone many times in the past."

For a time I had been having stomach problems. The Master remarked one day, "You had that trouble before, that's why."

When Norman left the ashram, the Master commented, "This is the first time in many lives that delusion has caught him."

I inquired of the Master shortly after I became a disciple, "Sir, was I a yogi before?"

"Many times," he replied. "You'd have had to be, to be living here now."

A number of the disciples asked him if they'd been with him when he was William the Conqueror. He answered them freely. (Curiously, I myself never asked that question, though it was being generally asked at the time. I've often wondered if he didn't prevent the question from surfacing in my mind.) To Norman he said, "You were my giant." (Norman has had a large body in this lifetime.) To Jerry he said, "You were good: You used to fight for me."

Henry and an old man, Ed Harding, who also was a disciple, had felt an instant antipathy toward one another.

They overcame it, but Henry asked the Master one day why they'd had such a feeling. "You were enemies in the past," was the Master's response.

Love is the power, usually, which brings people together life after life. So also is hate such a power. "When you see families that fight among themselves all the time," the Master said, "it is because they've been drawn together by their mutual animosity; that way, they get to work out their enmity at close quarters!"

My purpose in introducing this subject is to say that living with the Master made it natural for us to see life as a continuum, and the present life as only temporary. Eternity became more easily, for us, a daily reality.

"There are many great souls living here," the Master told me. Glancing out the window, he happened to see Louise Royston, an old woman, simple natured and very sincere, working on the grounds outside. "Even she," he commented with a smile. He then added to me with a chuckle, "You know, when she first came here she was just as ugly as she is now!"

I entered his sitting room one afternoon when one of the younger nuns, Corinne Forshee (who later received the monastic name, Mukti), was in there briefly, arranging papers on a table. She seemed to be paying no attention to the Master, and the criticism flashed through my mind, "She can't be a very devoted disciple to show so little interest in our Guru when she has the blessing of being in his presence."

After she'd left the room, the Master said to me with a beautiful smile, "What a *wonderful* soul she is!"

❧ 298 ☙

"I used to laugh a lot when I was a boy, because of my inner joy in God," the Master told us. "The saints I met, most of whom were outwardly grave, welcomed my laughter as coming from God.

"Badhuri Mahasaya (the 'levitating saint,' as I've described him in my *Autobiography*) enjoyed my laughter for the same reason. It upset a few of his disciples, however, to see me laugh in the presence of their ever-serious Master. One time he said to me, 'I understand, and appreciate, why you like to laugh, but as it disturbs some of these here, do you think, perhaps, you should be more serious for their sake?'

"'I understand what you mean,' I replied, 'but can they not see that it springs from the joy I feel in God, and in your company?'

"He relented. 'All right, laugh if you feel to. I will try to explain to them that it is from God.'"

☙ 299 ❧

I (Walter) once asked the Master, "Should I love people? Or ought I to reserve my love for God alone?"

"It is better," the Master answered, "to love God. In loving people you might get attached to them. What you must do, where others are concerned, is love God first, and then love Him *through them.*"

☙ 300 ❧

"You must work to establish your relationship with the Father, as a son," the Master said to us one day. "Think of Him as your own, dear Parent. Then talk to Him just as you would to your own Father or Mother. Make any request you have, or put to Him any question you like, in that spirit. Pray, for example, 'Father, I am Thy son. As Thy child, give me this or that.'"

☙ 301 ❧

A visitor once asked the Master, "What do you consider the most spiritual place in America?"

The Master replied, "I have always considered Los Angeles to be the Benares of America."

Interestingly, there is an esoteric tradition that in ancient times great spiritual masters lived here. Indeed, the spiritual vibrations of Southern California, and in the Los Angeles area particularly, are palpable to anyone who is sensitive, the moment he steps off the plane on his arrival there. People joke about the "goofiness" of the spiritual scene in Los Angeles, but one demonstrates his ignorance in the things he is interested in. I cannot but feel, also, that the Master's spiritual vibrations continue to permeate the whole atmosphere of that city.

꩜ 302 ꩜

At my first Christmas meditation in 1948, the Divine Mother came to Master and blessed the gathered devotees. To many of them he repeated Her wishes. To some, he said to give themselves unreservedly to God.

He then spoke openly with the Divine Mother, in such a way as to include all of us in his conversation. The conversation lasted a long time. Over and over, after a time, he repeated, "Oh, You are so beautiful!" At last he cried, "Don't go! You say that the material desires of these people are driving You away? Oh, come back! Don't leave!" All of us remained divinely uplifted, after that, for the rest of the day, savoring the joy She had left in our hearts.

How real God became for us, living with the Master! No longer, it seemed, was there a veil of *maya* separating us from the Infinite. Often it felt to me in his presence that God Himself was there, in our very midst.

๑๛ 303 ๛๑

Did the Master have any special traits or idiosyncrasies—such as one that was recorded by Samuel Johnson's biographer, Boswell: a habit of running the tip of his cane along the iron railings on a street? Little things, in other words?

In the Master's case, I can recall nothing of the sort. I don't say he had no mannerisms: I am simply not aware that he had.

I remember the reaction of Roy Benn, a radio announcer from Australia who visited Mount Washington during the early 1950s. I had said something to him about having seen the Master once drumming his fingers on the arm of his chair. Roy responded, "I wouldn't have thought the Master could have had a nervous habit like that." Reflecting on the matter afterward, I realized that the Master hadn't been showing nervousness at all. He had simply been "playing" rhythmically with his fingers to the accompaniment of a piece of music he was hearing in his head. He liked to play the Indian tablas (finger-played drums), and once remarked that he'd like it if more Indian music were played during our church services. (Sister Meera talked him out of it, insisting that in America it wouldn't be understood.)

Doctor Lewis once told me, "Nothing the Master ever did was out of habit. His every action was a conscious and deliberate exercise of free will." This was, to me, an astonishing statement.

"Not even when tying his shoelaces?" I inquired.

"Nothing," Doctor Lewis asseverated.

Indeed, as I look back I can recall no instance to indicate that Dr. Lewis might have been mistaken. Always, the Master seemed to be living completely in the moment—a "moment," however, that existed in eternity!

How was he in other ways, as a person? What was his appearance? How did he comport himself?

He seemed completely ageless. Physically he was not tall: about five feet six, as I've stated before. He was well built, slightly stocky, very firm looking. He left his hair long because his Guru had said he liked it so. From a wish to meet other aspects of American taste, however, he was clean-shaven. His two most notable features were his eyes and his smile, both of which were extraordinarily expressive. His eyes were deeply calm, and profoundly penetrating. Looking into them, one saw no glimmer of ego, or of any personal feelings at all: I often thought of them as windows onto infinity. His hands and feet were small. His complexion was rather dark, and full of vitality.

He always sat, stood, and walked with a straight back. Sometimes, in comportment, he appeared abstracted, but it was clear that his mind was actively occupied either with some deep, inner experience, or with reflections concerning a matter that was demanding his active attention. His powers of concentration were enormous. Whatever he did had his full focus. I never saw him vague, dull, or absent-minded; in this sense, though he was often deeply concentrated within, he was altogether different from the popular image of the "absent-minded" professor—one who looks about vaguely for his glasses, let us say, though they happen to be sitting on his nose! Indeed, the Master had fun, sometimes, over that classic "professorial" image.

"There was a philosopher," he said, "who flicked the ash of his cigarette down the back of his wife's dress. 'What are you doing!' she cried indignantly. 'Oh, sorry! sorry!' he replied with a cloudlike smile. 'I thought you were the wall.'"

Because of his spontaneity, I could never predict with any certainty how he would respond in any situation. He had no "set" attitudes. Whatever he did was exactly right *for that moment*.

One day I came to him, the bearer, I was sure, of good news. Happily I said, "Sir, we have a new man for the print shop!" We'd been needing someone there for months.

"Why do you tell me that?" he demanded indignantly. "First see if he has our spirit; then teach him how to deepen that spirit; only *then* see where he might be useful. Two others have already come and told me we have a candidate for the print shop. I never ask anyone first what he can do. I look at the spiritual side."

It took me years to understand that the Master viewed the organization itself as only a means to a higher, individual consciousness. Otherwise, the organization as such had no meaning for him. He used to say, firmly and with sincerity, "I could walk away from this work right now, and never look back."

"Believe me, Sir," I replied, abashed by his rebuke about the new man. "His spirit is my concern, too. I didn't say it, but it was certainly what I meant. Perhaps I should have reported first that he said to me, 'I'm glad to see that you all pray with such devotion.'" (I had invited him to my meditation room, and together we had listened to recordings of Hindu devotional singing. He loved them.)

"That is what I wanted to hear," said the Master approvingly.

I had yet to learn, however, to become more sensitive to the fact that he worked with intuitive insight, above all. This young man proved, on acquaintance, to be only superficially devotional. The Master was kind to him, and sometimes even teased him a little in a friendly way. Privately, however, he told me that he wasn't really suitable for this path. Not long afterward, our "new man for the print shop" left.

"When intuition develops," the Master said, "you don't always know why you say and do things differently, but when you are in that divine flow you are in tune with truth. Then, everything goes as it should.

"The other day," he added, "I invited some people to dinner. 'Come on Wednesday,' I said to them. They replied, 'Thursday would be better.' I didn't try to dissuade them, but as it happened, on Thursday it rained heavily."

More and more, as one lived with him, one learned to listen to even the nuances of his speech. For although he rarely insisted on anything, his mere hint, if one listened, was often a sufficient warning.

ᘛᘚ 304 ᘛᘚ

"In this way," the Master said, "one can develop intuition: After meditation, sit still for a long time, enjoying the inner peace. As you don't cook your food and then run off without eating it, but rather, sit down and enjoy it, so also the meditation techniques help to prepare the mind, but after them, sit quietly, enjoying the 'meal' you've prepared. Many people meditate till they feel a touch of peace, but jump up then and leave their meditation for their activities. That's all right, if you have important work waiting for you, for it is always better to meditate *before* any activity, that you may feel at least *some* peace as you work. Whenever possible, however, sit for a long time after your practice of the techniques. That is when the deepest enjoyment comes. Intuition is developed by continuously deepening that enjoyment, and, later on, by holding on to its calm aftereffect."

✥ 305 ✥

A visitor, who had read *Autobiography of a Yogi,* though he wasn't an SRF member, came to converse with the Master. I took notes at their meeting.

"May I ask, out of curiosity," the visitor said, "why, although you call this a 'Church of All Religions,' you place so much emphasis on the Christian religion?'

"Actually," the Master replied, "we place emphasis on *two* of the world's great religions: Christianity, and Hinduism. We concentrate especially on the teachings, rather than on the religions, of Jesus Christ and of Krishna. I do so because that was the wish of Babaji. He and Jesus Christ together sent this mission. They are the first in our line of gurus. The wish of them all was expressed to me by Babaji, particularly: to interpret the Christian New Testament, and the Hindu Bhagavad Gita, and thereby to demonstrate the essential oneness of the truths of both religions."

His visitor had, of course, implied something more also: Why didn't the Master teach *all* religions? On other occasions he answered this question also, though perhaps on the occasion I've described he didn't feel inspired to go more deeply into the matter with this particular person. To complete his meaning, therefore, I should explain that he said also that his mission was to show the *essence* of all religions. It was never his purpose to compare various scriptural passages intellectually, in order to show their similarity. In other words, he did not teach *syncretism*. That would have meant merely skimming the surface of truth.

His mission, and that of our line of gurus, was to show the *essential oneness of truth itself.* It is at their deepest level that all religions are one. For this purpose, it sufficed to show the oneness of only two of the great world religions.

Outwardly, Hinduism and Christianity are very different. Yet both have produced saints of high spiritual attainment. To know God is the eternal need of mankind. All people need to understand their need for *personal, direct communion* with the Lord.

"Self-realization," the Master predicted, "will someday be recognized as the essential truth of every religion in the world." His prediction referred not to his organization, Self-Realization *Fellowship,* except insofar as that organization promoted this ideal. What he was referring to was the eternal *principle* itself: Self-realization. This principle is destined, in the present Dwapara Yuga, to become accepted everywhere. The true purpose of religion, regardless of its diverse dogmas and "credos," is union with God, the eternal Self pervading the whole universe.

꧁ 306 ꧂

I seem to remember that it was the same guest—I have his question and the Master's answer in my notebook, but I've no other way of identifying him—who asked Master the following question: "I understand you have two classes of students: those who live in the world, and those who live in the monastery as renunciates. Which of these two ways do you consider the better, and why?"

"Good, better, and best," the Master replied, "are determined by the depth of one's love for God. Outside of divine devotion, nothing else matters.

"If one is in a position to leave everything and live only for God, why not do so outwardly also? Whether married or single, the important thing is to love Him deeply.

"The monastic life is for those who have the pure desire to live only for God, and who are also free of social entanglements."

ᗌᘏ 307 ᔕᘏ

Sometimes I (Walter), as the man in charge of the monks, accepted applicants mainly because it pained me to have to refuse anyone. Caroll Joliff was one such person. Though I accepted him for monastic training, I knew he was not suited to our way of life. He practically exuded worldly attitudes. I saw, however, that he sincerely wanted to change. The Master's comment to me, later, was, "I'm going to have to give you intuition!" (It is interesting to note that my intuition in these matters did improve markedly after he'd said those words.)

Months later, the Master was in his car, getting ready to go see Sister (Gyanamata) for the last time. Carroll was standing nearby. Seeing him, the Master paused to compliment him on the effort he'd been making. "How much you have changed," he remarked. "I left it up to your own will. But see: Isn't it much easier, really, to be good than bad? When one is bad, he is always afraid. When one is good, on the other hand, he is afraid of nothing and no one. The very gods, then, 'have to watch out,' as the saying is, for the Lord Himself is on his side! Just see how much better it is to live for God. You yourself know that you are happier!

"Everything is for God, anyway, only He doesn't let you see that. Man must first turn to God. Then only does he see God active everywhere."

Yogananda on a train circa 1925. The Master, during his years of "spiritual campaigning," traveled to many parts of the United States.

Carroll didn't remain long, as he himself surely realized he wouldn't. Being at Mount Washington, however, proved good for him, and must have been an important step in his spiritual evolution.

The Master stated also sometimes—and these words might have been a good addition to his reply to the guest in the foregoing conversation, had he felt to go into the matter more deeply: "It is more pleasing to God if you work consciously for Him, rather than for yourself. If one works in the world, and cares only for self and family, it is much more difficult to expand beyond the confines of ego-consciousness. Wise is he who views all humanity as his own greater family."

308

What, one may ask, was the Master's mission?

It was broadly based. Above all, it was intended for those, whether married or single, who understood the need to make truth, and therefore God, their priority. His mission also was to establish ideals of equal validity for both householders and renunciates. He came, again, and as I've indicated already, to show the underlying oneness of all religions, by emphasizing Self-realization in God.

His mission, however, like ripples on a pond into which some heavy object has been dropped, spread outward in all directions. For he came to uplift the whole of society. For example, another reason he came was to introduce into the schools a more balanced system of education, emphasizing spiritual training and character development rather than mundane facts that prepare youngsters for their future careers. He came to show people everywhere—in business, in the professions, in trade, in the arts—that the inclusion of spiritual principles in whatever they did would enable them to thrive, even financially.

He came to show that the arts both can and should be a means of inspiring people, and not merely of entertaining them.

He came to show that truth need not be declared in angry protest against some social injustice or error: that it can be revealed joyfully, as an aid toward people's own enlightenment.

In conclusion, his mission was to show all humanity that human life should be a divine service: that its true purpose is not self-aggrandizement, and not "living for number one," but living with self-expansive ideals. In short, his mission was by no means only to establish a monastery, as some people believe—an activity that he himself postponed for years in order to address more pressing needs, and that he left, finally, to be developed by others. His mission was to uplift and spiritualize all society.

For all these purposes, earnest workers were needed, and not only meditating monks and nuns. It was as though he viewed the high truths he had brought to the world as a flow downward from the spiritual heights: like the Ganges descending from the lofty Himalayas to the plains below, and from there on to the sea.

First in this downward flow was Babaji's commission to Lahiri Mahasaya. Babaji, though world-remote like the god Shiva, responded to people's desire for enlightenment in both East and West: vibrations that, he said, came to him "floodlike" from afar. The line of gurus brought the teachings out progressively into the world. That progression ended in Paramhansa Yogananda, who had the charge of bringing those divine teachings to society itself.

The Master told me of a discussion he'd had with his guru Swami Sri Yukteswar in 1935. "I saw how badly his ashram was in need of proper care. There was a loose tile on the roof which, my Master had said to me many years earlier, would be safe there 'as long as I'm alive.' (In fact, it fell down on the day of his death!) I offered, on my return to India, to pay for the needed repairs. 'Don't bother with them,' he answered. 'That is your world, out there. My world is here. See? I have my bed, and my meditation seat. That is all I need.'"

Swami Sri Yukteswar didn't intend this statement to be a criticism of his disciple. He wasn't accusing him of worldly attachment! Rather, the work his disciple was doing "out there" was his ordained duty; it was simply not his guru's own duty.

The Master emphasized the need for "workers in the field." To me, speaking of his school in Ranchi, he said, "I found that most of the boys, after receiving a spiritual education, went back to their families and to a worldly life. They took jobs, married, and became, to all intents, lost to this greater cause which they might otherwise have served. What we have now is better. People come to us of their own accord, after they've grown up and are free to make their own life decisions. In this way, we can train them wholly in our ideals. This is what the world needs now."

From these words, as well as from other conversations I had with him, I understood that his interest was not only in attracting souls with a desire to dedicate themselves to seeking God, but also those who would serve his mission. He made it clear to me that what he wanted of me, particularly, was active service, not withdrawal into the hermit's life for which, in fact, I had a deep longing.

"Your life," he told me, "will be one of intense activity and meditation." It is noteworthy that he placed meditation second. He also told me once, "God won't come to you until the end of life. Death itself is the final sacrifice you have to make." Often, at least in his talks with me, he referred to the spiritual life as "martyrdom."

Thus, we see that, for any real understanding of his mission on earth, we must see it in very broad, not in narrow terms, whether monastic or householder. He came, literally, for the world, and sought those also who wanted to help him serve all humanity. Obviously, he sought those above all who wanted enlightenment, but among these sincere seekers he hoped to find a few who were willing to seek enlightenment not only for themselves, but also for others—indeed, who thought in terms of *universal enlightenment.*

Thus, he said to me once, "Pray to God, 'Reveal Thyself that I may give Thee to all.' That is the highest prayer."

I have already quoted the words he addressed to me, "And you *mustn't* disappoint me!" His need was for willing workers to aid him with his mission, and not for those alone who wanted spiritual development for themselves.

309

The Master welcomed the discoveries of modern science. He pointed out, however, that science cannot really *invent* anything. Nor can artists really *create* anything. "All that man can do," he said, "is rearrange what is there already." The arts and sciences, like man himself, are not important in the great scheme of things except as they help to unfold the divine plan for the universe. Humility before God is the beginning of true understanding. And, as he said also, "Pride is the death of wisdom."

310

"How can people doubt God?" the Master asked. "I once said to a medical doctor, 'How is it that poison kills nearly everybody, yet nothing heals universally? Doesn't it seem as though "Someone" were at the controls? Einstein said, "Space looks very suspicious: We see everything coming out of it, and everything disappearing into it again." There seems to be everywhere a sort of " orderly disorder," which defies human expectations, yet has an undeniable if bewildering consistency. Man is not in control, no matter how much he'd like to believe he is. *Something,* or *Someone,* is certainly at the controls!'"

ॐ 311 ॐ

We had tried to grow edible melons in the desert, but had not been successful. Yet everywhere out there a type of melon, inedible or perhaps even poisonous, flourished in abundance. It grew on its own without help from anyone.

One day, the Master was walking past one of these weeds and, noticing it, remarked: "See, all this is a suggestion of God's. For no reason that man can see, and by the suggestion of consciousness alone, the bad melons grow here where no other melon will!"

His reference to those melons was to show that there is a conscious intention behind everything. That intention, applied to those melon-weeds, demonstrated also the presence of the satanic force. For Satan, he said, is that aspect of the Infinite Consciousness which might be called the Spoiler. Satan's handiwork is visible everywhere. He is the "villain of the piece." The Master obviously wasn't saying that the evils of this world, being suggestions of God, ought to be viewed as objects of worship! He was referring only to the amazing evidence all around us that there is *consciousness,* itself, everywhere at work.

᠃᠊᠎ 312 ᠃᠊᠎

"Evolution," the Master said, "is only a suggestion in the mind. Everything, in reality, is going on in the present tense. In God's consciousness there is no evolution, no change, no 'progress.' It is always and everywhere the same one Reality."

᠃᠊᠎ 313 ᠃᠊᠎

"My Master [Sri Yukteswar] used to refer, wryly, to the many responsibilities I would have someday. I answered him with a laugh: 'You don't have to rub it in. I know all about it!'"

᠃᠊᠎ 314 ᠃᠊᠎

Bernard told me something from which others, struggling toward inner victory, might find encouragement: "The Master once said to me, 'I don't ask you to overcome delusion. All I ask is that you *resist* it.'"

❧ 315 ❧

"Sir," I said to the Master one day, "Gene Haupt is discouraged because someone told him Ramakrishna said grace is only a sport of God's. To Gene, this statement means that a person might strive spiritually for years and get nowhere, whereas God might reveal Himself to any drunkard for no other reason than that He felt like doing so."

The Master was indignant at this suggestion. " Ramakrishna would *never* have said that!" he replied. "That is what happens when unenlightened people try to interpret the scriptures and the teachings of the masters. God is no creature of whims! It may of course *look* like sport, sometimes. That's because people can't see the effects of past karma. God works *within* the Law, however. He created the Law: Why would He go against it? Tell Haupt I said this is a serious misunderstanding on his part."

"I will, Sir," I replied. I paused, then continued, "Sir, won't you please speak with him? I think he has been going through a hard time, lately."

"Well," said the Master with a slight air of mental detachment, "Satan is testing the organization. Haupt is not the only one."

"Is that what the trouble has been?" I said. "It has seemed as though *something* were giving people a hard time."

346

"Quite a few heads will fall," he commented, sadly but acceptingly.

"Will it go on very long, Master?"

"Quite some time," he replied. After a pause, he continued, "It all started when that boy Jan left Encinitas. Then Smith left. Quite a few more will go."

༄ 316 ༄

At the Master's desert retreat in 1950, he spoke to me of the "larger picture."

"Lahiri Mahasaya," he said, "in a former incarnation was King Janaka.* That was why he took initiation from Babaji in a golden palace: He had lived in a palace before.

"Babaji, formerly, was Krishna."

The Master had already told us that, during Krishna's lifetime, he himself had been Arjuna. It seemed fitting, therefore, that what may have been his greatest literary work, his commentaries on the Bhagavad Gita, should have been destined for him to write.

"That," he added, "is why I am so close to Babaji in this life."

*The famous king in ancient India—a raja rishi, or royal and great sage. Janaka was the father of Sita, the wife of Rama. Sita is widely known as the heroine of the Ramayana, and as the ideal woman.

317

In May of 1950, after finishing his Gita commentaries, he exulted, "A new scripture has been born! Millions will find God through this book. Not just thousands—millions. I know it: I have seen it." He added, "Now I appreciate why my guru [Sri Yukteswar] would never let me read other Gita commentaries. He didn't want me to be influenced by the ideas of others. Instead, what I did was tune in to Byasa, the author of the Gita, and ask him to dictate it through me."

It was inspiring to watch how he dictated. He would gaze up into the spiritual eye, go deep within, and then only begin speaking.

"Other Gita interpretations," he continued, "are not fully rounded, as scriptures ought to be. Even Swami Shankaracharya's commentaries were one-sided in the sense that they completely rejected duality, though duality, for people living in this world, is a daily reality. That is why Krishna says in the Gita that the path of yoga is higher than the path of wisdom (which Shankaracharya taught). The path of yoga accepts *actual* human realities, and works with them as they are, instead of dismissing them as non-existent. They are illusory, certainly, but for all that duality exists, as a dream exists. It just isn't what it appears to be."

318

Humorously he once remarked, "How clever those great ones were to be born into this world while it was still at peace! Here I had to come at a time when there were *three* world wars!"

One cannot expect a master always to speak in abstruse *koans*. It is important, indeed, to know that our Master could also be lightly humorous. He meant the above words jocularly. They weren't really self-pitying or complaining! Yet he was also touching on issues which, to him, were important.

For he recognized the period into which he'd been born as a time of great unrest in the world. He wanted us to make an extra effort to live at our center within, and to try hard not to let ourselves be influenced by the emotions and excitement that swirl around us in these times. To him, indeed, the so-called "cold war"—the period of time following World War II—was a world war also. He was concerned also about the great tension that had been generated in the world by the determination of the Communist bloc to dominate people's understanding. He perceived this attempt as satanic.

He spoke very seriously of trials that he saw in store for mankind. Another holocaust would come, he said, far greater than anything the world had seen so far in this age. "No corner of the earth will be safe," he once remarked.

In addition, he spoke of a coming depression, which he said would be far greater than that which followed the 1929 stock market crash. I was present in the SRF Church in Hollywood one Sunday morning when he spoke, as he did often, of great economic hardships ahead. He urged people to do all they could to simplify their style of living, and even, if feasible, to move out to the country. At one point he interrupted what he was saying to declare with so much force that it seemed almost a shout: "You don't know what a *terrible cataclysm* is coming!"

Did he utter these words to underscore the importance of what he'd been saying? Or was he declaring an altogether new threat? The word, "cataclysm," usually implies a natural disaster, beyond human control: something geologic or even planetary. Clearly, in any case, he was not holding out the usual "olive branch" people extend after making dire predictions. He wasn't saying, "*If* people will learn to live together in harmony, *then,* maybe, everything will turn out well after all." He was saying, rather, "The time has passed for positive expectations regarding the near future. Matters are already out of control. Nothing can be done about them now, though we can always mitigate what comes if we practice spiritual principles. You *must* provide for your own safety, and plan to assist anyone you can."

In this context, I've reflected sometimes that his teachings were, in a sense, intended more as a guideline for future times, *after* the world has recovered from the disasters he saw in its more immediate future.

⁂ 319 ⁂

He spoke often, in the context of coming economic disaster, of people's need to gather together in what he called "world brotherhood colonies." Virtually every time he lectured in public during his last years, he harped on this theme. Elsewhere, I have written much on this subject of "world brotherhood colonies": it isn't necessary for me here, therefore, to elaborate on that theme. All that I've written on the subject has been based on his ideas. Here I want only to say that he urged everyone to take this concept *very seriously.*

One Sunday, he said, "I was thinking so much last night about world brotherhood colonies that my mind didn't want to meditate. Then I chanted a little bit, and my mind came back to me." From those few words alone, surely, one can see how deep were his feelings on this subject.

❧ 320 ❧

"James Coller was walking on the beach in Encinitas," the Master told us, "when I saw a light around him. Divine Mother was showing me that James is a saint. She told me, in fact, that he will be liberated in this lifetime. I don't know how," he continued with a laugh, "but Divine Mother says so, therefore it must be so!"

James was the disciple who, while driving back to Los Angeles from Phoenix, had eaten a hamburger (or was it two?)—a peccadillo for which the Master had gently reproached him. James wasn't particularly good at following rules. "He is most peculiar," the Master once said of him. "He phones me at any time of the day or night. He has strong devotion, however; that is what takes one to God. He is like a mouthful of hot molasses: too hot to swallow, but too sticky to spit out! Despite everything, he will be freed in this life."

What would James's "freedom" signify? This isn't a question for true devotees to ask. James's freedom, unless Master chose to volunteer the information, was between himself and God.

✑ 321 ✑

Several of us were talking about Kriya Yoga with the Master at his desert retreat. Bernard, who was present, told about a man who had come to him for counseling. The man had been practicing Kriya for sixteen years by breathing through his fists instead of directing his energy through the spine. (The fists are used only as an illustration, in teaching the technique.) The Master first looked incredulous, then laughed quietly with amusement, "Well, stupid people will never reach God!"

✑ 322 ✑

From 1950 onward, the Master spoke often of his imminent departure from this world. "My work is finished," he said. One day, I asked him, "Sir, when you are gone, will you still be as near to us as you are now?"

"To those who *think* me near," he replied, "I will be near." This he said in such a way as to suggest that the responsibility was ours, also.

༺ 323 ༻

Dr. de Radwan, an eminent psychologist, had several private meetings with the Master. He exclaimed during one of those meetings, "How fortunate it is that you came to America at this time in history. People are more ready to receive you, after the troubles the world has seen in this century."

The Master concurred. "Fifty years ago," he said, "they would have been indifferent."

༺ 324 ༻

To a doubting disciple the Master said, "Don't dwell on your doubts, or God won't keep you here. Many come expecting miracles, but those who have realized God never show their powers, unless God directs them to. People don't see that in that complete humility lies the greatest miracle! If I were to perform miracles in public, I could attract crowds of followers. But that isn't the way God wants it."

⚘ 325 ⚘

I (Walter) was having difficulty receiving the results in meditation that I wanted. One evening I found the Master alone, and said to him, "Sir, I keep trying and trying, but I'm not going deep. Am I not trying hard enough?"

The Master shook his head. "You are trying too hard," he said. "You are using too much will power. It becomes nervous. Just be natural. As long as you try 'hard' to meditate, you will not succeed—just as, if you try hard to fall asleep, you won't be able to do it. Will power should be applied gradually; otherwise it can be detrimental. That's why it is good in the beginning to emphasize relaxation."

⚘ 326 ⚘

For meditation he told us, "Relax the body. Don't be muscle-bound. In order to relax, first tense the body and inhale, then throw the breath out and relax. Repeat this practice several times. After that, sit perfectly still; dump your body in the Infinite!"

327

Another helpful hint he gave us for relaxing the body was to visualize one's skin as the outer earth surface; the muscles and internal organs as the continents; the bones as the underlying rock formations; the cities as one's teeming thoughts and mental tendencies. Visualize the heaving oceans, he said, as one's breath, the blood coursing in one's veins as the liquid lava flowing deep under the earth, and one's own heartbeat as the divine energy pumping life into the whole planet.

"Don't move a muscle, while meditating," said the Master, "Don't twitch a limb. Feel the life *inside* you, rather than your physical body, as your reality."

328

In 1950, he was planning to return to India. I asked him, "Sir, have you seen most of the people you saw waiting for you in America, during your 1920 vision in Ranchi?"

"Practically all of them," the Master answered.

Yogananda's elder brother Ananta having died years earlier, the Master selected a deeply spiritual woman, named Meera, as the bride for Ananta's son, Ramakrishna Ghosh, and performed their marriage ceremony.

329

"Sir," Clifford asked, "how can one become more humble?"

"Humility," the Master replied, "comes from seeing God, not yourself, as the Doer. When you see Him acting through you, how can you be proud of anything you do? I could sit here all day singing my own praises: It would mean nothing to me. I would know that I was giving praises only to God. Humility lies in the heart; it is not a 'put-up' job. You must *feel* that everything you do is accomplished by Him alone, through you."

An interesting memory of my experience with the Master was that I never saw in his eyes even a flicker of egoic self-awareness. The Self of which he was unceasingly aware was the Divine within him: selfhood expanded to Infinity.

A comment we heard frequently from him acquires special meaning from the foregoing observation: "I killed Yogananda long ago. No one dwells in this temple now but God."

～ 330 ～

In view of his words, "I killed Yogananda long ago," I recall another comment he made to us several times: "I won my liberation many lifetimes ago."

～ 331 ～

The absence of ego-consciousness does not mean that self-consciousness ceases to exist. Far from it! Rather, it is the sense of self made infinite. This great truth is described in his poem "*Samadhi*" in the following line: "Ever-present, all-flowing I, I, everywhere." Often, with great enjoyment, he told the following story to illustrate a master's complete lack of ego-consciousness:

"The gopis used to bring fresh cheese every morning to Krishna. Joyfully they would cross the river Jamuna to the other side, where Lord Krishna lived. He relished that cheese because of the devotion with which they brought it.

"One morning, to their great dismay, the river was in flood. How were they to cross it? One of them then had an inspiration.

"Byasa, a great disciple of Krishna's, lived on their own side of the Jamuna. This was the famous Byasa who, years later, wrote the Bhagavad Gita. 'Let us go and plead with him to perform a miracle,' the gopi cried. Eagerly they all rushed to the hut where Byasa lived.

"'Sir,' they cried, 'we've been taking cheese every morning to Lord Krishna. This morning, however, we can't get across: the Jamuna is in flood. Would you please help us?' They smiled at him winningly.

"'Krishna, Krishna!' shouted Byasa as if in anger. 'All I ever hear is "Krishna"! What about *me*? Does it never occur to you that *I*, too, might enjoy a little cheese?'

"Well, what a dilemma! They deeply respected Byasa, but after all this cheese was intended for Krishna. If, however, the only way to get it to him was with Byasa's help, what else could they do? 'Please, Sir,' they said, 'take a little of this cheese for yourself.'

"Well, Byasa took it. And then he ate—and ate—*and ate!* He didn't stop eating until he couldn't swallow any more. There was only a little portion of cheese left for Krishna! Byasa then hoisted himself to his feet, and somehow carried himself to the riverbank." (How I, Walter, smile at the memory of the Master's pantomiming that lumbering act!)

"'Jamuna!' Byasa cried on reaching the river, 'If I have not eaten anything, divide up and part!'

"'What on earth is he saying?' whispered the girls to one another. 'First he stuffs himself like a pig. And now he cries, "If I have not eaten." What a liar! What possible good can come of *this* adventure?'

"To their amazement, the river parted! A narrow opening formed between two great walls of water. The girls crossed hastily to the other side, not stopping to puzzle out this mystery. They hurried to Krishna's cottage, crying out, 'Lord Krishna! Lord Krishna!' Usually, he stood at the cottage door, eagerly awaiting their cheese. Today, however, there was no sign of him. 'Lord Krishna!' they cried, 'Where are you? What's the matter?'

"When they reached his front door, they peeked inside and saw Krishna stretched out on a couch, his mouth curved in a happy smile. To their anxious inquiries, he replied sleepily, 'Oh, I'm sorry, I just can't eat any more cheese today.'

"'But Lord, who fed you? No one else brings you cheese in the morning.'

"'Oh,' he replied, 'that fellow Byasa on the other side has fed me too much already.'

"Byasa, you see, had been thinking only of Krishna as he ate. His body swallowed the cheese, but Krishna got all the benefit.

"Thus," concluded the Master, "should one act in the world. Think always of God. Ask Him, in everything you do, to do it through you."

332

"Krishna gives this counsel in the Bhagavad Gita to his chief disciple: 'Oh, Arjuna, be thou a yogi!' One day Krishna said to Draupadi, heroine of the *Mahabharata,* 'Why don't you practice yoga meditation?'

"'I would love to, Lord,' Draupadi answered earnestly, 'but how can I do it? Every time I sit to practice the techniques, I become so absorbed in You that I forget everything else!'

"At those words, Krishna only smiled, blissfully."

333

The Master, after Sister Gyanamata's passing, was discussing her life with a few of us. "What a great soul she was!" he exclaimed. "The body is only a plate. Eat the feast of Spirit from it, as she did, while you still have the body. After that, what happens to the plate no longer matters."

334

Boone once told me, "I don't feel it would be right to submit completely to Master's will. It's important for me also to develop my own will. Otherwise, how would it be called free?"

I quoted these words to the Master later on, without mentioning Boone's name, to get his comments on the subject. Boone's idea seemed to me completely twisted.

The Master understood instantly to whom I was referring. He marveled, "But as long as he is bound by moods and desires, he is not free! I don't ask people to suppress their own will. Those who do what I say, however, find an *increase,* not a decrease, in their freedom, for what I show them is God's will. Freedom comes from tuning your will to the dictates of wisdom.

"Sister [Gyanamata] used to run up and down doing my will. One day, a few of the more rebellious sort said to her, 'Why do you always do what he says? You should express your own will!'

"'Don't you think,' Sister answered, 'that it's a little late for me to change? [She was an old woman by then.] And I must say, I have never been so happy in my life as I have been since coming here.'"

The Master chuckled, "They never bothered her again!"

335

My intention in writing this book has been to exclude, as much as possible, any autobiographical material. I find, however, that it isn't possible to do so entirely, for my life is closely connected with much that I have to say about my Guru. I quoted him above, for instance, as telling me I had "too much intellectual aloofness." As I mentioned in that conversation, I was working hard to overcome this defect.

In meditation one evening—I think it was in the early summer of 1951—I felt the power, finally, to cast ego forcefully out of my consciousness: to blast it, so to speak, into the Infinite. This strong act of will was succeeded by a great sense of release and inner freedom.

After that meditation I went out of doors, and there came upon the Master. He was standing silently above the Mount Washington tennis courts, gazing out across them at the twinkling lights of Los Angeles in the distance. I went to him, and, without saying anything, knelt to touch his feet. Silently I asked for a blessing. He touched me on the forehead and said quietly, "Very good."

That was not much of a conversation, some people might say! Yet in some ways it was the most important conversation we ever had. For from then on I never again felt a personal involvement in anything I did. My whole life became, inwardly, a conversation with him. Many people have attempted, since then, to strip me of that closeness. None have succeeded.

༄ 336 ༝

The Master almost never went to the movies. Occasionally in the past, however, he had done so—to divert his mind, I suspect, by becoming simply a spectator rather than the one responsible for so much of what happened around him. He once said to us, "I used sometimes to go to the movies to get away from interviews and telephone calls. As I was sitting in the theater, I went into *samadhi*. Afterward, people asked me, 'Did you enjoy the movie?' and I'd answer, 'Oh, very much!' I'd been watching the cosmic movies inside, with stars and planets whirling through space!"

༄ 337 ༝

He told us he'd once gone to see "The Song of Bernadette," a movie about the life of Saint Bernadette of Lourdes, France.

"I was deeply moved," he said, "for there were many similarities between her life and my own. And then I chanced to look up, and saw the light coming out of the projection booth. Everything taking place on the screen was an illusion, created by variations of shadows and light. Such is human existence. It is all God's light producing everything. Yet how completely real it all seems to human beings!"

❧ 338 ☙

I (Walter) once sat down on the floor in front of the Master with my toes curled under me, resting my weight on them.

"Don't sit like that," the Master told me.

I changed my position, but wondered why he'd said not to sit that way. He then explained, "It's bad for the eyes."

How strange, I thought, the subtle connections between the parts of the body, and between the body and the brain. I recalled photos I had seen of people in Japan, seated in that position. And I reflected that an unusually high proportion of them wore glasses.

339

"The simple thought that you are not free," the Master said one day, reiterating a thought he'd expressed earlier, "keeps you from being free. If you could only break that simple thought, you would go into *samadhi*.

"*Samadhi* is not something one needs to acquire. You have it already. Just think: Eternally you have been with God. For a few incarnations you live in delusion, but then again you are free in Him for eternity! Live always in that thought."

340

"It is helpful," the Master said, "to think of God as being forever with us: right here and right now, ever in the present tense. Ask yourself, at the same time, why are people so irresistibly drawn to living *for,* rather than *in,* the moment? In other words, to identify with the fleeting scenes and ever-fluctuating circumstances around them: changing events, endless streams of people, both enemies and friends. Unfortunately, it takes time to banish the mental hypnosis that all this, and that time itself, is a reality, focusing one on the desire for ephemeral sense-experiences."

Paramhansa Yogananda, in his profound explanation

of the *Rubaiyat* (quatrains) of Omar Khayyam, explained one of them as signifying that many souls who appeared in material form at the dawn of the present Day of Brahma will be still wandering in delusion at the end of that vast time period. This teaching is in Quatrain fifty-three of the translation by the English poet Edward FitzGerald. That version reads:

With Earth's first Clay They did the Last Man's knead,

And then of the Last Harvest sow'd the Seed:

Yea, the first Morning of Creation wrote

What the Last Dawn of Reckoning shall read.

ᘿ 341 ᘾ

A narrower and more immediate indication of the time it takes for the soul to find God may be seen from the following two stories:

Norman, who was inclined to be moody, once lamented to the Master, "I don't think I have very good karma, Sir."

"Remember this," the Master responded immediately, and very seriously: "It takes very, *very*, VERY good karma even to *want* to know God!"

How easy it is for even one desire, once fulfilled, to lead to others! They come in an unending procession, and tempt man to seek his fulfillment outwardly through the senses. One may wander as long as he elects to do so. How many mistakes get committed on the way, all of which end in broken dreams! How long it takes for an individual to realize that what he was always seeking was his own Self: the God-self within! As the Master answered me when I asked him how long I had been his disciple: "It has been a long time. That's all I will say."

Yet it needn't take any time at all! As he said also to the disciples, "I don't want to hear any of you moaning in despair, 'When will I find God?'—as if your own answer to that question were, 'Never!' You have Him already! You need only to *live* in that consciousness."

342

The Master often told this story to illustrate how the soul wanders on the long journey of countless incarnations, seeking perfect fulfillment:

"There was a man who loved God, and had achieved a little spiritual advancement, but who also had a few worldly desires left to fulfill. At the end of his life an angel appeared to him and asked, 'Is there anything you still want?'

"'Yes,' the man said, 'All my life I've been weak, thin, and unwell. I would like in my next life to have a strong, healthy body.'

"In his next life he was given a strong, large, and healthy body. He was poor, however, and found it difficult to keep that robust body properly fed. At last—still hungry—he lay dying. The angel appeared to him again and asked, 'Is there anything more you desire?'

"'Yes,' he replied. 'For my next life, I would like a strong, healthy body, and also a healthy bank account!'

"Well, the next time he had a strong, healthy body, and was also wealthy. In time, however, he began to grieve that he had no one with whom to share his good fortune. When death came, the angel asked, 'Is there anything else?'

"'Yes, please. Next time, I would like to be strong, healthy, and wealthy, and also to have a good woman for a wife.'

"Well, in his next life he was given all those blessings. His wife, too, was a good woman. Unfortunately, she died in her youth. For the rest of his days, he grieved at that loss. He worshiped her gloves, her shoes, and other memorabilia that were precious to him. As he lay dying of grief, the angel appeared to him again and said, 'What now?'

"'Next time,' said the man, 'I would like to be strong, healthy, and wealthy, and also to have a good wife who lives a long time.'

"'Are you sure you've covered everything?' demanded the angel.

"'Yes, I'm certain that's everything this time.'

"Well, in his next life he had all those things, including a good wife who lived a long time. The trouble was, she lived *too* long! As he grew older, he became infatuated with his beautiful young secretary, to the point where, finally, he left his good wife for that girl. As for the girl, all she wanted was his money. When she'd got her hands on it, she ran away with a much younger man. At last, as the man lay dying, the angel again appeared to him and demanded. 'Well, what is it this time?'

"'Nothing!' the man cried. 'Nothing ever again! I've learned my lesson. I see that, in every fulfillment, there is a catch. From now on, whether I'm rich or poor, healthy or unhealthy, married or single, whether here on this earth or in the astral plane, I want only my divine Beloved. Wherever God is, there alone lies perfection!'"

❧ 343 ❧

When Smith left the Master, forsaking his wife who chose to remain with her guru, the Master commented, "It takes incarnations of good karma to get such a good wife."

ᨃ 344 ᨃ

Often the Master compared this world to a movie, and the good and bad people in it to the heroes and villains on the screen. "There has to be a villain," he reminded us, "so we will learn to love the hero. If you imitate the villain's behavior, however, you will receive his punishment. It's all a dream, but ask yourselves, Why live a bad dream by creating bad karma? With good karma, you get to enjoy the dream. Good karma also makes you want, in time, to wake up from the dream. Bad karma, on the other hand, darkens the mind and keeps it bound to the dreaming process.

"From a mountaintop, one sees clearly the whole countryside, and also the open sky above. From the heights it is natural to want to soar even higher, far above the earth. In the fog-bound valley below, however, the most that one aspires to may be only to climb a bit higher."

ᨃ 345 ᨃ

The Master was far from indifferent to the world's sufferings. Quite the opposite, he had been reborn to help alleviate it. One day he remarked how terrible it is that whole nations keep the rest of mankind disrupted and suffering. Clifford—more out of indifference, I suspected, to the world's sufferings than because of any glowing faith in God (it was he who had confessed that he didn't practice Kriya)—said, "But Sir, isn't all that just part of the play of God?"

"Of course it is," the Master replied. "In God's movie, there have, as I've said, to be villains and heroes. Earth life *is* a movie. At present, however, we are speaking from the human point of view, not the divine."

I wondered if the Master wasn't also rebuking Clifford gently, not for his implied criticism—I never saw Master try to justify himself—but for pretending to a "cosmic aloofness" that he clearly didn't feel. The Master was extraordinarily sensitive to people's actual motives, and would never play along with any pretense on their part. A mere show of noble or lofty attitudes—foreign to a person's actual nature—he dismissed, knowing that it only covered up less noble feelings. He wanted to see us base our understanding on a realistic assessment of our actual realities. To affirm good health, for instance, is important for achieving it. Merely to say, however, "I am well," without putting forth the energy required to *become* well, is only wishful thinking. This is not the way to overcome delusion.

346

We were working on the grounds of SRF's newly acquired Lake Shrine in Pacific Palisades, getting it ready for its grand public opening. There were numerous little flies buzzing around our heads, getting into our eyes, ears, and nostrils. I exclaimed in exasperation to the Master, "Sir, here we have this beautiful setting. What a pity it is that it must be spoiled by such pests!"

The Master commented wryly, "That is the Lord's way of keeping us always moving toward Him."

347

During the Christmas meditation in 1949, the Master led us in chanting, "Do not dry the ocean of my love with the fires of my desires!" We sang it many times. "Christ is here today," he said. "Sing to him." Later he added, "If ever you feel delusion closing in upon you, sing this chant, and think of this occasion. Christ and Guru will come down themselves and save you, just because you sang this with me here today. Mark my words, for they are true."

❧ 348 ❧

What is superstition? It may sometimes be actually simply a deeper-than-usual sensitivity to interrelationships, or influences, of which most people are unaware. Sensitivity to solar radiation, for example, may seem superstitious to people if they know nothing about it. In modern times, science has discovered countless subtle influences that, even a few decades ago, would have struck people as imaginary. I don't intend to enlarge on this point here, so I'll leave it to my readers to decide for themselves whether the following notions, most of which the Master accepted from traditional Indian lore, should be classed as superstitions or as endorsed by his own intuitive awareness. These were beliefs that he not only held personally, but actually asked others to follow. They may strike some people as being contrary to common sense. I myself am in no position to judge, but I don't think they should be dismissed as "quaint idiosyncrasies," for if that is all they are, I never saw him display any others.

He told the disciples around him, for example, when they greeted him the first thing in the morning, not to close one eye in a squint as they came in. If one eye was closed, he told them to shut the other eye also. This "superstition" is widely held in India, where people say that if you greet someone in the morning with one eye closed, the two of you may quarrel that day.

When accepting gifts from people, the Master always received them with his right hand. He insisted that we do the same also. I often saw him insist on a gift being also given with the right hand, not with the left one. This is another universal practice in India, where it is held that the left hand is impure. I think, however, that the Master may have meant also that the magnetism of the left hand is passive, or negative, and less adapted therefore to whole-hearted giving or receiving.

When he saw a broom left out, he always insisted that it be put away. The monks who ate (some of them also lived) in the basement, tended to be lax in this regard until he said to them finally, "Brooms have a negative astral vibration." Did he say this only, as Sister Meera suggested to me, to induce us all to be neater? I simply don't know.

Once, when walking in the garden, he went around one side of a small tree. Several of the monks, trying to keep up with him, began going around the tree by the other side. The Master called them back and said, "Come by the way I took."

The Indian scriptures state that it is auspicious to arrive in a light rain, but inauspicious to leave in one. The Master, in *Autobiography of a Yogi,* mentions of his aborted flight to the Himalayas, "The memorable morning arrived with inauspicious rain."

I several times heard him state that Thursday afternoons are bad for initiating a long voyage. If one's conveyance was to leave in the afternoon, he suggested that one pack his bags and leave them outside the door so as to be able to say, technically, that his voyage had begun already.

Laurie Pratt, who practiced astrology, was incredulous when I repeated this last thought to her. I then said, "Master told us that this was 'according to the voice of God.'" She repeated that phrase wonderingly, even less credulously.

"But Thursday is ruled by Jupiter," she protested, "an auspicious planet. Jupiter is also the ruler of long voyages. It *can't* be wrong to start a long voyage on a Thursday." She wasn't dismissing his statement; simply expressing puzzlement. I, of course, knew nothing on the subject, having never so far read anything on it. Perhaps—this thought has occurred to me since then—because the sun is in its decline after noon, Jupiter's influence turns negative for long voyages. At any rate, the Master added, "According to the *voice* of God," not "according to the *word* of God," which he might have done had he read it in some scripture. I have it written as "*voice*" in my notebook, which I wrote in 1951, and in memory I can still hear him speak that word, "voice."

Another "superstition" may be seen in this example: Abie George, a disciple for whom the Master had great love for his pure heart, was asked by the Master to move to the Lake Shrine and take up his residence there. "Come on Tuesday," the Master instructed him, "before eleven o'clock."

⟨⟨ 349 ⟩⟩

"It is not easy to be spiritual," the Master once said, "but it is very easy if you will only follow a few rules. Begin by simplifying your life. Then, remain somewhat apart from others. If you want to find God, don't mix too much socially. I myself mix with others very little. When I am alone, I remain centered in the Self. 'Seclusion,' I often say to people, 'is the price of greatness.'"

⟨⟨ 350 ⟩⟩

Master had been telling me that a basic reason he was sent to the West was to reveal the basic truths underlying the Christian and the Hindu scriptures. This was after he'd just finished writing his commentary on the Bhagavad Gita. He had already written his commentaries on the New Testament.

"Sir," I protested, "isn't your work a new religion? Surely it isn't only to interpret past scriptures!"

"It is a new *expression,*" he replied. Thus, he succeeded in both confirming my statement and correcting it.

351

"There are so many things here in America that I wanted for my own impoverished country," the Master once said. "In time, however, I found that the people here are not so happy, on average, as the peasants in India—many of whom cannot afford more than one meal a day. Despite the material prosperity here, people haven't the same inner happiness. Americans are satiated with a plethora of sense pleasures. Happiness eludes them for the simple reason that they seek it everywhere except in themselves."

352

"It is God alone who acts through you, plays all the roles, directs all the action. It is Him alone you should really love—*through* others, when you love them. People aren't aware of that great, ever-comforting presence. They focus all their affection on one another. When someone whom they love dies, they think, 'Oh, how cruel!' But it was God alone all the time, playing at hide-and-seek with them!"

353

"It is not possible to attain happiness without non-attachment. Giving up attachments doesn't mean self-deprivation. When I was young, I practiced for a time deliberately watching myself as if from the outside: eating, bathing, walking, and so on. It was a bit strange at first, but that practice gave me, in the end, a wonderful sense of freedom."

354

"Of the several branches of yoga," a visitor asked, "which one do you teach?"

"All of them are basically the same," the Master answered. "They take the seeker by different paths, but their goal is the same: Self-realization.

"Most of the yoga branches, however, are based on different human temperaments, which may be primarily devotional, rational, or active. What we teach here is called *Raja Yoga*, the 'royal' yoga; it is so called because it is central to all of them, and is primarily concerned with what they are all meant to achieve, though they go less directly.

"The inner silence of communion is, in fact, the goal of every path of yoga. The others attain that goal less directly. We, in teaching *Raja Yoga,* don't ignore those other practices. We take a little bit from each of them, according to people's different temperaments, and show people how to direct their understanding toward that highest purpose: the stillness of inner communion.

"The goal of *Bhakti Yoga* [the path of devotion] is not to keep on singing to God. Every great *bhakta,* or devotee of God, has entered at last a state of silent communion with Him, where his devotion flows toward Him *inwardly.* All the great *karmis*—those who served God according to the principles of *Karma Yoga* [the path of selfless service]—have reached the point where they realized that the supreme service is to direct all one's energy *inwardly,* in silence, to God. And all the great *gyanis,* who follow the path of discrimination and wisdom, have realized at last that it isn't, in the end, by thinking that one achieves wisdom—that wisdom can only be *received,* in inner stillness.

"Thus, all the paths of yoga lead eventually, like tributary rivers, into the one, all-uniting river of *Raja Yoga.*"

ॐ 355 ॐ

A disciple was becoming somewhat proud of his success in developing devotion. The Master surprised him one day by saying, "If you love yourself, how can you love God?"

ॐ 356 ॐ

"Give both the good and the bad that you do to God. That doesn't mean, of course, that you should deliberately do bad things! When a habit is so strong, however, that you can't help yourself, affirm, 'God is acting through me.' By making Him responsible even for your mistakes, you break the constricting barriers of egoic self-identity. God alone dreamed you into existence, when He made you a separate ego. The very thought of that separation is a delusion."

In pondering this thought further, I (Walter) have come to realize that this is how great yogis must free themselves, through visions, of the karmas of their past lives. They see, in that superconscious state, that it was God alone performing all those actions *through* them. In this way, they can release any sense of personal responsibility for them.

357

I (Walter) took the blame on myself in a situation one time. As it turned out, this created problems for others; had I said nothing, those problems wouldn't have arisen. The Master said to me later, in a tone of rebuke: "You should be practical in your idealism."

358

"My Master [Sri Yukteswar] allowed me no superficiality when studying the scriptures. When we were studying the *Yoga Sutras* [aphorisms] of Patanjali, I would sometimes become a little impatient to move forward. He insisted, however, 'You haven't yet exhausted the full meaning of what we are studying.'

"For six months we studied only the first eight or nine aphorisms. When we'd plumbed to their depths about twelve of them, he closed the book and said, 'Now you don't need to study any further. You have the key in your hand. The meaning of any scripture passage you read will be revealed to you. Its secrets will be unlocked for you by your clear intuition.'

"Since then, every scripture I've read, no matter how abstruse, has been an 'open book' to me."

An interesting corroboration for that statement occurred in Sydney, Australia, in 1997. I (Walter) was lecturing on Yogananda's interpretation of the *Rubaiyat* (quatrains) of Omar Khayyam from his book, *The Rubaiyat of Omar Khayyam Explained.* A member of the audience raised his hand and challenged the Master's interpretation of one of the stanzas. According to him, it didn't correspond fully with Edward FitzGerald's translation into English. There happened to be a lady present from Iran. She too raised her hand, then informed us, "I've read what Yogananda wrote about that quatrain. It's true it doesn't correspond perfectly to FitzGerald's version. It does correspond *exactly,* however, to the original Persian of Omar Khayyam, with which I am familiar." Yogananda didn't know Persian. He had, as he himself stated in his introduction to the book, attuned himself directly with the consciousness of Omar Khayyam.

৯৫ 359 ৯৬

A concert had been given "under the stars" at the SRF Lake Shrine by several prominent musicians. The Master was speaking comfortably afterward with a small group of his disciples; the crowd had left. "Outsiders come and see only the surface," was his comment.

"They don't know what we have here, and leave. But those who are our own see beneath the surface. They never leave."

༄ 360 ༄

He referred briefly that same evening, however, to others who had left the ashram. "Someday," he told me, "those who have left here—Jan, David, et cetera, et cetera—will have their own groups."

༄ 361 ༄

The Master was at his desert retreat, attentively going over his Gita manuscript. I was seated on the floor, facing him, and thinking how wonderful it was to be his disciple. He continued to work, completely absorbed. When he'd finished working, he asked me to help him rise from his chair. When he was standing, he continued to hold my hands for an instant, gazed lovingly into my eyes, and said with shining eyes, "Just a bulge of the ocean." I knew he wanted me to understand that my love for him was for the ocean of Spirit which flowed through him.

362

"Life is, for most people, a great disappointment. Before forty, everything seems rosy and full of promise, but after forty most people's bodies begin to change. Engine troubles begin: The valves leak; the wiring system becomes frayed; the headlights grow dim as their vision fades; the radiator no longer works efficiently as their blood circulation weakens. People complain, 'I'm no longer the same person I was in my youth. How wonderful my body was then! Now, it is becoming a burden to my spirit.' They resent the change, but can do nothing about it.

"People ought to learn to view life from the beginning like long-distance runners. They should take better care of themselves in their youth: exercise properly, eat right, think good thoughts, and meditate daily. Old age won't be for them, then, a season of regret, but of increasing joy in God."

363

"Fools argue," the Master used to say, "but wise men discuss. How is discussion different from argument? When discussing, one approaches his subject constructively, with a view to reaching a conclusion. When people argue, they settle all the more firmly in their beliefs, and try to overwhelm others by fighting it out with them."

❧ 364 ☙

Leo made a practice of taking photograph after photograph of the Master. He would hang them on the walls of his bedroom; all the available space was covered with them. One day he asked the Master to pose for yet another photograph. This time, the Master said, "Why do you keep on taking pictures of this mortal frame? Get to know me in meditation. You will know me much better then. If you keep concentrating so much on this body, you will never get to know me as I really am."

❧ 365 ☙

"The Lord won't answer every prayer the way you want Him to, but if you pray with faith you will find Him giving you much *more* than you asked for."

~~ 366 ~~

"With all thy getting," says the Bible (Proverbs 4:7), "get understanding." What, people may ask, is the meaning of, "get understanding"? The understanding implied is wisdom. The Master explained that wisdom doesn't come from books. It comes with discrimination.

"Discrimination is necessary," he said, "and doesn't come by reasoning only, but by soul-intuition. Reason can help one to understand the *how* of things—that is, how they work, how they occur. It cannot, however, show one the subtle interrelationships between things. Nor can it, in a deeper way, show the *why* of things. Discrimination is an individual exercise. It is the wave aware that it is dancing on the ocean of Spirit. Wisdom comes with deepening one's perception of the Absolute. The understanding that is wisdom is universal."

~~ 367 ~~

A woman disciple had treated someone unkindly. The Master said to her, "You can't truly love God if you treat others that way. God is in everyone. You won't win His love, if you can't win the love of other people. You must place God first in your life, but reflect that other people, too, are His channels. They were given to you that you might learn to love Him in all."

༁༁ 368 ༁༁

Looking back, I see that Bernard never really comprehended Yogananda's spiritual mission. Indeed, he never even showed much interest in it. The Master tried repeatedly to get him to tune in to the deeper, more universal purpose of his work. Bernard once told me (Walter), "The Master wanted to get me interested in serving his work, so, after thinking about it, I came to him one day all fired up with new ideas for how to bring people flocking to us in large numbers. The Master replied, however, 'When *we* are ready, God will send to us those whom He wants to help.'"

To Bernard, this answer was incomprehensible. Hadn't the Master himself kept urging him to show a greater interest in the work? As I myself saw this story, however, the Master's answer suggested disappointment in Bernard's lack of understanding. Yogananda didn't see his work in terms of conversion. He saw it in terms of raising people's consciousness. As he used to say, "I prefer a soul to a crowd, and I love crowds of souls." He did want to see many souls devoted to the divine search, but he never thought of them in terms of mere numbers. As he said once, "I am not a merchant, looking to see how many people enter his shop."

Thus, to him, even organizing the work meant increasing our capacity, and our fitness, to serve. As far as I know, the Master never again tried to interest Bernard in these things. Evidently, he decided he was not *capable* of the necessary comprehension.

369

"Sir," I asked the Master one afternoon at his desert retreat, "how will I know your will, once you have left your body?"

"You already know my will," he reassured me, "at least in the important things."

Indeed, I've always done my best to carry out his will alone, and have always found it continuing to unfold in my mind as I followed his will as nearly as I was capable of understanding it.

370

"Behind every rosebush of pleasure," the Master used to say, "lies a rattlesnake of suffering, coiled and ready to strike. Be ever attentive not to be bitten, as can happen if you allow yourself to become attracted to anything that merely fans your infatuation."

371

The Master had been speaking of God and spiritual subjects one evening. Gradually, the talk shifted to political concerns. The Master paused, then said with a laugh, "From God to politics. Such is the power of His *maya* [cosmic illusion]!"

372

The Master used to tell us, "I suffer when you have moods, for then I see that Satan gets ahold of you."

373

"Extend help to those who are weak. But if you yourself are weak, remember, it is the greatest sin to spread that infection by making others weak."

≈ 374 ≈

"Don't pine for visions in meditation. In ecstasy, they become a disturbance. I have so much to see in meditation, I drive visions away!"

≈ 375 ≈

"God cannot escape if you catch Him in the net of divine meditation and divine service. One of these without the other, however, is spiritually dangerous. You need the balance."

≈ 376 ≈

The Master called me and two others into a separate room once, and gave us the following instructions:

"When watching the breath, I've previously taught not to control its flow. I wanted to tell you today, however, that that flow may be controlled to this extent: Between each breath, try, for that brief moment, to deepen the sense of release you feel from the need to breathe. Gradually, by natural degrees, those pauses will increase in length.

"You may, if you like, teach the technique this way to others."

❧ 377 ❧

I've mentioned earlier in this book also that he suggested practicing the mental repetition of the Hong-Sau mantra while watching the breath—but in the spine instead of in the nostrils. This was something he told me during my first month with him. "Watch," he told me, "without controlling the movement there in any way. This is an alternate practice to watching the flow of breath in the nostrils.

"The spine is the trunk of the 'tree of life.' God's joy is the 'sap' flowing through the trunk of the tree."

❧ 378 ❧

"If you want to become a master in this life, then, in addition to Kriya Yoga, you should practice Hong-Sau for at least two hours a day. I used to practice it as a boy, as long as seven hours at a time, until I went breathless."

The Master was not generally in favor of hypnotism. "It is all right sometimes, of course," he said, "for medical purposes. Otherwise, it is generally best to avoid it. Anything that causes a diminution of consciousness is not good. If the will is placed even temporarily under the control of another, it can become weakened. Magnetism is better; its influence is expansive to the consciousness. Magnetism is what yogis use when they help people."

There was a student of the Master's who practiced hypnosis—more or less for fun. The Master persuaded him to stop this practice.

"One day," the Master said, "we were both at a party. I happened to look over, and saw this man speaking to a group of people. I also saw a young woman who was evidently opposed to everything he said. Later on I saw this same woman following him about like a puppy. I said to him afterward, 'I thought you promised me not to do that anymore.'

"'I know,' he admitted, 'but she was heckling me. I got fed up with it! But I won't do it again.'" The Master laughed at this recollection, but warned us also to be respectful of the free will of others, even when they oppose us.

380

The Master was once speaking of a certain rich person. "There are two kinds of poverty," he remarked. "Some people wear rags because they can't afford better clothing. Others, however, even though they go in limousines, wear rags of spiritual poverty."

381

"Churches often do good work, but few nowadays emphasize inner, prayerful *communion* with God. That is the true essence of spiritual teaching. Those churches are like beehives without honey—or like restaurants without food. When working one should work also with the thought of God. Otherwise he may earn good karma, but he won't come closer to Him for whose sake the churches are, or ought to be, built. Churches that don't emphasize devotion and *inner* communion, by meditation, are social institutions, not houses of God. The church should be a spiritual oasis in the desert of mundane consciousness. It should be an active beehive, busy producing the honey of God's love."

⚜ 382 ⚜

"Notice lazy people, how, whether seated or moving about, they keep moaning and sighing. Watch yourselves: See that this tendency doesn't develop in you. Be energetically and *silently* active for God if you want to taste His joy, within."

⚜ 383 ⚜

"God answers all prayers. Restless prayers, however, He answers only a little bit. If you offer to others something that isn't yours to give, won't that be a merely empty gesture? If you pray to God, similarly, but lack control over your own thoughts, that prayer will be without power. Thoughts and feelings, both, must be focused when you pray. Otherwise God will meet your little trickle with another trickle of His own! He will dole His answers out to you in a teaspoon. Too often, prayer is more like the halfhearted mumbling of a beggar than the confident, loving demand of a friend."

﷽ 384 ﷽

"Was it for political reasons," a newcomer asked, "that you put Jesus Christ on your altar—because this is a mostly Christian country?"

"No, that was not the reason," the Master replied. "Jesus Christ is one of our line of five gurus."

"In what way?" pursued the newcomer. "And why have you placed him at the center?"

"It was Jesus Christ," the Master explained, "who appeared to Babaji in the Himalayas and asked him to send this message to the West. 'My followers,' he said, 'are doing good work, but they are forgetting inward communion with God. *Together* let us send someone to the West to teach them the art of meditation.'

"That is the reason I was sent. Jesus is at the center because this message to the West began with him. To the left of him is Babaji, then Babaji's disciple Lahiri Mahasaya. To the right is Swami Sri Yukteswarji, then *his* disciple—whom, as my Master told me, Babaji had sent to him for training."

❧ 385 ❧

"When this 'I' shall die," the Master once said, "then shall I know who am I. You must forget yourselves and any worries you have about your own importance. Tell yourselves always, 'Thou, Lord, only Thou!' God is dreaming through you. *He* is the sole reality."

❧ 386 ❧

"Our way of life in these colonies is more normal than extreme asceticism. Think of Diogenes, who—so we read—lived in a tub! I say to people: Make your heart a hermitage."

Often I (Walter) heard him quote from a poem by Richard Lovelace—slightly paraphrased to suit his own meaning:

Stone walls do not a prison make,
    Nor iron bars a cage;
Hearts innocent and quiet:
    Take that for a hermitage.

ᨦ 387 ᨦ

"Never count your faults. Just think whether you love God enough. He doesn't mind your faults. He minds your indifference."

ᨦ 388 ᨦ

"I go through your souls every day. I seldom tell what I see, though, because those things are sacred." The Master worked especially on raising our consciousness *from within,* if we were receptive to his vibrations, by helping us to change the direction of our thoughts and feelings. As someone once heard him say, "If you shut me out, how can I come in?"

ᨦ 389 ᨦ

The Master deplored the racial prejudice he found in certain sections of the country, as well as elsewhere in the world. "I don't see why they talk about white and black races," he said with a chuckle. "Without their skin, they are all red! In ourselves, similarly, we are all one."

"The actual races of man," he said, "if we choose to think of them as such, have nothing to do in any case with skin coloring. They are the four fundamental stages displayed by mankind in its spiritual refinement. In India, that is what was originally signified by the caste system.

"At his lowest level of refinement, man thinks not only of, but *with,* his physical body. Tradition typifies him as a farm laborer, though of course that is simplistic. Such a person belongs to the *sudra* caste.

"When a person begins to use his intellect, he first does so strictly for personal gain, thinking always, 'What's in this for me?' The obvious example of such a person is the greedy merchant. Again, this is simplistic, for by no means all merchants are greedy; many of them are very generous. This sort of person, in any case, belongs to what is known as the *vaishya* caste.

"When one develops further in spiritual refinement, he inclines to use his intelligence for the general good, rather than only for his own benefit. Such a person is typified as the soldier—not the marauding sort, but one who readily sacrifices his own life, if need be, for the sake of others. Such a person belongs to the *kshatriya* caste.

"Finally, when the individual evolves spiritually to the point where he wants only God, he is like idealized images of a priest. Such a person belongs to the *brahmin* caste.

"Society even in those days was not so simply stratified as to contain only peasants, merchants, soldiers, and priests! These were symbolic designations of the stages of spiritual refinement. They were not intended as social categories. And they were not intended to be hereditary.

"Things changed as the *yugas* [cycles of time] descended toward mental darkness. People in the higher castes wanted to make sure their children were accepted as members of their own caste. Thus, ego-identification caused them to freeze the ancient classifications into what is called the 'caste system.' Such was not the original intention. In obvious fact, however, the offspring of a *brahmin* may be a *sudra* by nature. And a peasant, sometimes, is a real saint."

༼༼ 390 ༽༽

"If you eat your dinner and then run, how will you expect to enjoy what you've eaten? Certainly your enjoyment will increase if you rest a little afterward.

"The same is true for your practice of Kriya Yoga: Don't jump up the moment you've done your Kriyas. Sit still awhile; enjoy the inner peace. That is how intuition is developed: Prolong and deepen as much as possible the peaceful aftereffects of practicing the techniques."

᚛ 391 ᚜

"You must be very joyous and happy, for this is God's dream. The little man and the big man are only projections of the Dreamer's consciousness. Take everything as it comes, and tell yourself that it is all coming from God. What comes of itself, let it come. Even when you feel you have to try to correct a wrong, try first to feel His inner guidance. Then when you act, do so on *His* behalf, and never with ego-inspired indignation."

᚛ 392 ᚜

"I scold those who listen," the Master used to say, "but not those who don't." His "scoldings" were always meant lovingly, and were never motivated by pique or personal displeasure. I always saw in his eyes, if he happened to take me to task, a deep regret—for my sake—at having to speak in that way.

᚛ 393 ᚜

"Don't be emotional when you pray. At the same time, don't be diplomatic. God is like a little child. You don't need to be tactful with Him. Talk to Him earnestly, with calm confidence. Tell Him sincerely how you *really* feel."

✽ 394 ✽

Horace Gray, a disciple in the Encinitas colony, had severe physical disabilities. It was difficult for him to walk, and even in speaking he had difficulty expressing himself, for almost every word was made painful to listen to by prolonged stuttering. The Master spoke of him highly one day. "Horace is very nearly there," he said. "The Lord is satisfied with his devotion."

James Coller, who was among us at the time, and (like the rest of us) knew what a simple soul Horace was, was seeking to reconcile this new image of "Saint Horace" with the person he knew. He said, "It must be a very simple kind of devotion, Master, isn't it?"

"Ah!" the Master smiled blissfully, "That is the kind God likes! He does not come to the prudent and the wise, but unto babes."

Our opinion of Horace took an upward leap from those words. We'd never had anything against this brother disciple, certainly; he was always pleasant to everybody. Institutionally, however, he was a nonentity, and contributed, as far as I knew, nothing whatever to the work. Master's words helped a number of us to re-alize how much a person's sanctity is entirely a matter *between him and God.* Always, it is a question of inner consciousness.

ᢙᢁ 395 ᢙᢁ

After a Christmas banquet, several of us were sitting with the Master in the office. Guests had arrived uninvited for the event, and some of the residents had relinquished their seats to make space for them. We briefly discussed this situation with Master. "Many," I remarked, "were vying for the privilege of giving up their seats."

"Ah!" the Master exclaimed blissfully, "These are the things which please me!"

ᢙᢁ 396 ᢙᢁ

"People want to escape sorrow not by overcoming it, but by avoiding it. They attempt—by drinking, or empty laughter, or excessive sleep, or other diversions—to for-get that any such effort to escape actually threatens their peace of mind. They 'drink to forget,' as the saying goes. This is a terrible practice. Although you may forget your problems for a little while, and may even feel a brief exhilaration during that escape, avoiding troubles doesn't mean they avoid you! They are with you still. Your escape, therefore, is illusory. It only blunts the mind, and makes it more difficult for you to deal with your troubles effectively, when circumstances force you to.

"Alcohol doesn't clear the mind: it addles it. The mind becomes like an automobile with dirty spark-plugs. Its engine misfires. Don't drink, even for the sake of a little fun. Drunkenness is Satanic ecstasy."

༂ 397 ༂

"There is great economic hardship coming to America and to the world. Partly for that reason, I urge all of you"—he was saying this in a public lecture—"to build world brotherhood colonies where you can produce your own vegetables and eggs, and, if possible, have your own fresh milk."

How often I heard him urge people in this direction! "Band together," he would cry, "those of you who can do so, in small, spiritual communities!" No matter what the topic of his sermon, during the years I knew him he would digress, urging people to embrace this concept.

ᦓ 398 ᦓ

A newcomer said to the Master, "Wine, sex, and money are, you've told us, the three greatest delusions. Why do you name these three, particularly?"

The Master replied: "They are delusions because, more than most things, they cloud the mind and confuse it. Moreover, they may actually seem, at first, to clarify it. Thus, their influence is doubly insidious.

"People imagine that drink helps them to clear their minds. '*In vino, veritas,*' is the ancient saying: 'Wine makes one truthful.' What it does, in fact, is make one incautious! Again, people see the possession of money as a support for their self-confidence. It gives them the courage to express themselves fearlessly. In their overconfidence, however, they often blind themselves to other people's realities and become increasingly insensitive and unaware. And as for sex, people say it releases them from mental tension and in that way it clears the mind. This release too, however, is temporary. Abuse of sex has nothing but deleterious effects.

"The long-range effect of all those so-called 'fulfillments' is that they dull the sensibilities. A mere glance into the eyes of those who are addicted to them is enough to reveal their mental confusion. They are unable to gauge things in correct proportion. Those three delusions are the greatest, finally, because, though man is subject to countless other delusions, these three, of them all, are the most addictive to the mind."

❧ 399 ❧

The Master was never opposed to marriage as such, although he may sometimes have seemed to be, because, in speaking with the monks, he tended to make light of the so-called fulfillment of "wedded bliss." On the occasion of our first meeting, he told me about a young couple he had known to whose wedding feast he'd been invited.

"Everyone around me was saying how ideally suited to one another these two were," he said. "I could see, however, that it was all a show. When someone next to me praised them too fulsomely, I said, 'Let me show you something.'

"A young woman disciple was attending the feast; she was quite attractive. I asked her to sit near the groom and gaze at him steadily, without saying a word. Pretty soon, the groom had eyes only for her. His bride at last rose to her feet, in extreme distress, and dragged him out of the room. He looked back and called out to this young woman, 'I'll see you again!' Everyone present was shocked. But what did it matter when the blow fell, really? It was bound to fall sooner or later.

"People who actually do find happiness in marriage don't find their happiness from one another. Always, it comes from *inside* themselves. How sad it is to see the suffering people go through, just because they base their expectations of happiness in other people!"

❧ 400 ❧

"I met a saint once in India," the Master told us, "who asked me if I was married. When I said I wasn't, he replied, 'You are on the safe side. Better stay that way! First, have God. After that, whatever happens to you, you'll be all right.

"'I myself am married,' the saint continued, 'My wife is very materialistic. Thank God, it no longer bothers me. I have fooled her: She doesn't know where I am!' Inside, he was always with God!"

❧ 401 ❧

"I met a Catholic monk once who was very devout. I asked him how long he had been seeking God. 'Many years,' he replied. I then asked if he had had any spiritual experiences. He was most surprised. 'When God wills it,' he said, 'He will reveal these things to me.' I said, 'That isn't true. You can have them *right now*, if you will make the right effort. It is because you pray mechanically that you've had no experience of Him.'

"Prayer must be offered with devotion, and never by mere rote."

༄ 402 ༄

"It is difficult to find one's way out of a labyrinth. When you enter it you may think, 'Oh, I'll find my way out easily, any time I want to.' But each time you think you've found the way out, you are only led into another blind alley. You need what Theseus had—Theseus, of Greek legend, who slew the minotaur. Ariadne gave him a thread to unreel as he was going in. That thread enabled him to retrace his steps back out. That thread symbolizes the Guru's advice, and your inner attunement with him. Even mental attunement will suffice to lead you to freedom. By that sacred thread, you will be led by God's grace."

403

The Master heard a disciple chanting in the chapel one evening, to the accompaniment of a harmonium. He paused during a conversation with several of the monks, then remarked with deep satisfaction, "*That* is what I like to hear in this hermitage of God!"

404

"It is very difficult," said the Master, "to find a right balance between work and meditation. You will achieve a good balance, however, if you work in the thought of God during the day, and meditate on Him deeply at night."

405

"You won't find God by making constant excuses: for example, saying, 'When I find a quiet place, I will meditate.' That is not at all the way to get there! If you tell yourself, however, 'Right *now* I will plunge into deep meditation!' you can be there in a moment. When you are really sleepy, you have no difficulty in sleeping no matter where you are. When a person is in love, he finds no difficulty in thinking of his beloved; rather, it is difficult *not* to think of her, even to the point of ignoring his work. Be in love with God! It is easy to meditate deeply, when your love for Him is deep enough."

⁓ 406 ⁓

"I never do anything with personal motivation. I don't do things because *I* want to. If people ask me, 'Why are you doing this, or that?' I say, 'Who is doing it? I am only carrying out *His* will. I have no personal concern.' Yogananda doesn't interest me any more. I want only to carry out His will."

⁓ 407 ⁓

"There is a legend that the gopis once grew jealous of Radha, who seemed to them more in Krishna's favor than the rest of them. One day he decided to teach them a lesson. Radha wasn't present. Krishna pretended to be seized by a terrible headache.

"'How can we help you, Lord?' the gopis all cried. 'Whatever we can do, we'll do it gladly.'

"Krishna, groaning, said, 'If one of you will only press her feet on my head, my headache will go away.'

"They were aghast. In India even to sit with one's feet pointed toward an older person, or toward someone revered, is considered an act of disrespect. To touch that person with one's feet is considered an insult. And to touch the Lord incarnate with one's feet, and—horror of horrors!—*on the head* would be almost the ultimate blasphemy! The gopis received his answer with the utmost dismay. Yet, meanwhile, Krishna's headache kept growing worse.

"Radha then appeared. When she learned of the Lord's distress, she ran to him crying, 'Can I help in any way?'

"'Yes,' he said, 'if you will only press your feet on my head, I will find relief.'

"'But of course, Lord,' she cried. 'Instantly!' Immediately she began pressing her feet on his head.

"The others cried out in horror at this outrage.

"'What is the matter?' she inquired.

"'You placed your feet on the head of the Lord of the universe. For such a great sin, you will go to hell!'

"'Is that all that's bothering you?' she scoffed. 'If putting my feet on his head will send me to hell, I will gladly go there. It will remain my joy that I gave the Lord even one moment of relief.'

"And then the others understood. They had been placing their own well-being ahead of Krishna's needs. Seeing Radha's absorption in the well-being of Krishna, even at the cost of her own salvation, they bowed humbly before her. They recognized now the greatness of her love, compared to their own."

408

"The mind is like a rubber band. The more you pull on it, the farther it will stretch."

409

"I sometimes wonder why people thank God for the 'gift of life'! What kind of gift is that? I tell Him, 'I didn't ask You to create me! But since You've done so, all I ask is, release me! Get me out of this mess You've put me in!' We didn't come into existence because of any *grace* of His. We are as eternal as He is! The soul is coexistent with the Spirit. Sometimes I like—lovingly, of course—to scold Him: 'Why did You force us to wander about in delusion?'

"He doesn't mind it when I talk to Him like that. He *has* to get us out, if we call to Him with deep love."

410

"Keep your devotion in a state of reason. Without reason, devotion becomes too easily emotional. But don't be *too* rational, either! Reason alone will never give you true understanding. It must be balanced with feeling. Understanding comes best when reason and feeling work together, each inspiring the other to flow upward.

"Look at a flower and ask, How come you to be so beautiful? How come you even to exist, and your beauty to exist? Surely, there is some greater intelligence at work behind you, forming you.

"And this great city of cells, your body: How did they come together into a homogeneous population? How do they work together so intelligently? Isn't there something *behind* the body, more than what the biologists claim? How can you have sprung into existence by mindless accident, as they teach? In these ways, reason can deepen and uplift your devotion."

ॐ 411 ॐ

I (Walter) was complaining mentally against a directive of the Master's. This happened a few months after I'd come to him. He had given me, I thought, a task that contradicted what he himself was constantly urging me to do: to develop devotion. What he was asking of me now was to write articles for our magazine. After my little mental rebellion, I wrote him a short note of apology.

In a response, he first demanded that I explain myself. When I had done so, he didn't explain to me carefully why he had given me that intellectual task. Instead, he answered quite brusquely, "Living for God is martyrdom!"

I was taken aback. He hadn't even tried to help me to resolve my dilemma. I resigned myself, however, to his answer, and decided he wanted me to have more faith in his guidance, as my guru. I understood, later, that in keeping me intellectually active he was saying he didn't want me to starve my intellect. Heart quality, in other words, should not be developed *at the expense of* the intellect. Feeling without reason, in fact, could lead me as far astray as I'd been misled by intellect.

I didn't want, at that time, to face—in fact, I rejected for years—the thought that what he was also asking of me was that I dedicate myself to a life of "intense activity," as he told me I must. My own deepest desire was to go deep in meditation. I didn't mind being active also, to any extent necessary, but what I really longed for was silent, inner communion with God.

What the Master had meant by "martyrdom" was that he wanted me to renounce even this desire. Perhaps there were other "martyrdoms" in my future, but clearly what he wanted in this instance—in fact, he said so—was that I surrender precious meditation time in order to write articles. *Karma Yoga*, evidently, not *Raja Yoga*, was my destined lot. It took me years to reconcile myself to this fact.

Yet, he had been sent to the West with a mission to accomplish. It was my great privilege, not my misfortune, that he wanted me to serve his work outwardly. Others had resisted his hopes in this regard. If I, by sacrificing my inner life, could serve him as others hadn't done, that was my great blessing. Indeed, by heeding the Guru's will I have found increasing inner joy.

Moreover, I recall my own thought the day I came to him: "This message is so wonderful, it should be known *everywhere!*" He knew, and appreciated, this deep desire. It was what had helped bring me onto the path.

✠ 412 ✠

On the evening when the Master recorded some of his "Cosmic Chants," I had to leave early to conduct the Wednesday evening service at the Hollywood Church. When I returned, the recording had been completed. I found the Master on the lawn outside, listening to one of the chants as it was played back over a loudspeaker: "What lightning flash glimmers in Thy face! Seeing Thee, I am thrilled through and through." The Master began almost to dance, his arms outstretched to the side, his eyes closed. He was swaying back and forth in ecstasy. "Play it again," he requested, then again and again. All of us, on that occasion, were deeply moved.

Afterward, as he was leaving, he said quietly, "I see all of you as images of light. Everything—the grass, the trees, the bushes—everything I see is made of light. You've no idea how beautiful it all is!"

413

"The more you do what your mind tells you," the Master told us, "the more you will become a slave. But the more you do Guru's will, the more you find yourself becoming inwardly freed." Taking this counsel to heart, I discovered for myself that it was true. Never had such a feeling of inner freedom been mine as came by attuning myself with his will.

414

Boone, under the spell of a violent delusion, wrote the Master a long, scathing letter filled with accusations of imaginary failings in the Master. This young man must have seen, later, that his missive had been—as such things always are—a projection of his own faults, for he didn't leave at that time, as his letter had announced that he would.

The Master, when he saw him next, referred only in passing to the letter. His comment held a note of sincere appreciation. "Boone, you should take up writing. That was the best letter Satan ever wrote me." His admiration was ungrudging, and a beautiful reflection on his own complete humility. Indeed, as he once said, "How can there even be humility, when there is no consciousness of self?"

417

𝓢𝓮 415 𝓼𝓮

"Keep your mind always engaged in serving God, whether meditating or serving Him through others. An idle mind is the workshop of the Devil."

𝓢𝓮 416 𝓼𝓮

"*Is* there a Devil, Master?" someone asked. "Many people say he exists only in the mind. The Christian Science teachings even insist, 'God does not know evil.'"

"God must be very stupid if He doesn't know something so obvious!" was the Master's wry comment. He then conceded that the belief, though mistaken, was not unreasonable. "I used," he said, "to think that Satan was only a figment of the mind. Since then, however, I have realized from personal experience, and now add my testimony to that of countless others before me, that Satan does exist. He is a conscious force, and works constantly to keep mankind bound to delusion."

417

"Is Satan, in that case, a part of God?" was that person's next question. "If God made everything, how could Satan exist apart from Him?"

"There are not two absolute causes in the universe," was the response. "Satan is a part of God's drama. He is necessary to it, as the villain is necessary in a stage play. Evil is the veil that conceals God, the magnet that tries to draw the mind away from Him. Good is that which helps to make God's hidden reality manifest: like the breeze, blowing away the smoke that hides a fire. Within the realm of duality, however, both good and evil exist. God, the Supreme Spirit, is beyond them both. Being omniscient, He knows them both equally—the evil as much as the good. Goodness, however, reveals more clearly to the mind the existence of bliss, which, since it is above relativity, may be described as goodness absolute. The satanic force, on the other hand, being conscious, tries deliberately to hide from man's gaze that ever-blazing light of divine bliss."

418

"The Christian Science teachings derive from an imperfect understanding of the Vedanta teachings. In denying the reality of evil, they open themselves to certain great errors.

"There was a child, whose mother was a Christian Scientist. The child came home from school one day, and said to his mother, 'Mommy, Sarah's mother is unwell.'

"'You mean, she *thinks* she is unwell,' responded his mother.

"The following day, the boy came home and said, 'Mommy, Sarah's mother is worse!'

"'You mean, she *thinks* she is worse,' came the inevitable reply.

"The third day, when the child returned home, his mother asked him, 'How is Sarah's mother today?'

"'Mommy,' he replied, 'She *thinks* she's dead'!

"Mrs. Eddy, the founder of Christian Science, was right in saying that her teachings were based on the teachings of Jesus Christ, for Jesus taught the same truths as are found in the Vedanta. Transcendentalism—a popular school of thought at the time in New England, where she lived—was actively influenced by the Vedanta teachings. Mrs. Eddy found that those teachings helped deepen her understanding of the teachings of Jesus. Neither Jesus nor the teachings of Vedanta, however, were the basis for her teaching on the nature of evil. Both those higher teachings are completely practical, whereas what Mrs. Eddy taught in this respect was not practical. She had 'figured out'—mistakenly in this respect—that evil was not of God, and therefore didn't exist. This was her own philosophy, a word that means 'love of wisdom.' It is not necessarily wisdom, itself. What both Jesus and the Vedanta taught were wisdom— the direct experience of truth."

๑ 419 ๑

"Master," a disciple inquired, "what is the best way to work out karma?"

"Karma," he replied, "is best worked out by meeting life's tests cheerfully and courageously. If you still fear something, that karma has not yet been worked out. To dissipate it, don't try to avoid the tests you have to face. Rise above them bravely, by dwelling in God's joy within."

๑ 420 ๑

"If you criticize others judgmentally, rather than simply commenting on their behavior impartially, that shows that you have their faults to work on in yourself. By criticizing others, moreover, you *increase* those faults in yourself. What you condemn in others, you will have to experience, someday, yourself. That is the karmic law. In that way, people are taught compassion."

~ 421 ~

"The company you keep cannot but influence you, especially if you keep that company by choice. My Master [Sri Yukteswar] used to say, therefore, 'Keep a spiritual bodyguard with you when mixing with others.' I have always obeyed his advice. I've made it a point to surround myself with a few spiritual souls. Most of the time, however, I prefer to be alone with God."

~ 422 ~

"The gardens of some people's minds are over-grown with weeds. And what a job it is to pull them all out! Just when you think the weeds have all been up-rooted, up come even more of them, as obstructive as ever! Their roots are very deep. It is very difficult to inspire such people to change."

~ 423 ~

The Master would sometimes speak to me about other spiritual teachers. Once he described a certain well-known teacher in India, who had been invited to participate in a religious congress in Chicago.

"He and fifteen of his followers were coming through Los Angeles on their way to Chicago. I invited him to Mount Washington, where we prepared a great banquet for them. At the last moment, there came a telegram from him in Hawaii. He had felt the inspiration, suddenly, to return to India." The Master looked at me with a look of mild disapproval. "No *master*," he remarked, "would have behaved in such a way!'"

People would do well to understand that the masters do not behave erratically, even though they are guided by the flow of inspiration. In dealing with this world, they honor its ways. And they are ever true to their word. Moreover, if they are obliged to mix socially with others, they are considerate of people's feelings. They are not, in other words, like rudderless ships driven hither and yon by the fickle winds of an imaginary "intuition."

❦ 424 ❦

I (Walter) asked Rev. Smith, during my first year as a disciple, "Is the Master *equally* conscious of *everything?*" The concept of being constantly in cosmic consciousness, even while acting in a physical body—the state Master called *nirbikalpa samadhi*—was, perhaps not surprisingly, quite beyond my comprehension. Rev. Smith, to whom I'd addressed the question, wanted others to think his explanations came from his own personal knowledge. Nevertheless, based on what he said, and matching it against what I heard later from the Master himself on this subject, I think the following is a fairly exact explanation of the Master's teachings on this subject:

"In cosmic consciousness, you are *inwardly* conscious of everything. Your human mind, however, must be aware of things specifically. When you yourself concentrate on one flower out of several, then, although you are aware of that one flower especially you are also aware that there are others. You see those others there, but to your present awareness they are peripheral.

"The case is similar in the case of a master. He is aware of everything, everywhere, but at the same time, whatever calls for his specific, human attention, since it is in his direct line of vision, he addresses particularly. His human mind functions in a human way. Inwardly, however, his inner consciousness embraces all existence."

Many were the opportunities I had to observe this dichotomy of awareness in Paramhansa Yogananda. He would know things, yet not always seem at first to be aware of them. I said to him once, "Master, please help [I named one of the monks; it wasn't Gene Haupt to whom I've referred earlier]; he seems to be going through a hard time." That monk was distant from us at the time.

"Oh-oh!" said the Master. Instantly he'd concentrated on this person, and had known what he was going through. That monk soon afterward left the monastery, in fact. The Master had been inwardly aware of the situation, and now responded to it because I had drawn it to his human attention. The monk himself, however, had not sought to draw that attention. He had lost his attunement, and had made no mental appeal for assistance.

The Master once told me, "It is very difficult to play these two roles together: the human and the divine."

Nowadays, when one simply reads about him, it may be easier, in a sense, to accept this distinction between his inner consciousness and his outer awareness. For us, however, who had to grapple with it in person, it wasn't always so easy. I remember that I was once standing near the Master, pondering this mystery.

"His body standing there," I was reminding myself earnestly, "isn't who he really is. He is everywhere. He is even inside me—as much so as in that body. But isn't he also *especially* in that body?" While I puzzled over this matter, the Master came over to me and, smiling quietly, gave me an apple. Nothing was said.

Once he said to me, "Those who are in tune, I know their every thought." The focus of his consciousness, as is obvious from that statement, was much broader than anything ordinary. Many times he showed me this amazing breadth of awareness.

Once, he reproached me slightly for something I'd said. I had tried to convince a skeptic, in ways that would only, unfortunately, have increased his skepticism.

The Master told me I should have shown more discrimination on that occasion. When I expressed surprise that he'd known about the episode, he replied, "I know every thought you think!"

Finally, I concluded that it was useless to try to understand him. Laurie Pratt once remarked to me, "Whenever I think I've understood Master, I discover that he's beyond what I understood." My own thought, when she said that, was, "Why even *try* to understand him! I'd rather simply deepen my attunement with him."

The Master's brother disciples used sometimes to complain they couldn't understand their guru Sri Yukteswar. To them, the youthful master replied, "Neither do you understand God!" My own job as a disciple, similarly, I realized, was to absorb as much wisdom and inspiration from him as I was capable of holding.

✺ 425 ✺

"A spiritual disease worse even than ignorance," the Master said, "is indifference. Linked to it is the habit of distracting the mind. As soon as you find yourself with a little leisure on your hands, you pick up a magazine, or turn on the radio. Such things can be poison. Anything that relaxes your vigilance is a threat to your spiritual life."

✤ 426 ✤

During the time of testing that preceded the Master's departure from his body, a number of the monks left their monastic calling. The Master counseled the rest of us, "Whenever you see someone leave, tell yourself inwardly, 'Men may come, and men may go, but I go on forever!' My Master [Sri Yukteswar] used to say, 'Satsanga's boat is calling. Who'll go? Who'll go? If no one else goes, *I* at least will go!"

I feared for my own spiritual safety. The path sometimes seemed to me almost like a game of musical chairs, in which the question of who gets to sit down when the music stops is a matter of pure luck. The Master, aware of my fear, consoled me, "As long as *you* make the effort, God will *never* let you down."

✤ 427 ✤

Sexual desires were, for the monks, the greatest temptation—especially for the younger ones. Master said to us once, "If the sexual impulse were taken away from you, you would realize you had lost your greatest friend. You would lose all interest in life. Sex was given to you to make you strong. The more you give in to it,

"For all who have come to me in this life, there has been a reason."

the weaker you become. But when you master it, you'll find that you've become a lion of happiness."

᷒ 428 ᷒

"Do not seek honor in God's work. Whoever seeks it will receive dishonor. If what you seek, however, is not honor but the glory of God, you will receive from His own hands His infinite blessedness."

᷒ 429 ᷒

"Sir," said James Coller on a visit from Phoenix, "I have such a great longing for God! *Why* does He take so long in coming?"

"Ah!" the Master replied with a blissful smile, "that is what makes it all the sweeter when He does come. That is the nature of His romance with the devotee!"

430

"Above everything else," the Master said, "be loyal to God. Devote more time to seeking Him. And be less concerned over lesser duties which, someday, won't exist anymore anyway. In those lesser preoccupations lies the greatest delusion. Never look upon them as, in themselves, important. Nothing is so pressingly important as your daily tryst with God."

431

"Because the sexual impulse is usually stronger in men, the spiritual path is harder for them than for women. Those men who get there, however, become very great."

432

To those, especially, who served in public roles, but also to all devotees of God, the Master counseled: "Devotion must not be displayed before others. As soon as you demonstrate it outwardly, that is the end of your devotion. To express such feelings deliberately to others is a blasphemy before God."

✧ 433 ✧

"One good way to begin overcoming bad habits is to start your self-discipline with food. For example, try eating a handful of hot chili peppers, and see if you can resist the thought that they are hot. A practice some devotees in India follow is to mix everything together that they are about to eat, before they even taste it. I practiced that for a while. It was a bit strange at first, and certainly the meal wasn't delicious with those items— sweet, pungent, bland—all tossed together! I found it helped, however, in gaining control over my palate."

✧ 434 ✧

Michael, who later was given the name "Bhaktananda," told us he had often repeated, during meditation, the words, "I love you, Guru." One day he met the Master in the garden at Encinitas. The Master smiled lovingly at his disciple and said, "I love you, too."

❧ 435 ❧

Across the dirt road from the Master's desert retreat stood a little house, hardly more than a shack. The man who owned it seemed, however, completely satisfied with life. Speaking of him, the Master said, "He is like a king in his palace! Such is the joy of simple living."

❧ 436 ❧

For weeks I (Walter) prayed to the Master, "Teach me to love you as you love me."

One day he looked at me and said, "How can the little cup hold the whole ocean of love? First it must be expanded to become as large as the ocean."

❧ 437 ❧

"Sir," I asked him once, "what is faith? And how can one develop it?"

"Faith," was his answer, "comes with direct, personal experience. That is what Saint Paul meant when he said, 'Faith is the proof of things unseen.' The deeper your *experience* of truth, the greater the faith you will have.

"There was a man who had read in the Bible that if a person has sufficient faith, he will be able to say to this mountain, 'Be thou moved into the sea,' and it will be so. 'How wonderful!' the man thought. 'It has always bothered me that there is a mountain outside my window that obscures the view I might have, otherwise, of that beautiful lake on the other side. Let me remove the mountain by faith.'

"That night, he prayed earnestly, 'Let the mountain be removed and cast into the sea.' He then went to bed. The next morning, the first thing he did was rush to the window to see what had happened. The mountain hadn't budged an inch.

"'I *knew* you'd still be there!' he cried.

"Such is the 'faith' of most people. Theirs isn't *faith*. It is merely belief."

ᔗᖇ 438 ᖇᔗ

A woman disciple often took unnecessary risks. People cautioned her to be more careful, but she justified herself with the declaration, "Whatever happens, Master will protect me."

"Of all things!" the Master exclaimed when these words were quoted to him. "Let her try driving off the cliff in Encinitas and see whether I'll protect her from the consequences of her foolish act! It is good to have faith, but one must also use common sense!"

439

Often Yogananda said of his disciples, however, that they did have protection. Once, when someone in the colonies was hurt, the Master said to him, "It would have been worse, had you not been living here." I saw this also in the case of Claude Pastori, a child six years old who had come to Encinitas with his mother. Claude lost a finger in an accident. Afterward, the Master said, "I saw, earlier, a dark cloud around him. He was protected from a much more serious karma."

440

Oliver Black, to whom the Master later gave the title *Yogacharya* (teacher of yoga), was the SRF center leader in Detroit, Michigan. The Master described Mr. Black to me as highly advanced, spiritually. Yogacharya Oliver told me the following story when I visited him at his home:

"I was visiting Encinitas. Master asked me one day to go out driving with him. Word came that he was just then going out the front door to get into his car. It had been raining hard, and when I received that summons I glanced out the window, a little apprehensively, and saw that the rain was pouring down heavily. This seemed hardly the ideal weather for a drive!

"Moments later, I, too, exited by the front door to join Master. To my astonishment, not only had the rain stopped completely, but the car and the driveway around it were all perfectly dry. The sun shone brightly in a blue sky. I looked around me unbelievingly for a few seconds. Then I looked at Master.

"'For you, Oliver,' he said with a quiet smile."

The Master once said to me, "God does not perform overt miracles for people as a rule, unless there is an obvious need, or for someone who is highly advanced."

441

The Master taught in his lessons that shaking hands with people creates an exchange of magnetism. That, no doubt, is why the traditional greeting in India is the palms-folded gesture, the *namaskar,* instead of the handshake.

Nevertheless, he had me stand outside the Hollywood Church after his Sunday services, and shake hands with the people as they left. Perhaps because they were drawing consciously from me, as his disciple, I felt dizzy and weak afterward. Later, I mentioned this problem to Master.

"That is because you are thinking of yourself," he replied. "Think of God, and feel His power flowing through you. Then you will be all right."

Following his advice, I never again felt drained of energy when shaking hands after the service. Rather, I felt more inspired.

꘍ 442 ꘏

A man came to Mount Washington and was accepted by the Master for training. The man received Kriya Yoga initiation, and practiced it with great fervor for a few months. Once, he told me, he meditated for forty hours without a break. Impatient, however, with the seeming slowness of his progress, he left the Master at last in discouragement.

Commenting later on this devotee, the Master told me, "He will *never* find God that way! He is like a merchant who says, 'Lord, I have given you so many Kriyas; now You have to keep Your side of the bargain and give me so much realization.' God never responds to such mercenary devotion! He accepts nothing less from us than our unconditional love."

I wondered if it wasn't of him that Master was thinking when he wrote, in his Gita commentaries, of some people who meditate with great will power, but without devotion, and who abandon their spiritual practices in time.

❧ 443 ☙

"Which is more spiritual?" a visitor inquired, "the sense of smell, or the sense of taste?"

"The sense of taste," was the reply.

One naturally asks, Why? I think the answer is that the sense of taste is situated closer to the heart's feelings.

❧ 444 ☙

"Visualize a ball of light," he once said. "Expand it with the speed of thought. You might go on expanding that light throughout eternity and *never* reach the point where you could say, 'Here are the boundaries of space.' Don't you see? It is all mental. This whole universe is only a dream. Scientists declare that, despite its vast size, the universe is finite. The only thing that cannot have *anything* beyond or outside it is an idea. Were God to expand that idea, the universe itself would expand with His thought. The moment you ask, 'What lies outside my idea?' you've expanded your thought of it."

Someone had said something derogatory about the "idol worship" practiced in India. The Master chuckled. "Westerners think of Hindus as idol worshipers, but what is it they themselves worship? Money and power—aren't those idols? There is nothing wrong or contrary to spiritual truth in using images as reminders of high principles. How many people are able to visualize such abstractions as love or wisdom? The Hindu images are not idols. They are symbols of different aspects of God. Their very variety shows a recognition of the fact that God is infinite.

"Westerners call Hindus heathens, and Hindus call Westerners heathens. Ignorance, I say, is fifty-fifty everywhere. When the wise meet, however, there is only harmony and understanding.

"When I visited the home of Therese Neumann of Konnersreuth, in Germany, she sent word down, 'I will see the man of God from India.' Her bishop had forbidden her to see anyone! Therese is a real saint." The Master revealed to us that she was Mary Magdalene, reincarnated.

I once asked him, "Has she attained liberation?"

"Not yet," he answered, "but she is in *nirbikalpa samadhi* [the highest *samadhi* state]. She is what they call in India a *jivan mukta*."

ᶩᶜ 446 ᶧᵌᵏ

A young Hindu had come to America for a year of study at a university. During the ship crossing, he saw in meditation a vision of Paramhansa Yogananda, of whom he had never before heard. He happened to meet the Master several months later, and recognized him from his vision.

This young man had a guru of his own in India. Debi Mukherjee, to whom I've referred earlier, became friends with this young man, and asked the Master why that youth had been vouchsafed such a vision, since he already had a guru of his own.

The Master replied, "That was because this is a special dispensation of God." There was no special significance in the vision. It didn't mean, for example, that the young man was being told to convert to the Master's teachings.

This story has helped me to understand that the mission of an *avatar,* especially, is to bring a new wave of consciousness into the world, and not only to provide a few people with an example of his own inspiring life. Indeed, I saw in him repeatedly this vast breadth of vision. Often he insisted to us, "We are not a sect." And of himself he said, as I quoted earlier, gazing blissfully into my eyes, "Just a bulge of the ocean." He urged us to be loyal to the path to which God had drawn us, but he never urged us to be bigoted. Quite the contrary.

"When you see any form of God in vision," he said, "behold in those eyes the consciousness of Infinity. It is a mistake to limit God to any form, to any definition, to any one religion."

447

To Debi Mukherjee the Master once said, "Someday, lionlike swamis will come from India and aid in spreading this message all over."

448

"A bent spine," the Master used to tell his students, "is the enemy of realization."

449

"What a divine soul Master Mahasaya was!" my Guru exclaimed to me once. Master Mahasaya was the disciple of Sri Ramakrishna who wrote *The Gospel of Sri Ramakrishna*. Yogananda, as a boy, had had so much love for this disciple that the saint had felt it necessary to remind him, "I am not your guru."

"Sometimes," the Master continued, "I would roll on the ground where he'd walked, so great was my love for him. I felt that even that ground had been sanctified."

⚜ 450 ⚜

"Tell your faults to no one," the Master counseled us, "for some day, in a fit of anger, the person you confide in may use them against you. Do tell your faults to God, however. From Him, one should conceal nothing."

⚜ 451 ⚜

"The greatest sin," the Master used to say, "is to call yourself a sinner. You are a child of God. Though gold be covered with mud for centuries, it remains gold. So the pure 'gold' of the soul can be covered over with the mud of delusion for aeons, but in its true nature it remains forever undefiled."

Ꮶᐸ 452 ᕼᏋ

"I once attended a service led by a famous woman evangelist. During her sermon she shouted, 'You are all sinners! Get down on your knees!'

"I was the only one present who remained standing," the Master ended with a smile. "I would not admit that I was a sinner."

People sometimes offer the following challenge to those words of the Master: "But Jesus himself *said* that we are sinners!" Yes, and Saint Francis and many other Christian saints have also called *themselves* sinners. So also for that matter, sometimes, did Yogananda, when he wanted to emphasize his human littleness before God. Self-deprecation with the purpose of emphasizing the greatness of the Infinite is altogether different from absorbing oneself in one's own imperfection. To emphasize one's own sinfulness, however, is an excuse many people use for *remaining* imperfect. We should remember that Jesus himself said, "Be ye therefore perfect, even as your Father which is in heaven is perfect."* Thus, Yogananda often said, "The greatest sin is to call oneself a sinner. It is a way of hypnotizing oneself with one's own weakness. Always affirm your strength in God—*His* strength, through you."

*Matthew 5:48

ᘓ 453 ᘔ

When Aimee Semple McPherson—who may have been the evangelist in the foregoing story—was reported "lost" for a time in the Mexican desert, malicious persons spread the gossip that she had disappeared for reasons not altogether praiseworthy. The Master defended her staunchly. "Look at the good she has done," he protested. "Let God be the judge, but let us be grateful also that she has done so much for others."

ᘓ 454 ᘔ

The Master often used this illustration to explain how to overcome error in oneself: "A room can be in darkness for thousands of years, but if you bring in light, the darkness will vanish as though it had never been. So is it when the light of God illuminates the soul: The darkness of incarnations vanishes in an instant.

"Never say that you are a sinner. Don't, in that way, affirm your limitations. Dwell instead on the thought that you were made in God's image—that in your soul, in your true Self, the darkness of delusion cannot exist."

455

"Twenty-five percent of spiritual success," the Master told us, "comes by the devotee's effort. Twenty-five percent comes by the Guru's effort on his behalf. And fifty percent comes by the grace of God."

456

Referring to the universal need for yoga, and particularly for Kriya Yoga, which guides the energy into, and up, the spine, Yogananda once said, "You can be in a room twenty years, trying to get out through the walls, the ceiling, the floor. It is when you finally discover the door that you find your way out. That's how it is with the soul. The average devotee may struggle his whole life trying to escape the bodily limitations by unscientific means, and by the paths only of devotion or discrimination. By Kriya Yoga, however, if he is sincere, he can escape quickly. Kriya Yoga takes one to God by the universal highway: the spine."

It seemed to be my fate to have to report things to the Master, when others didn't dare to speak. Some people had been speaking against Dr. Lewis, saying that he had let the Master down in certain important ways. The criticisms were valid, and I spoke to the Master about them. The highest value to him, however, was loyalty. He was deeply loyal to his friends, even when they disappointed him. Thus I, as the messenger, had to bear his indignant response:

"When you have been tested through many years, as he has, *then* you will have earned the right to speak these things!" Master surely knew I didn't hold those attitudes personally, but he felt it necessary to make that point in front of many others. He then went upstairs and telephoned Dr. Lewis, simply to affirm his deep friendship for him. The truth is, Doctor had his little foibles, and had indeed let the Master down in certain important matters concerning the work. The Master, however, like Jesus, was saying essentially, "Let him who is without sin cast the first stone." Even today, Dr. Lewis is criticized by many. I myself know that he had things to overcome. But as the expression has it among Jews in America: "So what else is new?" We are all struggling toward perfection. Only after one has achieved it has he a right to criticize: And, having once attained perfection, one finds that perfection itself eliminates the very desire to criticize anyone!

⊰ 458 ⊱

A disciple was having difficulty going breathless. "What can I do about it, Master?" he asked.

"It is a question," replied the Master, "of persuading the mind that your *natural* state is freedom from the body. At first, the devotee is like a bird that has lived in a cage for twenty years. Someone opens the cage door, and the bird thinks, 'Oh! that wide, terrible world!' and, trembling fearfully, it retreats to the rear of its little cage to which it has grown accustomed. The mind, similarly, at its first taste of inner freedom, becomes frightened and clings to body-consciousness.

"Reflect, however, that it is natural for the bird to fly. It is natural also for the soul to soar in omnipresence."

⊰ 459 ⊱

The Master loved to relate this story: "Saint Teresa of Avila was crossing a stream with a few nuns. They were on their way to found a new convent. Teresa by this time was old and infirm.

"Suddenly the horse she was on was swept away in the stream, which was swollen by heavy rains. Her nuns were helpless to save her from drowning. They were sure she was lost.

"Teresa suddenly beheld Jesus Christ on the opposite bank. In no time, she found herself standing before him, completely dry.

"'Be of good cheer, Teresa!' Jesus said to her. 'This is how I treat all my friends.'

"Teresa answered joyfully, 'That, my Lord, is why You have so few!'

"That was a witty answer, but what a true one!"

ꕥ 460 ꕥ

"Saint Anthony spent years meditating in a tomb in the desert. For much of that time he was tormented by devils. At last Satan himself threatened to destroy him if he didn't give up his search for God. The walls of the tomb began to crack, and threatened to fall in upon him, crushing him. The friezes of animals on the walls assumed living shapes and converged upon him to devour him. Anthony gazed up once more and called to Christ.

"All at once, a great light appeared. Jesus himself stood there, looking down. The tomb resumed its former appearance. The darkness vanished. In the ecstasy of divine awakening, Anthony remembered all the incarnations he had been seeking God.

"Oh! I know that experience: What joy comes with it! And Anthony cried out from the depths of his soul, 'Lord, where were you all those years that I was crying out for you?'

"And Jesus, smiling with deep love, answered, 'Anthony, I was all the time with you!'"

৵৵ 461 ৵৵

"Once," the Master told us, "when I was in my Guru's ashram, I mentioned another spiritual organization, comparing it to our own.

"'Why do you make comparisons?' my Guru asked. 'This is the way the Lord wants to play through you and me. Let us follow faithfully the path to which He has drawn us.'

"How it thrilled me, to think that God was playing through me in a particular way."

The Gospel of Saint John in the Bible ends with the words, "And there are also many other things which Jesus did, the which, if they should be written every one, I suppose that even the world itself could not contain the books that should be written." Those words echo my own sentiments perfectly. There was much, much more I could have written. I feel, however, that I have brought together enough Conversations with Yogananda to give the reader some slight idea of the thrill and inspiration we all felt, who knew him. I have sought in these pages to make him at least a little bit real for those readers who had not the blessing to know him personally.

My final message, dear reader, touches you intimately: Paramhansa Yogananda is still alive. You will find him in your own heart, if you will but seek him there.

And *his* message to everyone is this: For every problem you confront in life there is a way out. That way is to find God: to realize your own Self as, in essence, one with the Supreme Spirit, *Satchidanandam*.

The Master, seated with his disciples at Mount Washington for the
Christmas banquet, December 25, 1951. Seated at his left and right side,
respectively, are Dr. M. W. Lewis and Rajarsi Janakananda.
Serving Rajarsi is Mrs. Mildred Lewis, wife of Dr. Lewis. I am the one
standing behind the Master, serving the guests.

Index

The references in this index list the page number, followed by the "conversation" number in parentheses. For example, the citation 405 (410) refers to page 405, conversation number 410.

desire: action free of, 264 (232); as spiritual obstacle, 106–7 (86), 168 (145), 240 (212). *See also* God, desire for

destiny, 244 (214). *See also* predestination

Devil, 418 (416). *See also* Satan

devotion: developing, 414 (411); displayed inwardly vs. outwardly, 335 (306), 414 (410), 430 (432); vs. emotion, 39–40 (25); importance on spiritual path, 46 (33), 67 (46), 96 (75), 138 (114), 261 (229), 265 (232), 284 (248), 290 (259), 436–37 (442). *See also Bhakti Yoga*

Dhirananda, Swami, 113 (90), 193–94 (162)

diabetes, man with, 305 (275)

diet, 46–48 (33–34), 130 (104), 209 (178), 234 (205). *See also* vegetarianism

differences, outward, 219 (188)

Diogenes, 397 (386)

directionality, 275 (240), 294–95 (263)

disasters, predicted, 349–51 (318–319)

disciples, 112 (90), 318 (290); guru and (*see* guru and disciples; Yogananda)

discipline, 81 (59). *See also* self-discipline

discrimination: conceptual, 388 (366); racial (*see* racial prejudice)

disease: origin and causes of, 296–97 (264–265). *See also* illness

diversity, accepting, 92 (69)

Divine Mother: aspect of God, 145 (119), 147 (121), 187 (157), 210 (179), 223 (193), 311 (281), 327 (302); will of, 239 (211), 282 (245), 352 (320)

Divine Power, 159 (136)

divorce, 25–26 (13), 84 (62)

doctors, 132 (106)

doubt, 240 (212), 354 (324)

drama, 310 (280)

Draupadi, 362 (332)

dreaming, 43 (28)

dreams, contact with deceased relatives in, 202–3 (172)

dress. *See* appearance

drunkenness, 404 (396)

duality(ies), 419 (417); principle of, 267 (235). *See also* polarities

Durbasha, 179 (152)

Durga (Florina Darling), 224 (194)

duties, hierarchy of, 26 (13), 28 (15)

Dwapara Yuga, 55–58 (40), 189 (159), 223 (192), 294 (263), 335 (305)

Earth, cycles and evolution of, 52–53 (40)

Eastern culture and spirituality, 87–88 (65)

ecstasy, 122 (98), 249 (220–21). *See also* bliss; *samadhi*

Eddy, Mrs., 420 (418)

ego(-consciousness), 400 (389); bringing it to heel, 71–76 (48–52); freedom from, 128 (102), 219 (188), 338 (307), 358–59 (329–331), 398 (385) (*see also* self-transcendence); and ignorance, 16 (2); origin, 32 (18); perfection and, 125 (101); problems resulting from, 16 (3), 20 (10), 35 (21), 51 (39); purpose, 17 (4); suicide and, 32 (18); thwarting crosscurrents of, 39 (24); what to do with, 70 (47), 71 (48), 364 (335) (*see also* self-transcendence). *See also* honor; individuality; pride; self-consciousness

embarrassment, overcoming, 72–75 (48–51), 117–18 (94)

emotion, 95–96 (75), 156 (132), 180 (153), 402 (392); transformed into devotion, 94–95 (73). *See also* feeling

emotional devotion and religion, 39–40 (25)

emptiness, 236 (207)

energization exercises, 71–72 (48)

energy, 54 (40), 60 (40), 61 (40); projected by people, 44 (30)

enlightenment, 16 (2), 19 (8), 293 (262); universal, 342 (308). *See also* awakening

error in oneself, how to overcome, 443 (454)

Essence of Self-Realization, The (Yogananda), 8, 9

Evans, Michelle, 85 (63)

evil, 296 (264), 297 (265), 304 (274), 418–20 (416–418); absence of true joy as, 257–58 (224–225); purpose, 43 (29); rejection of God as, 258 (225); seeing it in others, 171–74 (149). *See also* demons; Satan; sin(s)

evolution, 345 (312); spiritual, 16 (2), 50–51 (39), 63 (41)

existence, 51 (39), 365–66 (337)

exorcism, 111 (88)

expectations, 240 (212)

experience, 17 (5)

faddists, 130 (104)

faith, 34–35 (21), 165–66 (143), 432–34 (437–438)

father, one's true 285 (249)

"Father Divine," 40 (26)

faults, 398 (387), 441 (450)

fear, 240 (212); of loss (*see* attachment)

feeling: reason and, 414–15 (410). *See also* emotion

feet placed on elder's head, 411–12 (407)

fish, eating, 163–65 (140–142)

FitzGerald, Edward, 367–68 (340), 383–84 (358)

focus, 153–55 (130–131). See also concentration

food, 46–48 (33–35), 234–35 (205), 253–54 (224), 431 (433). See also fish; silence, at mealtimes

forgiveness, 167–68 (144), 273 (237)

Forshee, Corinne (Mukti), 324–25 (297)

Francis of Assisi, Saint, 36 (22), 131 (105), 442 (452)

Frederick, Clifford, 197 (166), 300 (268), 358 (329), 372–73 (345)

free-thinking, 259 (226)

free will, 21 (10), 45 (31), 70 (47), 114 (90), 363 (334), 394 (379). See also will

freedom: how to find, 21–22 (10), 51 (39); liberated saints, 111 (87); Yogananda's guidance for disciples, 75 (52), 114 (90), 115 (91), 119 (95), 352 (320), 363 (334), 367 (339), 446 (458). See also liberation

friendships, 93 (70). See also companionship

Frost, Karle, 132–33 (107)

fundamentalism. See religious fundamentalism

galaxies, 50–51 (39), 60 (40)

Galli-Curci, Amelita, 25–26 (13), 31–33 (18–19), 182 (154)

Gandhi, Mahatma, 57 (40), 297 (266)

Garden of Eden, 51 (39), 302 (271)

generosity, 101–2 (79–80), 251–52 (222)

Genesis, Book of, 294 (263), 302 (271)

Genghis Khan: Stalin as reincarnation of, 43 (29), 317 (289)

George, Abie, 378 (348)

Germany, 90 (66)

Ghosh, Mrinalkanti, 311 (281)

Ghosh, Sananda Lal, 139 (115), 147 (121), 189 (159)

gifts, receiving, 375–78 (348)

giving, 48 (35)

goals: pursued to completion, 129 (103)

God, 31 (17); "airplane route" vs. "bullock cart" method of seeking, 66 (46), 71 (47); anthropomorphic concepts of, 56–57 (40), 62 (41); being released by, 21 (10); belief in, 34–35 (21); consciousness of, 49 (37), 440 (446); crying out to, 95–96 (75); desire for, 21–22 (10), 63 (41), 136 (112), 145 (119),

171 (149), 429 (429); focusing on, 22 (10); as forever with us, 367 (340); His higher aspect vs. His show, 21 (10); living/giving life for, 79–81 (57–58), 197–98 (166), 211 (180), 381–82 (354–356), 411 (406), 414–15 (411); love for, 45 (31), 86 (64), 93 (71), 128 (102), 326 (299), 381 (355), 388 (367), 399 (387), 436–37 (442); love of, 114 (90); loyalty as greatest law of, 290 (258); loyalty to, 430 (430); making love to, 319 (291); man as made in image of, 16 (3); nature of, 21 (10), 32 (18), 37 (23), 40 (25), 44 (29), 419 (417); as parent, 326 (300); placing everything in his hands, 165–66 (143); plan of, 62 (41); reaching, 19 (9), 22 (10), 319 (291); rejecting/turning away from, 258–59 (225); seeking, 17 (4), 114 (90), 218 (188), 262 (229), 367–69 (340–341), 368 (341), 447 (460); seeking to please, 201–2 (171), 265 (232), 338 (307); teachings, 45 (31); "tempting," 166 (143); unity with, 20 (10), 22 (10), 237 (209), 270 (236), 276 (240), 382 (356); will never let you down, 427 (426); will of, 45 (31)

God-realization, 130 (104). See also Self-realization

good, 419 (417); in others, seeing, 171–74 (149)

gopis, 198-201 (168–69)

gossip and rumors, 113 (90), 121–22 (98), 262–63 (230), 274 (239)

Gray, Horace, 403-4 (394)

Great Depression, 350 (318)

"Great Mother," 81–82 (60)

greed, 399 (389)

gunas, 50 (39), 182 (154)

guru and disciples: difference between, 15–16 (2); relationship between, 19 (8), 28–29 (16), 34 (21), 105–6 (84), 112 (90), 133–34 (109), 318 (290), 417 (412). See also under Yogananda

guru(s), 397 (384); having faith in, 206–7 (178); need for, 111 (88); as spiritual doctor, 19 (8), 34 (21), 85 (63). See also masters

Gyanamata, Sister, 31 (17), 275–77 (240), 336 (307), 362 (333), 363 (334)

gyanis, 381 (354)

habits, 287 (251), 329 (303), 382 (356), 431 (433)

handshaking, 435–36 (441)

happiness, 172 (149), 257–59 (224–225), 379 (351–353), 401 (390); is found from inside self, 407 (399)

Harding, Ed, 323–24 (297)

Haridas, Sadhu, 113–14 (90), 273 (237)

hate, 324 (297)

Recommended Books, Music & DVDs

Books by Paramhansa Yogananda

Autobiography of a Yogi (original 1946 edition)

One of the great spiritual classics of this century. This is a verbatim reprinting of the original 1946 edition. Yogananda was the first yoga master of India whose mission is was to live and teach in the West. This book, first published in 1946, helped to launch, and continues to inspire, a spiritual revolution in the West.

The Essence of Self-Realization

Recorded and Compiled by His Disciple, Swami Kriyananda

"A wonderful book! To find a previously unknown message from Yogananda now is an extraordinary gift." Body, Mind, Spirit Magazine

The Rubaiyat of Omar Khayyam Explained

Edited by Swami Kriyananda

Yogananda discovered a scripture previously unknown to the world. It was hidden in the beautiful imagery of the beloved poem, The Rubaiyat of Omar Khayyam. His commentary reveals the profound spiritual mystery behind this world famous love poem. showing deep allegory of the soul's romance with God.

Books by Swami Kriyananda (J. Donald Walters)

God Is for Everyone

This book is the core of Yogananda's teachings. It presents a concept of God and spiritual meaning that will broadly appeal to everyone, from the most uncertain agnostic to the most fervent believer. Clearly and simply written, thoroughly nonsectarian and non-dogmatic in its approach, it is the perfect introduction to the spiritual path.

The Path

One Man's Quest on the Only Path There Is

This is a moving story of Kriyananda's years with Yogananda. *The Path* completes Yogananda's life story and includes more then 400 never-before-published stories about the great master.

Music by Swami Kriyananda (Donald Walters)

Relax:Meditations for Flute & Cello
CD, 7-98499-50272-2
This CD is specifically designed to slow respiration and heart rate, bringing listeners to their calm center. This recording features 15 melodies on flute and cello, accompanied by harp, guitar, keyboard, and strings.

Mantra of Eternity, AUM
CD, 7-98499-50102-2
AUM is a Sanskrit word meaning peace and oneness of spirit.
"Highly recommended for meditation, yoga practice or work with sound healing therapy." Lee Starky, East West Book Shop, California

Music for Yoga
3 CD Box Set
CD, 7-98499-50262-3
The music in this set is ideal for any style of yoga practice. Each CD has been enthusiastically tested and approved by yoga teachers and practitioners throughout the USA and Europe. Musical selections are drawn from both Eastern and Western traditions and offer a variety of moods and rhythms that will keep your practice fresh.

For more information or a free catalog contact:

Crystal Clarity Publishers
Clarity Sound & Light
800.424.1055
530.478.7600
fax 530.478.7610
www.crystalclarity.com
clarity@crystalclarity.com